KT-407-769

Studying Abroad

X400 000003 5379

Studying Abroad:
A guide for UK students

5th edition

trotman | **t**

	Wolverhampton City Council	
	X400 000003 5379	
	Askews & Holts	05-Sep-2016
		£14.99
		ALL

Studying Abroad: A Guide for UK Students

This fifth edition published in 2016 by Trotman Education, a division of Crimson Publishing Ltd, Westminster House, Kew Road, Richmond, TW9 2ND
BA1 1HX

© Trotman Education 2016

Compiled and edited by: Miranda ...

Previous editions published in 2012, 2013, 2014, 2015.

Author: Cerys Evans

All rights reserved. This book is sold subject to the condition that it shall not, by way of trade or otherwise, be lent, resold, hired out or otherwise circulated without the publisher's prior written consent in any form of binding or cover other than that in which it is published and without a similar condition including this condition being imposed on the subsequent purchaser. No part of this publication may be reproduced, stored in a retrieval system or transmitted in any form or by any means, electronic and mechanical, photocopying, recording or otherwise without prior permission of Crimson Publishing.

European Union Referendum: This edition was compiled prior to the referendum on 23 June, 2016 regarding the UK's continued membership of the European Union, and the information was correct at the time of writing. At the time of going to press, the UK remains a constituent member of the Union, which allows the free movement of people, capital, goods and services across the 28 Member States. Formal proceedings for negotiating the terms of the UK's withdrawal from the Union can only commence when the UK government triggers Article 50 of the Lisbon Treaty and, at the time of going to press, information was not available regarding the projected timescale for this process. Until that time, the information provided on the European Union remains valid.

British Library Cataloguing in Publication Data

A catalogue record for this book is available from the British Library

ISBN 978 1 84455 640 3

Typeset by IDSUK (DataConnection) Ltd

Printed and bound by TJ International Ltd, Padstow, UK

Acknowledgements

This fifth edition has been compiled and edited by Miranda Lim. The publishers acknowledge Cerys Evans as the author of the first four editions of the book.

The publisher would like to thank the following third party copyright holders for their kind permission to reproduce their material: UNESCO Institute for Statistics (UIS), the OCED, The British Council, the European Parliament (Policy Department for Structural and Cohesion Policies), Think Global, StudyPortals, ACA, University of Florida, UCAS, The Complete University Guide and i-graduate. Particular thanks go to David Mannion (US-UK Fulbright Commission) for his guidance and supplying a profile on studying in the USA, as well as for putting us in touch with students. We would also like to thank Mark Huntington (A Star Future) for liaising with students and supplying extra context on study in Europe; as well as all the students (Laura Bowker, Jordan Clark, Elizabeth Edwards, Catherine Foreshaw, Matthew Green, Vincent Hendricks, Jade Knight, Charlie Roscoe and Katherine Taylor) who have helpfully provided new case studies and quotes for use in the book.

European Union Referendum

The information in this fifth edition was correct at the time of writing, however the publisher acknowledges that the information provided in the book on the European Union may be subject to change following the UK's decision to leave the European Union. At the time of going to press, the UK remains a Member State of the Union and will continue to be subject to its obligations under EU law until it has finalised the terms of its withdrawal with the other 27 Member States.

Contents

Contents

Contents

Introduction

Britain has a long tradition of welcoming international students to its universities, yet far fewer UK students venture overseas to study. All that is changing and there has never been so much interest in the possibility of studying abroad.

The increased tuition fees and changes to funding in parts of the UK has prompted some young people to start looking for alternative, affordable ways to study. Many UK students are unaware of the degrees available to them overseas that are taught in English, and at a range of prices. Students will be able to find comparably priced, and sometimes cheaper, opportunities than those available at home. Elsewhere in Europe, for instance, UK students can even find free university courses available at both undergraduate and postgraduate level.

But price alone is not enough to drive people to study overseas. A more competitive marketplace for graduate employment is leading students to make themselves more attractive to potential employers, and studying overseas provides the opportunity to produce a more dynamic CV.

However, choosing to study overseas is not a decision that should be made lightly. There are many aspects to consider and many questions to ask before reaching that stage. Higher education is a global market and, although there is a lot of information available online, the challenge is making sense of it, ensuring that it is genuine and being in a position to make meaningful comparisons between the different options available.

This book will help you to determine whether studying for a degree abroad is the right option for you. It will tackle the costs, risks and benefits of studying abroad. It will enable you to compare the merits of different countries and their education systems. You can read about the trials and the tribulations of a variety of students, as well as learning about their overseas study highlights. The book will assist you in navigating the plethora of information available, guiding you through the decision-making process by providing answers to essential questions.

This book is merely the starting point of what could be a life-changing educational and cultural adventure.

Note

The following exchange rates were used throughout the book (sourced in April 2016, prior to the UK's decision to leave the European Union):

- £1 to €1.29 **(Euro)**
- £1 to $1.45 **(US Dollar)**
- £1 to C$1.84 **(Canadian Dollar)**
- £1 to A$1.88 **(Australian Dollar)**
- £1 to NZ$2.11 **(New Zealand Dollar)**
- £1 to DKK 9.59 **(Danish Krone)**
- £1 to CZK34.83 **(Czech Koruna)**
- £1 to NOK11.91 **(Norwegian Krone)**
- £1 to SEK11.80 **(Swedish Krona)**

- £1 to CHF1.42 **(Swiss Franc)**
- £1 to S$1.97 **(Singapore Dollar)**
- £1 to HK$11.29 **(Hong Kong Dollar)**
- £1 to ¥9.45 **(Chinese Yuan Renminbi)**
- £1 to JPY161.37 **(Japanese Yen)**
- £1 to ZAR21.07 **(South African Rand)**
- £1 to MYR5.71 **(Malaysian Ringgit)**
- £1 to JA$178.03 **(Jamaican Dollar)**
- £1 to QAR5.30 **(Qatari Riyal)**
- £1 to BRL5.17 **(Brazilian Real)**.

Student testimonial, A Star Future
Charlie Roscoe
University: Stenden University of Applied Sciences, the Netherlands
Course: International Business Management Studies
Year: First year
Hometown: Shropshire, England

1. Why go abroad?

I went travelling to Thailand, Laos and Cambodia after leaving school and while I was there I was offered a job as a sales representative for a tour guide company in Asia. So I ended up living and working in Bangkok for six months. This experience made me realise how much I love travelling and that I wanted to study at a university abroad rather than in the UK.

The IBMS degree at Stenden also gives me the opportunity to travel on a student exchange and also to do my internship in another country too. I am constantly in a diverse multicultural environment – something I really enjoy.

2. How would you rate the assistance of the university before you arrived (the application process, finding accommodation, sorting out financial matters)?

Stenden University of Applied Sciences' admission team was very helpful with the application process and financial matters. I had regular email contact with the university and they provided a lot of information. I did not need help with arranging accommodation as I live with my Dutch boyfriend.

3. Orientation/Making friends

When I arrived at Stenden the students and teachers were very helpful. Everyone made me feel welcome. The university arranged a study start week where we were given a buddy to look after us and provide support. During the study start week I got to know the other students on my course and we also went camping together on an island.

4. Lifestyle and culture

I felt prepared for an international setting as I had already travelled a lot; however, I was not prepared for some of the organisational procedures I had to go through. For example, arranging study finance, registering at the municipality and sorting out health insurance all took time. I would recommend other students research these things beforehand if they have time.

5. How would you rate the learning environment (teaching style, studying with other international students, non-native English-speaking lecturers)?

The learning environment at Stenden is very good and the teachers always try to help the students who show they are keen to learn and are dedicated to their studies. There are a few occasions when teachers use American English rather than UK English but this does not cause learning problems.

The IBMS course involves a lot of teamwork and collaboration. It is really fun as I get to work with people from different cultures; we also study many topics within business such as economics, law and culture. International students also have the chance to learn Dutch – something that's really useful when you've committed to staying in the Netherlands for four years to complete the IBMS degree.

6. Would you recommend studying abroad to a 17–18-year-old Brit who might never have thought about it before?

Yes, I would because it will increase self-confidence as you'll find yourself in situations where you have to interact and work with people from many different cultures. You'll also experience so much more – for example, learning a language and exploring a new country ... and you'll have plenty of time to experience the country's sights without feeling rushed.

Studying in an international setting provides you with so many more opportunities too after you graduate, as potential employers can see that you adapt well.

The Netherlands is a great place to study. It's not an expensive place to live and there is always something to do. Transport is very good so you can easily visit other cities on weekends. The majority of people also speak English and this makes communicating a lot easier.

However, you have to be prepared to work hard, as you have to get enough credits in order to be able to continue on to the second year of the degree.

7. Is there anything you wish someone had told you at the time you applied?

I wish that there had been more detailed information about what I would be studying within each module and also information about the grading system in the Netherlands. It's a credit system, so quite different from the UK, and takes a bit of getting used to. I recommend researching this beforehand.

8. Would you recommend your course, university, city to British students?

I would recommend the IBMS course to other British students because it is such a broad course; you learn everything that you need to in business, such as law and accounting. Each module is different and they are always interesting. The university also provides additional information. There are also clubs such as Enactus, which is a charity committee; this is also another way to meet new people. It is hard work, but it is fun, as you are constantly working with new people.

I have no regrets about studying in the Netherlands; it is one of the best decisions I have made!

Tuition fees are €1,984 in 2016/17 as for nearly all Dutch university degrees. Tuition fee loans are available from the Dutch government.

As mandatory elements of her degree, Charlie will study abroad for a semester and gain work experience (usually paid). She works part time as a student ambassador for the university already.

Chapter 1
Why study abroad?

UK students don't traditionally study abroad. Far more international students come to the UK than leave its shores to study. According to a study published in 2016 by the United Nations Educational, Scientific and Cultural Organization (UNESCO) Institute for Statistics, 416,693 international students came to the UK to study in 2013, while just 27,377 British students opted to study abroad. (Global Flow of Tertiary-Level Students, UNESCO Institute for Statistics (UIS), 2013, www.uis. unesco.org/datacentre.) International study might be a relatively new concept for UK students, but across much of the world it is far more common. China recorded the highest number of mobile students, with 717,157 students choosing to pursue higher education abroad, according to the UNESCO study.

The number of international students around the world has increased significantly in recent years: indeed, the Organisation for Economic Co-operation and Development (OECD) tells us that the number of students going abroad to study increased by 50% between 2005 and 2012 alone. However, in its latest report, the OECD has suggested that student mobility may slow in light of the current economic climate, which has seen a decrease in the level of financial support available to students, in the form of scholarships and grants (OECD (2015) *Education at a Glance 2015: OECD Indicators*, OECD Publishing, Paris, DOI: http://dx.doi.org/10.1787/ eag-2015-en.

Nonetheless, higher education institutions across the world are more eager than ever to recruit foreign students, and are taking steps to try to increase student mobility by offering educational programmes that integrate an international, cultural or global dimension, according to a 2015 report from the European Parliament's Committee on Culture and Education. To this end, a number of countries, which includes the UK, are leading the way in the internationalisation of higher education, and therefore offer an attractive prospect for students considering study abroad; these countries include France, Germany, Italy, the Netherlands, Norway, Spain, the USA, Canada, Australia, Japan, Malaysia and South Africa. (European Parliament (ed.) (2015). *Internationalisation of Higher Education*. Study upon the request of the Committee on Culture and Education. Retrieved from http://www.europarl.europa.eu/RegData/etudes/STUD/2015/540370/IPOL_STU(2015)540370_EN.pdf.)

Despite the relatively low figures with regard to UK student mobility, the number of UK students interested in studying abroad has risen in recent years. In its Broadening Horizons 2015 report, the British Council conducted a survey of 2,856 full-time UK students: of those surveyed, 34% expressed an interest in studying abroad. This is an increase of 14% from 2013's findings, where only 20% of respondents indicated that they were considering studying abroad (Broadening Horizons 2015: The value of the overseas experience, British Council, https://www.britishcouncil.org/sites/default/files/6.3_broadening-horizons-2015.pdf, 2015).

If you mention studying abroad, a common response is that we already have a world-class university system, so why look elsewhere? The answer is that there are numerous benefits of moving country to go to university, which is why UK students are starting to look at study options further afield, and in increasing numbers. There are plenty of reasons why study abroad might be beneficial: maybe you want to avoid higher tuition fees, to benefit from a rich cultural or educational experience or to gain a place at one of the top universities in the world.

Interest in overseas study has been steadily growing since the introduction of the fee increases in the UK. Studying abroad may seem an attractive prospect, but it is not necessarily an adequate enough reason to set sail for foreign shores. Things are changing so fast that it is hard to know what the economic, employment or educational landscape will look like in a year or two, while you might still be part-way through your overseas degree. So, it makes sense to consider overseas study in far more depth as part of your wider and longer-term plans; you will need to look carefully at the pros and cons of living and studying in another country before you make your decision.

The global market

As you walk around schools and colleges in other European countries, it is normal to see international opportunities on the notice boards; summer schools, study exchanges and overseas degrees are far more commonplace than in the UK. Young people in many other countries have come to expect international study experiences, and this gives them the opportunity to broaden their horizons and acquire a more global outlook.

This is not always the case in the UK and, unless young people begin to think more globally, we may risk being left behind, according to a recent report into the global skills gap, which highlights the growing gulf between what students currently learn in school and the global knowledge and skills needed to survive and succeed in a globalised world. The report, entitled

Bridging the Global Skills Gap, draws on data taken from a survey of 753 teachers, conducted by YouGov on behalf of Think Global. Of those teachers surveyed, 85% agreed that schools should prepare students to cope with a fast-changing, globalised world, but only 16% felt that this was currently being achieved by the school system, with two-thirds admitting to being worried that young people's horizons are not broad enough to operate in a global economy and society. In addition, according to another YouGov report, which surveyed undergraduates between the ages of 19 and 21 studying at UK universities, only 48% of respondents said that they believed an international outlook was beneficial to their work prospects (Bridging the Global Skills Gap: Teachers' views on how to prepare a Global Generation for the challenges ahead, © Think Global, http://think- global.org.uk/wp-content/uploads/dea/documents/Bridging%20the%20Global%20Skills%20Gap.pdf, 2013).

The British Chambers of Commerce carried out a survey of over 8,000 UK businesses, exploring barriers to exporting and international trade. The British Chambers of Commerce concluded that future business owners should be 'born global' and possess strong foreign language abilities.

Picture yourself having finished university and ready to look for work. If you consider the global marketplace when looking for jobs, then you will not only be competing against UK graduates, but against the brightest and best from across the world. And while the number of graduates from Western countries is starting to plateau, countries like China and India are producing more young graduates, many of whom choose to pursue international higher education. The market is becoming increasingly crowded and competitive.

Many organisations now do business or seek clients in more than one country, so job applicants with international experience, with the increased cultural awareness that this brings, have added value. Some students choose study abroad as the first step towards an international career. For example, those graduates who have spent a summer school in the States, or an exchange to Sweden as part of their first degree, followed by postgraduate study in Malaysia, have a head start.

> **❝** I feel I am having a much more international experience here than I ever would have had in England. I am studying in a diverse environment which is reflected in the debates and classes that we take part in. My class has such a range of nationalities that makes the lessons more dynamic, but it also has a real effect on personal development. By being in these classes you develop a more tolerant attitude and change your outlook completely on some things. **❞**
>
> *Clare Higgins, The Hague University of Applied Sciences, the Netherlands*

A 2011 report from the Association of Graduate Recruiters (AGR), Council for Industry and Higher Education (CIHE) and CFE (research and consultancy specialists in employment and skills) examines how global graduates can be developed. 'Students have a role to play in acquiring global competencies and choosing appropriate pathways to enable them to develop a global mindset. Experience of working outside their home country and immersion in a different culture can catapult a graduate into being considered for rewarding and challenging roles.'

The report's authors worked with multinational employers based in the UK to identify the most important qualities a global graduate will need. 'Global graduates require a blend of knowledge, competencies and corresponding attributes spanning global mindset, cultural agility and relationship management and must be able to apply them flexibly.'

Studying abroad can not only give you the opportunity to study in a new country, but also to choose a degree with an international focus, while studying alongside a group of students from across the world. Consider how all these aspects can help you to develop the global mindset that will prepare you for the international job market and the global economy.

Competition in the UK

Competition for university places

UCAS reports that in 2015, more students than ever before were offered places at UK universities. In total, 532,300 students enrolled on to higher education courses in the UK, an increase of 3.9% on the previous year (2015 End of Cycle Report, UCAS, www.ucas.com/end-of-cycle-reports).

Up until last year, a cap on the number of places available in England meant that for many popular courses, the demand outstripped the supply, meaning universities were able to pick and choose their candidates and ask for higher and higher requirements.

As of 2015 entry, the cap on places has been lifted, meaning that universities are now able to admit considerably more home students for most undergraduate courses.

Now that the cap has been lifted, competition has increased between universities in a bid to recruit students, with universities making 1.9 million offers to students in 2015, according to UCAS data (2015 End of Cycle Report, UCAS, www.ucas.com/end-of-cycle-reports). Last year also saw a record number of unconditional offers being made in light of the reforms, even among the highly selective Russell Group universities, with the University of Birmingham unveiling a new unconditional offer scheme in order to attract highly talented applicants.

Nonetheless, higher education institutions in the UK continue to place great importance on predicted grades and high academic achievement, and for some of the most competitive courses in the UK, such as medicine or veterinary science, there are tens of applications per place. Yet there are internationally recognised universities offering the same opportunities in the Caribbean and parts of Europe. Although you still need to demonstrate academic excellence and the right aptitude and attitude, the level of competition for places on these courses is not as extreme as it is in the UK. It is not surprising that applicants, frustrated by the limits in the UK, are looking for alternatives.

Some countries will accept you provided that you have achieved three A levels (or equivalent) but are less concerned about grades. This doesn't mean that they are less stringent in their entry processes; in some cases, they are more concerned with how you actually perform at university – if you don't achieve satisfactorily in your first year, they may ask you to leave.

A number of countries don't have a coordinated central application process like UCAS. On the downside, this may mean having to complete more application forms. On the positive side, it also means that you aren't limited in the number of applications you make, which can help you to keep your options open. You can even apply through UCAS at the same time as applying to overseas universities, all the while gathering the information you need to decide which option suits you best. Indeed, some students use an international university as a back-up option for their UK plans.

Competition for jobs

Many current students and recent graduates understand all too clearly the effects of the upsurge in numbers in higher education over the past decade. The increase in numbers of graduates, exacerbated by the recent economic challenges, is creating a very crowded graduate job market. Yet the more graduates there are, the more pressure there is to get a degree, in order to compete with other jobseekers. A degree has become essential yet, conversely, a degree alone is not enough. Students are looking for ways in which to stand out and to get an edge over the competition. Studying abroad can be a way to achieve all these things.

> ❝ Global leaders need to be willing to work in different locations as an integral part of their career but many employers have difficulty recruiting graduates willing to travel or relocate. Employers felt that graduates with a global mindset would be more likely to embrace international immersion and relish the opportunity to work in different countries. It is essential that leaders are positioned where they are most needed and thus able to respond to market demands. ❞
>
> (Diamond, A., Walkley, L. et al., Global Graduates into Global Leaders, www.ncub.co.uk/reports/global-graduates-into-global-leaders.html [Online] accessed May 2016.)

As Dr Jo Beall, British Council's Executive Board member with responsibility for Education and Society, explains: 'The good news is that people are beginning to recognise how vital international skills are for enhancing their career. Research last year revealed that more UK employers look for international awareness and experience alongside academic qualifications. But the bad news is that not enough people in the UK are taking opportunities to gain international experience. That needs to change for the UK to successfully compete in the global economy. Our recent research showed that while almost two-thirds of students felt they had an international outlook, they failed to see the potential career advantages to be gained from international experiences.'

Financial benefits

Tuition fees of up to £9,000 per year are charged in England for undergraduate courses. Fees will continue to be charged at these rates for students starting university in 2016. However, tuition fees may be subject to further increases from autumn 2017: in May 2016, the government published its white paper, *Success as a Knowledge Economy*, outlining proposals that would allow English universities offering high-quality teaching to raise tuition fees above £9,000, in line with inflation.

At undergraduate level, in Wales, tuition fees of up to £9,000 per year are charged. Students from Wales can apply for a tuition fee loan of up to £3,805; if their university fees are higher than this amount, they are also eligible to receive a fee grant of up to £5,100 to cover the remaining balance. Fees in Northern Ireland (for students from Northern Ireland) are capped at £3,925. Undergraduate study in Scotland remains free for Scottish students, although students from the rest of the UK studying in Scotland will pay fees of up to £9,000 per year.

On top of the increasing fees, repayment options for student loans are also looking less appealing. Currently, in England and Wales, an interest rate of RPI plus 3% (making a total of 3.9% for 2015–2016) will be charged on your loan from day one, with variable rates charged once you graduate, depending on your earnings. The UK is not a cheap place to live at the moment either, with the cost of living remaining fairly high. So, in addition to hefty debts from fees, you could face less reasonable terms on your loan and high costs of living on graduation.

Unsurprisingly, students and parents are now wondering whether there might be a more financially attractive proposition elsewhere. There are public universities in some countries, such as Germany and Norway, where tuition is free, regardless of nationality. Many overseas public universities charge less than England, Wales and Northern Ireland – in countries such as France and Ireland, for example. There are countries with considerably cheaper costs of living (the Czech Republic or Malaysia, for example) and there are universities with generous scholarships and sources of student financial support (for example, the USA and the Netherlands). Graduates from certain overseas universities may come home with the ideal situation of no debt (or at least smaller debt), as well as many of the other benefits introduced in this chapter.

> **66** Belgium offered a world-renowned university at the heart of Europe for a fraction of the tuition price at American and British institutions. **99**
>
> *Tom Aitchison, KU Leuven, Belgium*

Academic benefits

There can be academic benefits to studying abroad: for example, the chance to try out a number of subjects before specialising; or the opportunity to study new subjects or specialist options that are not available in the UK. Some countries are world leaders in specific subjects: Australia, for example, is known for its geology and marine biology courses, among others. Other countries offer a different perspective on familiar subjects, such as veterinary medicine or history. Or, perhaps you relish the opportunity to study a subject in its natural setting – Arctic studies or American literature, for example.

> **❝** The style of learning is very similar to A levels in that you are taking multiple subjects at once. Because of this, each of my classes feels very interdisciplinary. For example, there is a Math major in my English class, who brings a different perspective to the texts compared to a History major, for example. **❞**
>
> *Stephanie Addenbrooke, Yale University, USA*

Studying abroad may give you a more realistic chance of studying at a world-class university; outside the UK, some of the best universities in the world can be more accessible in terms of the grades they expect and in the scholarships they offer. Individual countries place different importance on entrance exams, face-to-face interviews, exam results, and hobbies and interests. You may find that what is required by other universities across the world plays to your strengths better than what the UK asks of you.

You will have the chance to experience a different academic environment, with access to various types of campus and university facilities. Some universities offer much smaller classes than in the UK, better tutor-contact time or high-profile internships; finding out exactly what is on offer is an essential part of your research.

You may even find that the styles of teaching and learning outside the UK suit you better. For example, in Australia teaching is often more informal and lecturers are approachable and accessible; in Denmark, meanwhile, much is made of problem-based learning.

Personal benefits

Studying abroad can be a great adventure, as it broadens your horizons and throws up new and unexpected challenges. It is hardly surprising that so many students come home from time overseas feeling more confident, mature and independent. Understanding that there are different ways of doing things can make you more flexible. Learning to cope in an unfamiliar situation reinforces your adaptability and ability to use your initiative. Most universities arrange lots of events to let international students meet one another and get settled in, so your social skills will get some practice too.

International experience helps individuals to develop communication, problem-solving, critical-thinking and analytical skills, in addition to supporting personal development, according to a 2015 study conducted by CFE Research and LSE Enterprise on behalf of the British Council, which surveyed 1,148 UK residents, of whom 712 had studied, worked or travelled abroad. Of those who had attended university overseas, over half felt the experience had helped them to find a job that they were interested in, with 76% saying that they were confident in their ability to

communicate with people from other countries and cultures
as a result of their experience studying abroad, and two-thirds
reporting that their experience played a key part in helping them
to develop a creative mindset.

> **" "** The values and memories that studying abroad
> gives you are always worth it and they equip you
> with skills to do it again or adapt to similar alien situations
> in the future. **" "**
>
> *Tom Aitchison, KU Leuven, Belgium*
>
> **" "** Difficulties aside, the positive aspects of living
> abroad far outweigh the negative in terms of what
> internationals gain in experience and open-mindedness, and
> the rich multicultural friendships that they make along the
> way. **" "**
>
> *Elizabeth Edwards, Otto-Friedrich-Universität,*
> *Bamberg, Germany*

The report's authors concluded that 'people who had travelled,
worked or studied abroad indicated that as a result of the experience
they had increased confidence and improved verbal communication
and analytical and critical thinking skills. They reported an
increased understanding of foreign cultures and an awareness of
international affairs. They felt they were more tolerant of difference
and were more confident in their ability to adapt to new and
unfamiliar situations. The experience also helped them to clarify
their personal priorities.' In addition, the research showed that
'participation in international opportunities can support individuals
developing fulfilling career paths'. (A world of experience: How
international opportunities benefit individuals and employers and

support UK prosperity, British Council, www.britishcouncil.org/
sites/default/files/_a_world_of_experience.pdf, 2015.)

The list of personal benefits goes on and on. Many courses
delivered in English attract a wide and varied mix of international
students, not just those from English-speaking countries. The
chance to make friends from across the world will make you more
culturally aware, but also means a wider network of contacts for
future life and work.

Even if you are being taught in English, studying in a non-
English-speaking country means that you will need to develop
your language skills in order to be able to communicate effectively.
Most institutions will offer language courses to their students to
supplement their studies. Language skills can make you more
employable; Britain lags behind the rest of Europe with regard to
its foreign-language skills: in its 2013 report, 'Languages for the
Future', the British Council highlighted the language deficit that
exists in the UK, and the need for the UK to improve its linguistic
capabilities. According to the study, the level of achievement
of pupils in England in the European Survey on Language
Competences was lower than that of all other participating
countries, while the number of students taking languages at
A level has been decreasing year on year, with fewer than one
in every twenty-six students progressing beyond a basic level
in a foreign language. In addition, the report cites a survey of
businesses carried out by the Confederation of British Industry in
2013, which reveals that among the businesses surveyed, only 36%
were satisfied with their employees' language abilities, with seven
out of ten businesses stating the value they place on language skills
in their employees. (Languages for the Future: which languages
the UK needs most and why, British Council, www.britishcouncil.
org/sites/default/files/languages-for-the-future-report.pdf, 2013.)

Think how beneficial language skills could be to your future prospects.

> **❝** My plan is to return to the UK with two new languages in my repertoire (Dutch and an understanding of German) and an experience which would rival that of any graduate from the UK. **❞**
>
> *Simran Gill, Fontys University of Applied Sciences,*
> *the Netherlands*

Studying in another country can also give you access to lifestyle options that aren't accessible or affordable in the UK. If you fancy a sauna in your apartment building, try Finland. Or how about surfing before lectures in Australia? If you're looking for a great place to ski, parts of the USA or Canada have much to offer.

You might get the chance to work overseas too, perhaps part time, alongside your studies, or as part of an internship, co-op programme or placement related to your subject. Essentially, you will get the chance to develop an international outlook, which is so important in today's global society.

The employer's view

When considering overseas study as part of a longer-term plan, you need to be sure of your prospects when you return to the UK. So what kinds of competencies could you develop through overseas study that would be attractive to employers back in the UK? Here are the views of some top employers.

> **66** Cultural dexterity is important: an ability not to impose one's own culture on another one, to be sensitive to other cultures and how to do business in different environments. There are certain ways of working with clients in the Middle East that you wouldn't adopt in Japan. **99**
>
> *PWC*

> **66** Adaptability and self-awareness are probably the two things that we find the toughest to find ... we want our graduates to feel they fit with our culture and hit the ground running. **99**
>
> *HSBC*

> **66** If you have people that can integrate with local teams, or who are able to move globally and take with them their experience in a seamless way, I think that can only help the business move forward. A lot of our work is very dependent on engaging with local governments [and] other local and national oil companies, and we need to be able to work with them effectively. **99**
>
> *BP*

> **66** You need the mindset that says, 'The person I'm talking to isn't like me and I need to understand what they are like and then work with them.' It isn't only about having the technical knowledge, it's also necessary to understand the values, customs, cultures and behaviours that are significant to them. **99**
>
> *National Grid (Source: Diamond, A., Walkley, L. et al., Global Graduates into Global Leaders, www.ncub.co.uk/ reports/global-graduates-into-global-leaders.html, [Online] accessed May 2016.)*

A 2013 British Council report, Culture at Work, considered the views of recruitment specialists at 360 large organisations from nine countries, including the UK. The employers could clearly see the benefits that intercultural skills could bring to a company's earnings. They also identified the risks, including financial risk, of not having employees with these skills, which included:

- loss of clients
- damage to an organisation's reputation
- team conflict.

(Culture at Work: The value of intercultural skills in the workplace, British Council, https://www.britishcouncil.org/sites/default/files/culture-at-work-report-v2.pdf, 2013.)

If you choose to study overseas, you should develop many of the qualities that these organisations are looking for, but you will still need to be sure that you can articulate these strengths to potential employers. Think about how you could sell your international experiences, your ability in foreign languages and your intercultural skills at interview.

Why *not* go?

Of course, studying abroad isn't the right choice for everyone and there are a number of reasons why you might not choose to take this option. Some of the reasons that make international study ideal for one person (the chance to have an adventure or take a leap into the unknown, for example) might make it a daunting prospect for another.

In the British Council's Broadening Horizons report, students were asked about the main concerns they had regarding overseas study, and were told to choose from a range of options. Some of the most common responses included:

- 'I am concerned about access to quality healthcare.'
- 'I find it difficult to leave my family/parents.'
- 'Overseas tuition fees are high.'
- 'I am not confident about my language ability.'
- 'I am concerned about getting a visa.'
- 'Overseas degrees are not recognised in the UK.'
- 'I don't want to leave my home country.'

(Broadening Horizons 2015: The value of the overseas experience, British Council, https://www.britishcouncil.org/sites/default/files/6.3_broadening-horizons-2015.pdf, 2015.)

You do need a certain amount of confidence to take this step. It is a braver move than simply following the crowd and it does involve certain risks. You are further from home if things go wrong, although many students overseas talk of the support network they build up of university staff, room-mates and fellow students.

> **❝** I was surprised at how friendly every single person I met was; people I didn't know would say hello to me all the time, which is also part of being such a small institution – there are fewer than 700 students here. **❞**
>
> *Katherine Taylor, Bennington College, USA*

The need for thorough preparation and research

Ideally, you need to be fully prepared to take this step. Getting a place through Clearing in the UK can be a stressful process and

can lead to students feeling the pressure to accept courses or
institutions for which they are not suited. Imagine how it feels
when you end up in a different country. After A level results day in
August there is often great interest in late opportunities overseas,
but not always the time and space to make an informed decision.
A rushed decision doesn't always end up being a negative one, but
there are benefits from taking your time with this process.

> 66 The Dutch universities start earlier so I had not
> even enrolled, had no financial aid or plan, don't
> speak any Dutch and had no accommodation, so I felt very
> unprepared. 99
>
> *Clare Higgins, The Hague University of*
> *Applied Sciences, the Netherlands*

When considering an unfamiliar education system, you need to
find out far more about the type and reputation of an institution,
the way you will be taught and assessed, the qualifications you
will gain, the grading system and so on; you can't assume that
anything will be the same as in the UK.

Financial reasons

One of the downsides to overseas study is the lack of UK student
financial support you can access. With no loans from the UK
government for full-time study abroad, you will need to find some
money to cover fees and living costs before you go.

That being said, as of 2014, the Scottish government has
been trialling the Portability Pilot scheme, in a bid to open up
opportunities abroad to Scottish students. Under the scheme,
students who choose to study at specific institutions in Europe

have access to the same type of financial support (based on household income) that they would receive if they were to attend university in Scotland. All the eligible universities in the scheme offer undergraduate courses that are taught in English. These are:

- University of Maastricht, the Netherlands
- University of Groningen, the Netherlands
- Rhine-Waal University of Applied Sciences, Germany
- University of Southern Denmark, Denmark
- Malmo University, Sweden.

The pilot is being evaluated by the Scottish government over the course of a three-year intake (2014–2017), and is due to finish at the end of the academic year 2016–2017. However, funding will continue to be available after summer 2017, so Scottish students interested in the scheme will receive support for the full duration of their undergraduate degree. For the latest information on the progress of the scheme going forwards, check the website for the Student Awards Agency for Scotland at www.saas.gov.uk.

If you need to apply for a visa, you will need to provide evidence that you have sufficient funds for study. Don't forget to factor in additional costs for application fees, travel, admissions tests, visa applications or insurance, for example.

> **"** Remember that start-up costs are a lot. Whether it is desk lamps or mattresses, it soon spirals. Your first month's living costs will likely be twice as high as a normal month. **"**
>
> *Tom Aitchison, KU Leuven, Belgium*

There may be some opportunities for scholarships, and occasionally even grants and loans, from your host country. Even if you're lucky enough to get a scholarship or financial support from the country where you study, chances are that you'll need additional funds to supplement living and studying in the country and to be prepared in case of an emergency. If you plan to work to fund your studies, don't bank on getting work straight away, particularly if you don't yet speak the language.

Language barrier

If you are studying in a country where English isn't an official language, even though your course may be taught in English, you will still need to manage away from the university. A rental agreement for accommodation or an application for a bank account, for example, will be in another language, so you will need to consider how you might cope. If most of your fellow students don't speak English as a first language, you may feel isolated in social situations.

Learning a new language is likely to be highly beneficial, but it is another commitment on top of your studies. If you are concerned about the language barrier, it is worth finding out how widely English is spoken in your chosen country and whether the institution takes many students from English-speaking countries.

> **66** Whether the population is bilingual in English or not, always make an effort to learn the language. It is probably the biggest barrier to forming new friendships, which are much more important when living away from home. **99**
>
> *Catherine Foreshaw, University of Malta*

Adjusting

You will need to be prepared to make adjustments if you decide to study abroad.

Education

Teaching and learning can vary considerably from country to country and between individual institutions (as you'll learn in Chapters 5 to 11). Expectations about what you should achieve in your first year can be very high, often determining whether you are allowed to stay on into the second year. The workload may be heavier than you would expect in the UK and terminology may be unfamiliar.

It will be a steep learning curve, so you will need to use your initiative and seek help to avoid falling behind.

Lifestyle

Moving abroad means that your normal way of life will be thrown into disarray. The familiar and comforting will have disappeared, replaced by the new and strange, and the life you expect to lead at university may not always be realised. You may spend a disproportionate amount of time studying, adjusting to the new education system and working (rather than socialising). You may find that other home students from the host country are older or living at home. There will be cultural and social differences in terms of the ways you spend your time and you will be far away from your normal support network of family and friends. In combination, these factors often lead to feelings of culture shock and homesickness. It is quite normal to feel this way, but it is an adjustment that you will need to consider.

Risks

Although many people love their experience of studying abroad, it is not risk-free. You might be concerned about whether you will get a visa, how you will manage financially, or worry about the distance from family and friends. International study can bring a degree of flexibility, but there may be more restrictions in the choices that you make, particularly if you need a visa. It can be problematic to change institution or course once you start. It is not always possible to change your reason for being in a country, from studying to full-time work, for example, so you need to be fairly sure of your plans before you depart.

> **66** There is a big restaurant scene in Doha, but a limited number of bars and they are all located in hotels. Much of student life when we are not working revolves around cultural events, socialising at the souqs, or going to the beach and malls. **99**
>
> *Benedict Leigh, UCL Qatar, Qatar*
>
> **66** Read up on the culture before you get there. Malta is a very Catholic country and the culture is completely different to what I've grown up with – embrace it and love it, as their way of life is actually a lot more fun than ours! **99**
>
> *Catherine Foreshaw, University of Malta*

No matter how thoroughly you plan and research, you cannot know what you will be faced with when you come to leave university, so you cannot assume that the opportunities of today will still be there tomorrow. You may find that employers do not recognise or understand your degree, even if it is equivalent to those available in the UK. Even if you're attending a world-ranked university, UK employers may fail to recognise its status. Perhaps you initially planned to stay on in a country, but economic conditions made that difficult. Courses that meet certain professional standards today might not fit the bill tomorrow, so it is worth considering a back-up plan, where possible.

Finally, international education is big business, so there are people out there trying to make money from bogus institutions, low-quality education provision and non-existent accommodation. Be on your guard and use some of the tips and reputable sources of information found in this book.

Having gathered and considered all the information that you need, you may just get the feeling that studying abroad is not the right option for you. If it isn't the right step right now, you don't necessarily need to rule it out for ever. You might want to consider alternatives to taking your full degree abroad (see page 71) or you might choose to study or work abroad at a later stage in life.

Many of the trailblazing students who have already taken the step of taking their full degree overseas have additional reasons for going. Some have already spent some time abroad, have family members who live overseas or have personal links to a country before they decide to study there. This is changing: as a degree overseas has started to become more common, more attractive and more understood in the UK, students are now making the move without necessarily having those personal links beforehand.

If you're looking for ...

- If you're looking for some of the cheapest fees, try **Europe** (Chapter 5).
- If you're looking for a similar student lifestyle to that of the UK, try **Ireland** (page 156), **the Netherlands** (page 168) and many of the **US campus universities** (Chapter 6).

- If you're looking for accelerated degrees or tailor-made education, try a **private university** (page 37).
- If you're looking for a low cost of living, try **eastern Europe** (Chapter 5), **South Africa** (page 345) or **Malaysia** (page 322).
- If you're looking for the best in the world, try the **USA** (Chapter 6).
- If you're looking for a different culture, try **Qatar** (page 336), **Hong Kong** (page 311) or **Japan** (page 317).
- If you're looking for no tuition fees, try **Germany** (page 149) or **Norway** (page 175).
- If you're looking for outdoor activities, try **Canada** (Chapter 7), **Australia** (Chapter 8) or **New Zealand** (Chapter 9).
- If you're looking for the opportunity to stay on after study, try **Europe** (Chapter 5), **Canada** (page 260), **Australia** (page 280) or **New Zealand** (page 304).

Student testimonial, A Star Future
Vincent Hendricks
University: Bocconi University, Italy
Course: International Economics and Management (BIEM)
Year: Second year
School attended in the UK: Bournemouth Collegiate School, Bournemouth

1. Why go abroad?

I have an international background and only moved to the UK when I was 15 to do my A levels. Having spent three years in England for school, it felt like studying in England at university level would not add more value to me as a person (from an experience, personal development and academic point of view). Bocconi seemed to be the perfect fit. Why? Because it gives you the right balance between cultural experience (quality of life) and top-class academic education, which ultimately is what every determined student should look for when choosing a university destination.

2. How would you rate the assistance of the university before you arrived (the application process, finding accommodation, sorting out financial matters)?

All application procedures are explained on the website. Sometimes the language (Italian) seemed to be an issue (by the way, the application process is completely in English; however, some parts, such as financial, were in Italian), but the admission office responded quickly to any emails sent regarding assistance. It is all online, so accessible from all over the world, and works similar to UCAS. If candidates are not wiling to sit ACT or SAT standardised tests, students should come over to Milan to sit the "Bocconi Test", which can also be a great opportunity to combine a visit to the university and the city.

The university provides plenty of accommodation possibilities, which can be booked very easily (recommended for freshers).

Financial matters are easy to sort, and are mostly communicated online. Scholarships (merit-based) are assigned based on the outcome of the selection process, so no long application for that is required. Need-based scholarships do require a bit more paperwork filling.

3. How would you rate the assistance of the university when you arrived (orientation, etc.)?

Welcome week included social events and crash courses (maths and Italian). A lot of 'indirect' (email, offices, etc.) assistance is available if needed.

4. Did you feel prepared when you arrived and/or what surprised you?

Moving to a completely new environment is always accompanied with some minor issues (e.g. bank accounts, tax codes, phone contracts, etc.); however, the university is in partnership with an on-campus bank, and all essential shops are in the area. Language is also not an issue.

5. How would you rate the learning environment (teaching style, studying with other international students, non-native English-speaking lecturers)?

The international academic standards are really good and continue to improve every year. All lecture notes are also available online (e-learning platform). The mix of nationalities in the classes (which consist of approximately 100 students per class) is well distributed, with around 40% Italians (with high English-speaking standards) and 60% internationals from all over the world (important contacts for life). Professors, too, come from many different countries, or are Italians who have worked and studied abroad. There is also the option to catch up on lectures independently online at home.

6. Would you recommend studying abroad to a 17–18-year-old Brit who might never have thought about it before?

I always ask myself 'why stay here if there is a whole world of opportunities out there to explore?'. Sure, moving abroad is not an easy choice and will require some determination during the first weeks of arrivals; however, it is an investment for your future, it makes you stand out from your friends who stay in the UK and it teaches you essential attributes for life. It is the right step in the right direction for those students who aim to have a successful international future.

7. Is there anything you wish someone had told you at the time you applied?

Make sure you compare all the different courses (in detail, subjects they include, credits, etc.) that each university offers, so you can be certain that the course, which you will spend three years of your life doing, is the right one for you.

8. Would you recommend your course, university, city to British students?

Living in one of the most prestigious cities in the world, with the seaside and Alps each two hours away (perfect for weekend trips) and gaining a higher education at one of the top five universities in Europe for the course speaks for itself. You can have a great time here if you are up for the challenge (and willing to adapt).

Università Bocconi is the highest-ranked non-US or -UK university for economics in the world: www.topuniversities.com/ university-rankings/university-subject-rankings/2015/economics-econometrics.

Tuition fees are variable. Vincent provides some information above but for British students they will be in the range of €5,200 to €11,600. These are dependent on family income. A student's family would need to earn more than approximately £93,000 a year before they would pay the full fees. In addition to this financial support, merit-based awards are also available and for international students, this might result in a 100% reduction in tuition. While no student loans are automatically available to British students in Italy, all Bocconi students can apply for a bank loan from Intesa Sanpaolo but only from the second year onwards, while German passport holders can apply for a special loan from Deutsche Bank.

Chapter 2

What you need to know before you go

It is normal to have concerns and to feel some anxiety about whether studying abroad is the right step for you. As we have already seen in Chapter 1, common worries include the cost of fees and access to finance; the prospect of leaving family and friends; concerns about getting a visa; whether your qualifications will be recognised when you return home; and fear of adjusting to another country, culture or language.

This chapter aims to put your mind at rest by addressing some of the questions you may have about making the move overseas.

Education

Don't assume that education overseas will be just like the system in the UK. There are lots of questions that need to be addressed: When does the academic year start? How long do bachelor's degrees take? How do I know if my university or course is genuine?

Length of study and academic year

When you start to look at the options for overseas study, it is important to understand that many countries operate a four-year bachelor's degree and a two-year master's degree. When comparing the academic experience and the cost of fees and living, an extra year can make a significant difference.

Other countries may also differ in terms of when their academic year begins and when you can join a course. Many European universities start in late August or early September, which will require early application, or may even mean you having to defer your place until the following year. However, some universities offer more than one start date during the year, which can save you having to wait a full year for the next intake.

Differences in teaching and learning

Education systems vary across the world, so you will encounter some differences when you study in another country. University in the UK requires independent study and critical thinking. In some countries (although less so in Europe and the Western world) university education can be more tutor-led, following set texts. You need to know how education works in your chosen country (and institution, see Different types of institution on page 37) and how you will be taught and assessed. If you study in a country where every course is assessed by means of an exam, you need to be able to cope under exam pressure. Before you apply, you should check whether the style of education suits your method of learning. Finding out what to expect will help you prepare for any differences when you arrive. Your university will be able to tell you more.

To prepare yourself and improve your chances of success, find out as much as you can about what to expect. Read through the course information and make a start on any recommended reading before you get there. See the chapters on 'Studying in ...' for more details.

> 66 I would say that education in Brazil is much more tutor-led; Brazilian students have their hands held much more than in the UK. 99
>
> *Justin Axel-Berg, University of São Paulo, Brazil*

> 66 Teachers are always addressed by their surnames and generally keep a distance from their students, tending not to treat them as equals. I am used to a more informal relationship with my teachers, so this is something that I have had to become accustomed to. 99
>
> *Elizabeth Edwards, Otto-Friedrich-Universität,*
> *Bamberg, Germany*

> 66 I found academically McGill was fairly different to my regular university, Edinburgh. There is a very competitive and driven atmosphere around the university, and the policies of almost continuous exams and testing, with mid-term exams dotted throughout the semester as well as finals and assignments, means that you have to work incredibly hard. 99
>
> *Laura Bowker, McGill University, Canada*

> 66 I have a very close relationship with all of my professors. Classes rarely, if ever, exceed 30 students. 99
>
> *Joshua Jackson, SP Jain School of Global Management,*
> *Singapore and Australia*

Different types of institution

Having local knowledge can be reassuring; in the UK, you may already understand which universities are considered to be the best, which have strong vocational backgrounds or which are seen to be weaker. It is much more difficult to make these comparisons on an international scale, particularly where the education system is unfamiliar.

As you research your chosen countries, find out about the various types of institution and how they differ. In Finland, and in a number of other European countries, universities offer research-based education, while universities of applied science offer work-related education. In the USA, you can choose between university and community college. The reputation (but also cost and competitiveness) of the different types of institution may vary.

Although there are only a handful of private institutions with UK degree-awarding powers, it is a different case overseas. The USA has many private providers, and there are plenty to be found across the rest of the world too. Private universities offer a variety of different features: they tend to have higher fees, but often offer more generous scholarships and financial aid. They may provide a more supported or bespoke service, with accelerated programmes, low student–teacher ratio and personalised tuition and internships. Don't rule private universities out on a cost basis alone; in some cases they might end up the better-value option, due to the financial support available and the opportunities to choose a tailor-made education.

University rankings

If you are seeking a particular type of institution, you might like to compare potential overseas universities to those that you are familiar with in the UK. Use worldwide university rankings to get an idea of how your chosen institutions fare on the world stage and how they compare to institutions that you know from the UK. Look at which international universities choose to work in partnership with a familiar university back home; it is likely that partner institutions will share some characteristics. For example, the University of Manchester has links with universities in a number of other countries, including Australia, Canada, Hong Kong, Japan, New Zealand, Singapore and the USA, while the University of Birmingham has partner institutions in China, India and Brazil.

Here in the UK, you are probably familiar with the national league tables, but you might not know so much about worldwide rankings. Pay attention to worldwide league tables (Times Higher Education World University Rankings, QS Top Universities, and Academic Ranking of World Universities, for example) to see how your chosen UK university measures up against the global competition. Many universities that we might not recognise as household names are outperforming UK universities: for example, the USA's Northwestern University, Tsinghua University in China and the Swiss Federal Institute of Technology in Zurich are all rated more highly than the University of Manchester and the University of Bristol in the Times Higher Education World University Rankings 2015–2016.

Try some of the following league tables:

- **Times Higher Education World University Rankings:**
  www.timeshighereducation.com/world-university-rankings
- **Academic Ranking of World Universities (ARWU):**
  www.shanghairanking.com
- **QS Top Universities:**
  www.topuniversities.com/university-rankings
- **Financial Times Business School Rankings:**
  http://rankings.ft.com/businessschoolrankings/rankings.

If you are going to use league tables as part of your research, make sure you don't use them in isolation and that you understand what they are measuring. In this book, we use the Times Higher Education World University Rankings 2015–2016 throughout; however, if world rankings are likely to play a part in helping you to narrow down your options, it is important to bear in mind that each league table sets its own criteria when assessing institutions, so the rankings may vary considerably between different tables. For instance, for 2015–2016, the Australian National University features in the top 20 of the QS World University Rankings, but it is ranked at number 52 in the Times Higher Education table.

What is more, a league table can't tell you whether a university is the right choice for you. The methods used to rank universities mean that large, research-based, English-speaking universities tend to do best. It is worth noting that many of the universities that don't make it into the top few hundred in the world can still offer you a good-quality education that might suit your needs perfectly.

An alternative to the traditional league tables is U-Multirank (www.u-multirank.eu), a resource that allows you to compare universities based on a range of different data. On the site, you are given two options: the first allows you to compare 'like with like' by viewing similar universities side-by-side, based on your preferred type of institution. If you choose this option, you will be either able to compare by subject area, or compare the universities as a whole. Alternatively, you can research a specific university, and then filter your search by choosing from a range of options, including research and international orientation. Once you have made your selection, U-Multirank will find similar universities for comparison.

UK equivalence

There are two aspects to consider in regard to the equivalence of qualifications. Will your qualifications be accepted by your chosen overseas institution? And, when your studies are over, will a degree from your institution be recognised when you return to the UK?

The International Baccalaureate and A levels tend to be well-recognised overseas and often meet the minimum entry requirements of international universities. In some cases, they exceed the requirements. In the USA, for example, you may be able to join an associate degree course at a community college without A levels; you can find out more in Chapter 6, Studying in the USA.

Other qualifications, such as Scottish Highers, or vocational qualifications, such as BTEC Diplomas, may need to be verified by a centre of academic recognition. Overseas universities don't tend to include Highers or vocational qualifications within their published entry criteria, but you shouldn't assume that these qualifications won't be accepted. Each country has its own system for comparing international qualifications to those in a student's home country. Go to ENIC-NARIC (European Network of Information Centres – National Academic Recognition Information Centres in the EU) at www.enic-naric.net to find out about the academic recognition process in the country where you wish to study. For countries that are not listed, try their Ministry of Education.

For all of the countries listed within this book, degrees at undergraduate and postgraduate level taken at accredited universities are equivalent to the level offered in the UK; this means that you should be able to use them to access further study or graduate-level employment on your return to the UK.

However, you will need to do further checks to ensure that your qualifications meet any professional requirements; see Professional recognition below for more information.

Most UK degrees are classed as honours degrees, which represent a minimum of 360 credits of full-time study completed over three years, and often involve a dissertation or project in the final year. Although an honours degree is the norm in England, Wales and Northern Ireland, many countries outside the UK don't offer honours degrees as standard; they might offer an ordinary or general bachelor's degree instead. Where honours degrees are available, they might require an additional year of study, in addition to the preparation of a dissertation or thesis. You will need to check whether your degree is classed as an honours degree or not, as this may have a bearing on your future plans, particularly if you intend to undertake further study.

A number of the students featured in this book have decided to stay on in their chosen country or move to a new country for further study or work. If you decide to do the same, you may also need to check how your qualification compares to the academic standards in your new country of residence. You can do this through one of the National Academic Recognition Information Centres (NARIC); for a list of national centres, go to www.enic-naric.net. If your country isn't listed, your university's international office or the Ministry of Education in your chosen country will be able to advise further.

Professional recognition

If you intend to practise a particular profession on your return to the UK, or plan to undertake further study to fulfil this aim, it is essential that your qualification is accepted, otherwise you will have wasted precious time and money.

If you know that you want to move into a particular field, you should check with the relevant professional organisations in the country where you hope to practise. So, if you want to be a doctor in the UK, you could check your qualifications with the General Medical Council, while prospective architects should contact the Architects Registration Board.

The National Contact Point for Professional Qualifications in the UK (UKNCP) www.ecctis.co.uk/uk%20ncp, aids the mobility of professionals across Europe. If you return to the UK with a professional qualification, UKNCP can advise you on any regulations in your profession and outline the steps you will need to take before finding employment. They can also direct you to the relevant authorities in other countries across Europe. To find professional bodies outside Europe, you should speak to your overseas university's careers service.

A list of UK-regulated professions and contact details for the professional bodies can be found on the UKNCP website. These bodies should have clear guidelines on acceptable qualifications. Check before you go and keep checking as you continue your studies. There is a risk that changes may be made to these guidelines while you are midway through your studies; some students have been affected in this way. Should this happen, there may be options for further study to make up any shortfall in knowledge or expertise.

Quality and reputation

One natural concern for many students is about the quality of the education they will receive overseas. The UK has its own systems for quality assurance, but how do you check whether international universities meet the same stringent standards? When you are making decisions from a distance, how can you be sure that your university even exists, let alone that it is a genuine provider of quality education?

There is money to be made from international students, so you need to be aware of potential scams and discrepancies between what an institution says it will offer and what it actually delivers. You want to be sure that any money you spend is going towards a good-quality education that will deliver what you expect.

You can verify that your institution is recognised with education authorities or similar government bodies in your chosen country by using www.enic-naric.net, which features a list of recognised universities from over 50 countries, as well as information on their education systems. Bear in mind that if you need to apply for a visa, there may well be a requirement for you to attend a recognised university. You are safer and better protected within an accredited and recognised university.

Ask your university about inspection or quality assurance procedures. Most countries will have national (or regional) organisations that ensure that universities meet the required standards. You may be able to read their inspection reports online. You can find further information on the quality assurance systems for higher education at www.enic-naric.net.

Using reliable and official websites, such as those included in this book, should help you to find accredited and quality-assured universities. Use common sense when trawling through information and be suspicious of some of the following points:

- a purportedly official website full of errors, adverts or broken links
- an institution offering courses at rock-bottom prices
- if entry requirements are much lower than comparable institutions
- if you are being offered the chance to gain a qualification much more quickly than normal.

How to apply

Most countries don't have the equivalent of UCAS, i.e., a centralised admissions system, so give yourself time to complete multiple applications. You may have to apply on paper, rather than online, so allow time for your application to be delivered (and make copies, in case it gets lost in the post). Make note of the deadlines included in Chapters 5 to 11, so you don't miss the chance to have your application considered.

Countries operating centralised applications include Denmark, Finland, the Netherlands, Sweden and (for some courses) Germany.

 Studielink, Holland's equivalent of UCAS, is simple to navigate and free. 99
Simran Gill, Fontys University of Applied Sciences,
the Netherlands

There may be entrance exams and additional tests that you need to sit in order to be considered for a place. These might include the Scholastic Assessment Test (SAT), Graduate Record Exam (GRE) revised General Test or Graduate Australian Medical Schools Admission Test (GAMSAT). If English is your first language and you will be studying in English, you are unlikely to be tested on your English-language skills. Check with your institution, or see Chapters 5 to 11 for more details. Once you have been offered a place, and where fees are payable, you may then need to pay a deposit to secure your place.

Costs

Fees vary widely and depend on the country where you choose to study; where you are from; the type of institution you are attending; and the level of your course. Public universities in Germany offer free tuition at undergraduate level, regardless of your nationality, although you will still incur nominal fees per semester; for more details, see Chapter 5. Countries such as France, Spain and Italy, meanwhile, charge relatively low fees.

> **❝❝** In countries from the European Union and the European Economic Area (EEA), the same tuition fees are charged for nationals and students from the EU and EEA countries. In Austria, for example, the average tuition fees charged by public institutions for students who are not citizens of EU or European Economic Area (EEA) countries are twice the fees charged for citizens of these countries (for bachelor, master and doctorate programmes in public institutions). Similar policies are found in Australia, Belgium (French and Flemish communities), Canada, Chile, the Czech Republic, Denmark (as of 2006–07), Estonia, Ireland, the Netherlands, New Zealand (except for foreign PhD students), Poland, Portugal, the Russian Federation, Sweden (as of 2011), Turkey, the United Kingdom and the United States. **❞❞**
>
> (OECD (2015) *Education at a Glance 2015: OECD Indicators*, OECD Publishing, Paris, DOI: http://dx.doi.org/10.1787/eag-2015-en)

Currently, the UK remains a member of the EU, and the information above still applies to British citizens. The fee agreement for British students in EU and EEA countries is to be arranged as part of the UK's exit negotiations with the EU. Be sure to check with your university at the time of applying.

Further afield, some countries, such as Japan and South Korea, tend to charge the same fees for domestic and international students. Most countries will charge higher fees for international students than for domestic students: this list includes Australia, Canada, the USA and New Zealand (except for students on advanced research programmes, who pay domestic fees).

Fees are not the only consideration. Some countries have high fees, but extensive financial support systems (particularly for those who demonstrate academic excellence or who come from a low-income background). Other countries have high fees but a lower cost of living. Some countries that have a lower cost of living than the UK may still have variations within pricing, perhaps high prices for accommodation, internet access or even alcohol. If you had to pay three or four months' rent to secure accommodation, as is the case in some countries, how would it affect your finances? Other costs include visas, travel and application fees. Consider all these factors when calculating the cost of study and remember that exchange-rate fluctuations can have a great impact on any cost calculations.

Paying for your studies

One of the challenges for a student choosing to study overseas is how to fund it. The UK's financial support system is only applicable to students studying for full-time degrees in the UK, with the exception of short-term study abroad programmes of up to a year, whereby students are entitled to receive a maintenance loan based on household income. Although the terms of UK student loans are no longer as attractive as they once were, they do solve the problem of having to find the money to pay for tuition fees upfront; in certain countries, such as Australia, tuition fees are partially payable in advance, and you will need to pay a deposit before you can apply for a visa.

Financial support when studying overseas will need to come from:

- financial support from the host country
- scholarships
- bursaries
- savings
- earnings.

In most cases, international students have to fund themselves. Scholarships are often highly competitive. Jobs may be hard to come by, particularly if you don't yet speak the language, and some visas may restrict or deny you the opportunity to work. If you are applying for a visa, you are likely to have to prove that you have the necessary funds; you need to consider how you will support yourself before you apply. See page 53 for more information on visas.

It is recommended to have some money saved. Mark Huntington, of A Star Future, advises young people on overseas study. 'We recommend that even those who plan to work while abroad should have at least a semester's worth of living expenses covered before they go.'

While living costs and tuition fees might not always be as high as they are in the UK, they still have to be paid for. International students often use a combination of sources to pay for their studies: savings or personal loans, income from work, and scholarships.

Financial support from the host country
Ask the Ministry of Education or your chosen institution about any opportunities for grants, loans or other benefits for students. In some countries, fees may include a free or discounted travel pass or free language lessons.

Scholarships

Scholarships are available, although competition can be fierce. Scholarship funding tends to be more widely available for postgraduate than for undergraduate study. You should apply early, often a year in advance, following all instructions to the letter. Bear in mind that many applicants are unsuccessful in gaining scholarships and, even if you are successful, many scholarships do not cover the full costs of study, so consider how you will cover any shortfall.

The Ministry of Education or embassy in your chosen country should have information about government scholarships, while your institution is the best source of information for local sources of funding. See Chapters 5 to 11 for more information. You can also search for scholarships through websites such as http://www.scholarshipportal.com, www.hotcoursesabroad.com/study/international-scholarships.html and www.iefa.org.

Other sources of funding include:

- **US-UK Fulbright Commission:** www.fulbright.org.uk
- **Endeavour Scholarships and Fellowships:** https://internationaleducation.gov.au/endeavour%20program/scholarships-and-fellowships/international-applicants/pages/international-applicants.aspx
- **The Leverhulme Trust:** www.leverhulme.ac.uk/funding/funding.cfm
- **Research Councils UK:** www.rcuk.ac.uk
- **UNESCO Fellowships:** www.unesco.org/new/en/fellowships
- **British Transatlantic Exchange Association:** www.butex.ac.uk/students/useful-organisations

- **ISIC Global Study Awards:** www.isic.org/the-global-study-awards-expand-your-horizons
- **Erasmus+ Master Loans:** http://ec.europa.eu/programmes/erasmus-plus/sites/erasmusplus/files/library//erasmus-plus-master-loan_en.pdf (make sure to check the website before applying).

> Take out an International Student Identity Card (ISIC, www.isic.org) to enjoy student discounts and benefits across the world.

Charities and trusts

In the UK, a range of charities and trusts offer varying levels of funding. Each has their own eligibility criteria, deadlines and application procedures. A good place to start is the Educational Grants Services, www.family-action.org.uk/what-we-do/grants.

If you are looking for postgraduate funding, approach your university, which should have a copy of the Grants Register, a worldwide guide to postgraduate funding. Alternatively, you can search online for funding opportunities at www.prospects.ac.uk/postgraduate-study/funding-postgraduate-study.

Professional and Career Development Loans

If you are studying overseas because your course is not available closer to home, and you intend to return to the UK to work after your studies, it may be possible to get a Professional and Career Development Loan. Your institution overseas will need to register your chosen course with the Skills Funding Agency in the UK before you can apply for your loan, unless they have already done so for another student. Your course must help towards your intended career, though it does not necessarily have to lead to a qualification. You can borrow up to £10,000 for up to two years of study, or three, if your course includes a year's work experience, so it would be more appropriate for postgraduate students. Repayments and interest payments start one month after you complete your course, regardless of your situation. For more information, go to www.gov.uk/career-development-loans/overview.

Life overseas

Whether you will be living 100 or 10,000 miles away from home, it is important to know that you will be supported. Finding out the basics before you go can help to ease the adjustment process. Who's going to be there to help you out? What are the essentials you need to know about moving and living overseas?

Support available

The international office at your chosen university is likely to be your first, and probably your best, source of support throughout the process, from when and how to apply for a visa to finding the cheapest place to buy groceries. They should support you throughout the research and application process and will also be there to help you settle in once you arrive.

In addition to assistance from your international office and your department, making friends with other students makes settling in a lot easier and also provides a source of much-needed support. Orientation week, welcome week, *nollning* or frosh week activities can be a great place to start meeting new friends. In the UK, we know it as freshers' week, but different countries have their own names and traditions.

> **❝** Every question under the sun was answered by email, with quick replies. The admissions department are great. Also, upon arrival at an open day, I was welcomed with open arms, despite arriving four hours late! **❞**
>
> *Jacob Matthias Kummer, IE University, Spain*

> **❝** I received a lot of key information and support via email. I received a list of books and resources that I had to buy as well as details of where to buy them. I was sent an online orientation module to complete and this was very helpful as it included local transport and how to access your timetables and accommodation. **❞**
>
> *Anwar Hussain Nadat, University of Auckland,*
> *New Zealand*

> **❝** I settled in very quickly on my year abroad, which is largely thanks to the very competent and helpful international office at the university. Among other things, they sorted out accommodation for me in the private student halls. There is usually quite a long waiting list for the various student halls in the town, so I am very grateful for their help. **❞**
>
> *Elizabeth Edwards, Otto-Friedrich-Universität,*
> *Bamberg, Germany*

Your university might offer special activities and events to help you meet students from across the world. Try to take the opportunity to meet domestic students as well as international students. Local students will give you a different perspective on life and culture in their home country; they will also have more insight into where to go, where to shop and what not to miss. International friendships are important too and may help to ease your homesickness and culture shock, as you see other people adjusting to their new environment.

> 66 McGill offered a number of great orientation events, which were great ways to meet new people and get to know your way around the university and city. The most anticipated is 'Frosh' – a fresher's week equivalent, which consisted of a week jam-packed with activities and nights out. This was an excellent way to meet lots of new people. 99
>
> *Laura Bowker, McGill University, Canada*

There will normally be a team of staff to support you at university; this team might include careers advisers, counsellors and welfare officers. Support will vary from country to country and between institutions. If you have a disability, a learning difficulty or any health problems, you should discuss these with your university before you apply, to ensure that they can support you adequately.

Getting a visa

If you are studying outside Europe, you are likely to need a visa. You can apply for a visa once you have the offer of a place. Where possible, use the services of your university to assist you; if they recruit lots of international students, they should be experienced in supporting students through the process. They will also understand the reasons why some people are declined, so make sure to follow their advice. If you aren't able to receive this type of support from your university, you should contact the nearest national embassy, consulate or High Commission.

In many cases, visas are declined because of lack of correct evidence or because of insufficient finances; in other cases, if the immigration office doesn't believe that you are a genuine student and that you intend to return home after completing your studies. Never lie or falsify information on a visa application; if discovered, your application will be declined and future attempts to apply will be affected. Some health conditions (TB, for example) and key criminal convictions (violent offences or drugs charges, for example) can also affect your chances.

Visa applications can be complex; it is essential to follow each step to the letter, ensuring that you provide all the evidence required.

> **"** Applying for a visa to study in Montreal was a fairly long process. It required applying for a Canadian Study Permit and a Provincial document specifically for studying in Quebec (CAQ). I would recommend starting this process as soon as possible. It's very time-consuming to complete all the documentation and the processing time was a couple of months. It's not something to leave last minute! **"**
>
> *Laura Bowker, McGill University, Canada*

Registering within Europe

Following the European Union referendum on 23 June, 2016, in which the UK voted to leave the EU, arrangements for British students studying at European institutions are to be negotiated as part of wider discussions with the EU. Currently, while the UK is still a member of the EU, UK citizens will continue to have free movement within EU countries, though there may be some red tape to go through when you first move to another European country. In many cases, EU citizens have to register with a local government office. You should usually do this within the first week or two of arrival; your university will explain what you need to do.

EU countries

Austria, Belgium, Bulgaria, Croatia, Republic of Cyprus, Czech Republic, Denmark, Estonia, Finland, France, Germany, Greece, Hungary, Ireland, Italy, Latvia, Lithuania, Luxembourg, Malta, the Netherlands, Poland, Portugal, Romania, Slovakia, Slovenia, Spain and Sweden. The UK has voted to leave the EU, however at the time of going to press, it remains a Member State until exit proceedings have been finalised with the 27 other Member States.

EEA countries

The EEA is made up of all the countries in the EU plus Iceland, Liechtenstein and Norway. Although not within the EEA, Switzerland offers some rights to EEA citizens.

Accommodation

Safe and acceptable accommodation is essential to enable you to settle in and start adjusting to life overseas. The good news is that most universities with international students do their utmost to place them in suitable housing, often giving them priority. To enhance your chances of finding adequate accommodation, remember to:

- apply well in advance
- be realistic about the rent you are prepared to pay
- be flexible about where you are prepared to live.

Most students want good quality, affordable accommodation in a convenient location; you may find that there is not enough to go round, so it is worth considering what you are prepared to compromise on.

Types of student accommodation

If you're counting on university-run halls of residence, you may be surprised; some countries don't offer this option for accommodation. Some universities have campus-based halls run by private companies, while others have no accommodation at all. Alternatives on offer include temporary or short-term accommodation, rental property or home-stay with a local host family.

Finding accommodation from the UK

In some university towns there is a shortage of student accommodation, so some international students, particularly late applicants, find themselves in the position of leaving the UK without having secured long-term accommodation. Arranging private accommodation from a distance can be risky. You shouldn't pay a deposit to a private landlord for a property you haven't seen.

Seek the advice of your university's international or accommodation office on the safest and most reliable options when finding accommodation from the UK. They might discuss reputable short-term options with you, perhaps a bed and breakfast, local hostel or home-stay. Home-stay involves living with a local family; it can be a great way to give you time to adjust and help you to learn about life in your chosen country, as well as boosting your language skills. Securing short-term accommodation like this should then give you time to find suitable longer-term accommodation when you get there.

> ❝ The university cannot guarantee accommodation because of the size of the student body, but private sector provision is excellent and catered towards students in either 'republicas' (shared houses) or individual kitchenettes or studio flats both next to the campus and further into the city. It'll be very hard to sort anything out before you arrive though, so plan on starting in a hostel for a couple of weeks. ❞
>
> *Justin Axel-Berg, University of São Paulo, Brazil*

> ❝ The university provided a database for housing and the opportunity to apply for halls. While halls primarily go to undergraduates, there is always a chance for postgraduate students. Housing in Leuven is a mixture of studios, rooms and shared apartments. The database is made up of registered landlords who sign up to a university-drafted contract, giving you full support if anything was to go wrong. ❞
>
> *Tom Aitchison, KU Leuven, Belgium*

Check what's included

Whichever accommodation option you choose, remember to clarify what will and won't be included in your rent (water, electricity, gas, any kind of local rates, internet) and factor in travel costs; that way, you can make a more meaningful comparison between properties. Check whether you will need to buy things like cooking utensils and bedding when you get there.

Practicalities

As you prepare to make the big move, you're going to need to know about the cheapest ways to phone home; how to open a bank account; how to navigate the area by public transport; the system for paying tax on your earnings; and much more. Talk to your university's international office or check out expat websites, such as Just Landed, www.justlanded.com. You can also ask questions on online message boards for prospective students, some of which are filled with information about accommodation, buying bikes and so on.

> **❝** Before you leave home, make sure you sort how your finances are going to work from your bank back home, and how you can withdraw money abroad. **❞**
>
> *Tudor Etchells, IE University, Spain*

Once you arrive, you can start to use the network of friends that you make. This is where local students, and those who've already studied there for a while, become invaluable. Most people are more than happy to help.

Insurance: health and belongings

It is important to make sure that you and your belongings are adequately insured from the time you leave the UK until your return.

Following the EU referendum result, UK students are still currently able to use the EHIC and, as yet, no changes to the EHIC scheme have been announced. Until the terms of the UK's exit from the EU have been finalised, you should continue to apply for the EHIC as set out below and keep checking the NHS website for the latest information.

If you are planning to study within the EEA or Switzerland, you should take out a European Health Insurance Card (EHIC). The

EHIC is free and easily obtainable, normally arriving within seven to ten days after you have made your application, which can be done online or over the phone. The card entitles you to receive state healthcare in your host country, either for free, or at a reduced cost. It will cover you for treatment that you need in order to be able to continue your stay in your host country until you return to the UK, as well as treatment for pre-existing conditions. Conditions will vary depending on your country of study, so be sure to check any time limits or restrictions carefully by using the EHIC country-by-country guide on the NHS website. For full details, see www.nhs.uk/NHSEngland/Healthcareabroad/ EHIC/Pages/about-the-ehic.aspx.

You will need to take out additional insurance for travel and health to cover you while you are away; if you are applying for a visa, it is likely that you will be required to give evidence of adequate travel and medical insurance in order for your application to be approved. A number of UK providers offer study-abroad insurance policies, including Endsleigh (www.endsleigh.co.uk/ personal/travel-insurance/study-abroad-insurance) and STA Travel (www.statravel.co.uk/travel-insurance.htm). Alternatively, you could take out a policy in your host country. If you are working alongside your studies, you may be required to purchase additional insurance. Your international office should be able to advise further.

There may be vaccinations or preventive measures, such as malaria tablets, that you need to take before you travel. Talk to your GP and see the Travel Health pages of the Foreign and Commonwealth Office (www.fco.gov.uk). You may need to demonstrate that you are fit and well in order to obtain a visa; this may involve a medical examination.

> **❝** Our school provided us with health insurance
> policies in both Singapore and Sydney. In Sydney it
> was mandatory to have health insurance to get the visa. **❞**
> *Joshua Jackson, SP Jain School of Global Management,*
> *Singapore and Australia*

Personal safety

Although studying abroad is not, in itself, a dangerous activity,
visiting other countries carries certain risks. The Foreign
and Commonwealth Office has useful information for Britons
travelling and living overseas, including travel advice by country.
Find out about safety and security, health issues, local laws and
customs or natural disasters before you go. The Foreign and
Commonwealth Office also has a useful travel checklist: see
www.gov.uk/foreign-travel-checklist.

Follow the advice of your international office; they have a vested
interest in keeping you safe and have an understanding of
potential risks in the local area. However, you do have to take
responsibility for your own safety, much as you would if you were
leaving home to study in the UK.

According to a 2016 survey of 177 countries conducted
by Statistic Brain Research Institute, some of the safest
places to study include Japan, Taiwan, Hong Kong, South
Korea, Luxembourg, Singapore, Iceland, Germany, Estonia,
Norway, Qatar and China. ('Safest Countries to Live in the
World – Statistic Brain.' Statistic Brain Research Institute,
publishing as Statistic Brain. Accessed 29 April 2016. www.
statisticbrain.com/safest-countries-to-live-in-the-world.)

Top tips for staying safe include the following.

- Get to know your local area.
- Make yourself familiar with the transport system, and be sure you know how to get home, especially when travelling late at night.
- Find out when the last transport links run.
- Have a few local taxi numbers to hand.
- Make a note of useful numbers, such as the police and local consulate or embassy.
- Drink sensibly.
- Tell people where you are going.
- Make sure you have a phone that works abroad and keep in contact.
- Don't flash valuables and cash.

> **❝❝** Pickpocketing, having food stolen while on a train and witnessing mass brawls have all occurred in the two years I have spent in China. However, providing you are aware of risks and use some common sense you should be fine. On the whole, China is probably the country that I have felt safest in for travelling, living and walking home late at night. **❞❞**
>
> *Lewis McCarthy, University of Shanghai Jiao Tong, China*
>
> **❝❝** Despite São Paulo's violent reputation, it's really quite a safe place. I've lived here for three years now, travelling all over the city at all times of night and day and never come to harm anywhere. **❞❞**
>
> *Justin Axel-Berg, University of São Paulo, Brazil*

Language and cultural issues

However much you prepare yourself and find out about what to expect, there are going to be some adjustments to make when you move abroad. Differences in language, lifestyle, culture and cuisine may bring unexpected challenges.

Culture shock is a common side effect of spending time overseas, away from family, friends and the familiarity of your own culture. It takes time to adjust and you will need to be open-minded and flexible as you get used to the changes a new country brings.

Your university will provide orientation events to help you to adjust and make new friends. Most universities have a range of support services (student welfare staff, counsellors, health professionals and so on) to help you if you find the adjustment process particularly challenging. If you look after yourself by eating well, taking exercise and sleeping well, you will feel in a stronger position to tackle any challenges.

> **"** Embrace the lifestyle and culture. Live it. I admit I take a fair few siestas here in Spain and have whole meals of tapas! **"**
>
> *Tudor Etchells, IE University, Spain*

> **"** The lifestyle in Singapore is very metropolitan, busy, and Asian; they are more traditional, hierarchical and family oriented. It is definitely a hybrid between typical Western and Eastern lifestyles, a good stepping stone between England and Malaysia, for example. **"**
>
> *Joshua Jackson, SP Jain School of Global Management,*
> *Singapore and Australia*

Other tips to help you deal with culture shock include:

- keeping in touch with family and friends back home.
- getting involved with familiar activities, such as sports or cultural activities you enjoy.
- displaying personal items and mementoes to make your room feel homely.
- making an effort to meet other international students.
- getting to know students from the host country.

> ❝ Malta doesn't have a particularly strong Students' Union in terms of societies, etc., so make sure you make an effort to find clubs or groups outside university – these are mostly full of university students and young people. I joined a netball team and everyone was so friendly and excited to meet an English person! ❞
>
> *Catherine Foreshaw, University of Malta*

> ❝ I took part in lots of different societies and activities at McGill, from playing on a basketball team and writing for the newspaper to volunteering in a community café. My favourite society was the McGill Outdoors Club, which was an amazing way to meet people and see lots of the beautiful Canadian countryside. ❞
>
> *Laura Bowker, McGill University, Canada*

> ❝ I've had little difficulty adjusting to life here, which I feel is largely because of the strong community aspect at Northwestern. I live in an all freshman dorm, which made the process of making friends easy, and the clubs and societies I've joined have become little families. ❞
>
> *Jordan Clark, Northwestern University, USA*

Staying on after study

After spending three or four years in your host country, you may start to wonder whether you want to return to grey old Britain.

So, which countries offer the most attractive prospect for students who want to stay on? Canada, Australia and New Zealand give extra points in their immigration systems to students who have studied at their universities; this can make it easier to apply to stay on temporarily for work, or even permanently. In many other countries, working-visa and temporary-residence systems have been simplified for international students; you may find that you have the right to stay on and work for a period of time, for example.

Other options that can aid integration include opportunities to learn the local language, work permits and internship opportunities. See the 'Studying in ...' chapters for more information on staying on after study.

Returning to the UK

Coming back to the UK after your new experiences is not always as positive as you might anticipate. Reverse culture shock can be an unexpected side effect of spending time away. It can impact on the way you relate to friends and family and affect the way you adjust back to life at home. Try to remember how you managed to adjust to your new life overseas; you may well need to use these same skills to settle back in on your return. Don't assume that returning home will be seamless; allow yourself time to come to terms with the changes.

You will need to consider how to highlight the benefits of your experience and how to sell yourself to potential employers (or educational establishments). Think about how you might articulate what you can offer an employer, what you have learned and the skills you have developed. Consider how you would explain to an employer the type of institution you attended and how your degree compares to those on offer in the UK (or your chosen destination country). You can work with your university's careers service to prepare for this long before you leave university. Use their support to search for job vacancies and other schemes for graduates or postgraduates. Make sure that you get hold of references from teaching staff and from employers; it is much easier to do this before you leave.

There will be some loose ends to tie up before you leave, such as giving notice to your landlord, notifying your utilities' suppliers and reclaiming any deposits you have paid. Let your bank know that you are leaving and close your account; this might take a couple of weeks to finalise.

A break in residency?

If you return to the UK having been overseas for three months or more, this could be considered to be a break in UK residency, which can prevent you from gaining immediate access to certain services on your return. When you return to the UK, you may have to satisfy the conditions of a habitual residence test (HRT) before you are able to make a claim for certain means-tested benefits. 'Habitual residence' means that you intend to settle in the UK, Ireland, Isle of Man or Channel Islands (known as the 'common travel area') and make one of these your home for the present.

The HRT looks at what you are doing to make the UK the centre of your life and the ties you currently have in the UK, such as a UK base and close family. The Department of Work and Pensions, HM Revenue & Customs or your local authority will decide the point at which you can be considered habitually resident, which will depend on how long you have been away, why you went abroad and what ties you kept up with the UK during your break in residency. Advice centres, such as Citizens Advice Bureau (www.citizensadvice.org.uk), will be able to advise further, as this can be a complicated subject with legal implications.

Tax

Whether your absence is considered temporary or not will also affect the tax you will need to pay. When you return to the UK after studying abroad on a short-term placement, you'll usually be classed as a UK resident again. You remain a UK resident if you are abroad less than a full tax year (6 April to 5 April the following year). You're automatically resident if you've spent 183 or more days in the UK during the tax year and your sole home was in the UK, provided you have lived in it for at least 91 days and spent at least 30 days there in the tax year.

Your UK residence status also affects whether you need to pay tax on foreign income that you receive while you are away; if you remain a UK resident while overseas, you will normally have to pay UK tax on any foreign income earned. If you return to the UK within four years of moving overseas, you also may have to pay tax on any foreign income that you brought to the UK while you were non-resident; for example, if you transferred the income into a UK bank account while abroad, you may have to pay tax on these earnings. However, if you are not classed as a UK resident, then, on your return, you only pay UK tax on UK income.

This information can be complex and is subject to change, so you should make contact with HM Revenue & Customs at www.hmrc. gov.uk for the most up-to-date information.

You are also likely to be taxed by your host country on any money earned while overseas, though some countries have treaties preventing the need to pay double tax. To find out the rules on tax and whether you should be paying it, talk to your overseas university; they should be able to direct you to any specialist advice you need.

Support and networking after you leave

If you want to keep in touch with your wider network of friends from university, you could join an alumni organisation. This should also keep you up to date with events and developments. Other university services may still be available to you after you leave, including careers services.

Student testimonial, A Star Future
Jade Knight
University: Tilburg University, the Netherlands
Course: Global Law
Year: Second year
Hometown in UK: Plymouth

1. Why did you choose to study abroad?
I chose to study abroad because I felt like I needed a challenge and to push myself out of my comfort zone. Additionally, with the fees for university and the living costs in England skyrocketing in recent years, I felt the need to search for alternative opportunities that would not involve such a huge debt.

2. How would you rate the assistance of the university before you arrived (the application process, finding accommodation, sorting out financial matters)?

The university was incredibly helpful in answering all of your questions before arrival (current students phoned to answer any questions or concerns you may have, it was a really nice touch). Everything was very straightforward and if you had questions with regards to the application process you would receive a swift reply as to what you should do. Accommodation was very much your own responsibility; coming from England it is very different in the sense that there is no university accommodation, and so you have to be proactive in that sense. However, websites were readily distributed to help you find your accommodation.

3. How would you rate the assistance of the university when you arrived (orientation, etc.)?

Incredibly helpful, everything was organised and arranged over a few days and you were helped with all matters, for example setting up a bank account.

4. Did you feel prepared when you arrived and/or what surprised you?

I felt prepared for moving to the Netherlands; the university ensured you had complied with all of the bureaucratic aspects of moving to a new country, for example, signing up at the town hall, etc.

5. How would you rate the learning environment (teaching style, studying with other international students, non-native English-speaking lecturers)?

The learning environment is far more suited to the nature of the course; due to my program being quite new, there are only around 60 students in lectures, and so you really are able to contribute and have your questions answered by the lecturer. Studying with international students is invaluable. With the outlook of the course being global, having a global classroom helps to bring into perspective alternative points of view, which is of course incredibly interesting. The quality of the English spoken by both the lecturers as well as the students is very high; I have not had any trouble with communication at all.

6. Would you recommend studying abroad to a 17–18-year-old Brit who might never have thought about it before?

Yes, absolutely! The Netherlands is a really nice country and English is so widely spoken that you will never feel out of your depth. Moving to a new country is quite a big step I understand, and I myself was very nervous before I came. But honestly, I do not believe that I would have received the same quality of education and opportunities anywhere else. Moving abroad during your studies is a safe way to try something different, and in an age where going to university is becoming the norm, doing something different can really set you apart.

7. Working while studying

If you are considering getting a job whilst at university be aware that most do require you to speak Dutch. Tilburg University does provide you with two language course opportunities, which can include Dutch. But if you require a job from the beginning of the school year, I would suggest learning the basics before you come.

8. Would you recommend your course, university, city to British students?

I would definitely recommend my course and university to fellow British students. The course helps you to really consider your future and the options open to you, and studying with such motivated students helps to propel your own studies. The university campus, and the university as an institute, is incredibly student friendly. Lecturers are always ready to answer any questions, and the lecturers of Global Law are all invested in the program itself, and you really feel that. If I am to be brutally honest, Tilburg is not how you anticipate student life when compared to back in England! Of course the city is what you make of it, but it is really a place to study and do well, as opposed to having huge nights out. Of course the Netherlands is very small and so travelling to another city is incredibly doable for that.

Jade is studying an LLB in Global Law, which is excellent preparation for a career in global law but it is not the same as an LLB from an English university. If she intends to practise in England she will need to take a conversion course. This will extend her studies but ultimately, she will almost certainly be better prepared for a career in international law than a UK-trained graduate.

Chapter 3
Alternative options

If you feel that a full degree overseas is not right for you, you need not necessarily rule out studying outside your home country. Whatever the reasons swaying you against taking a full degree abroad, there may be an alternative choice for you to consider.

'I don't feel ready to take my full degree overseas'

Studying for a full degree overseas is a big step, but have you considered taking part of your UK degree course overseas instead? There are a range of schemes offering you the chance to study abroad without always lengthening your degree; some of these choices even bring their own financial benefits.

As you research UK universities, look into the types of study-abroad option they offer. Perhaps you like the look of the University of Bath's BSc Chemistry, which features a year in Europe, North America, Asia, Australia or New Zealand; MMath Mathematics at the University of Sheffield, which offers two pathways: 'Study in Europe' or 'The Year Abroad', with placements in English-speaking countries, including Australia, Canada and the USA; or maybe LLB European Law at the University of Warwick, with a year in France or Germany. It is important to find out whether your degree course will be lengthened by this experience and which years of study count towards your final degree classification.

> **“** I love to travel and I have always wanted to see the world. I chose my university partly based on whether they offered study abroad or exchange opportunities as I knew that I would like to go abroad for part of my degree. I enjoy experiencing new cultures and going to new places, and studying overseas just makes it convenient. **”**
>
> *Angela Minvalla, exchange student at RMIT*
> *University, Australia*
>
> **“** I wanted to do an exchange, because I feel that it offers a chance to be immersed in a new culture in a way that is very different to any other way of being abroad. **”**
>
> *Katherine Taylor, Bennington College, USA*

Many UK universities now have overseas campuses offering courses taught in English and mirroring some of the courses available back in the UK. Recent figures from the UK Higher Education International Unit suggest that around half a million students are studying for a UK degree overseas. These campuses are often set up to attract international students, but an added benefit for UK students could be the chance to study for a semester or a year at an international campus.

Check out which courses and in which countries enable you to study this way. For example, University College London (UCL) has campuses in Qatar and Australia, and the University of Middlesex has branches in Dubai, Malta and Mauritius; while Newcastle

University, the University of Southampton and the University of Reading all have a presence in EduCity, Malaysia. The University of Nottingham, the University of Central Lancashire and Heriot-Watt University also have a number of campuses overseas. The UK government is keen to see UK universities establish teaching outposts abroad, so there may be even greater choice for UK students in the future.

If you prefer the familiarity of a UK university name on your degree certificate, you could always opt for a full degree course at a UK overseas campus. Fees might be the same or a little lower than you'd expect at home, but the costs of living are often considerably less. In some cases, you might even gain a degree from the UK and from the country you will be studying in.

> **❝** My tutor at University of Birmingham will come out to visit after a few months to see if we are happy with the work and our lifestyles. He also asks for a summary update every couple of months. **❞**
>
> *Madeleine Prince, Cawthron Institute (professional placement abroad), New Zealand*

What will I pay?

If you are studying overseas for part of your course, you will often continue to pay tuition fees to your university at home, rather than to your overseas university. If you choose to spend a year at certain US universities, for example, this may mean studying at a fraction of the full cost of tuition. If you are studying for a full year overseas, your UK tuition fees should be reduced. The rules vary from country to country, with a maximum of 15% of the full-time fee caps charged in England and a percentage payable in Wales, Scotland and Northern Ireland. Your UK university will be able to tell you more.

You will still be able to access the normal UK system of loans, with maintenance loans available for short-term overseas study. In some cases, you may be able to apply for a travel grant to assist with the costs of travel, medical insurance, visas and so on. There may be additional bursaries or scholarships which you can apply for. For example, the British Universities Transatlantic Exchange Association (BUTEX) offers awards to undergraduate students studying abroad or on an exchange for at least one semester. The placement should not be eligible for an Erasmus grant, and you will need to check whether your university is registered as a BUTEX institution. For more details, visit www.butex.ac.uk/scholarships/are-you-eligible. Alternatively, Third Year Abroad has suggestions for other sources of funding: www.thirdyearabroad.com/before-you-go/money-matters.

Find out more from your UK university or from your national organisation for student finance:

- **Student Finance England:** www.gov.uk/student-finance/overview
- **Student Awards Agency for Scotland:** www.saas.gov.uk
- **Student Finance Wales:** www.studentfinancewales.co.uk
- **Student Finance NI:** www.studentfinanceni.co.uk.

If you are studying outside Europe, you are still likely to need a visa in the same way as if you were taking your full degree course; your university will be able to get you started with this process.

> 66 As tuition in Scotland is free, the cost of tuition on
> my year abroad was covered by the Scottish
> government. Living costs proved to be far less expensive in
> the south, so the only real expense was the flights (as well as
> all the travelling I did in the USA). 99
>
> *Rosie Hodgart, University of South Carolina*
> *(exchange), USA*

With these options, you can gain a degree from a familiar university, with the added benefits of an international experience, but without so many of the risks. You may get some financial support throughout the process, with the advantage of personal support from both institutions, too. It should be reasonably straightforward to transfer any credits achieved internationally back to the UK; your university should have planned for this to happen.

Erasmus+

Following the UK's decision to leave the EU, the UK's future access to the Erasmus+ scheme has yet to be determined. However, in June 2016 the Government issued a statement to confirm that the referendum result will not affect current students studying in the EU, recipients of Erasmus+, or those who are thinking of applying in 2017. Students considering applying after 2017 are advised to keep an eye on the websites of Erasmus+ (www.erasmusplus.org. uk) and the British Council (www.britishcouncil.org), as well as university websites, for the most up-to-date information. While the UK remains a member of the EU, the information provided below is still applicable to British students; going forwards, the terms of the UK's continued participation in the Erasmus+ scheme are to be negotiated as part of wider discussions with the EU.

Through the European Union Erasmus+ scheme, outside the UK, you have the opportunity to study in one of 32 countries in Europe and beyond for between three and twelve months. This is completed as a part of your course.

You will receive an Erasmus grant to put towards the additional costs of studying abroad, but you will still be expected to fund your own living expenses. In 2015–2016, students were able to receive an Erasmus grant ranging from €250–€300 (£194–£232) per month to contribute towards living and accommodation costs, with extra funding available for students with special needs, and for those who qualified for additional higher education support. For the latest information on funding, visit www.britishcouncil. org/study-work-create/opportunity/study-abroad/erasmus and www.erasmusplus.org.uk.

You will not be expected to pay fees to your host university and you should pay reduced tuition fees back home. In some cases, if you opt for a full year overseas, you won't pay tuition fees at all, although this ruling varies from year to year. Some universities offer additional bursaries to students opting for an Erasmus placement. The Erasmus representative at your UK university will be able to advise you on funding information and which fees (if any) are payable to your home university during your study abroad placement.

The Erasmus+ Joint Master's degree scheme allows students to study internationally recognised joint programmes at postgraduate level in multiple countries, some outside the EU. Certain scholarships are available; however, individual scholarships will vary considerably depending on the course, host country and cost of tuition. Find out more at www.erasmusplus. org.uk and www.britishcouncil.org/study-work-create/opportunity/ study-abroad/erasmus-joint-masters-degree.

> ❝ The Erasmus scheme is really big in Denmark –
> they have a market where previous international
> students sell their furniture or Danish-plug electronic items,
> and they organise trips to see tourist attractions around
> Denmark. ❞
>
> *Hannah Burrows, University of Southern Denmark*

English-language assistant

Once you have two years' worth of higher education under
your belt, you could consider working as an English-language
assistant. These opportunities are normally open to language
students in the UK, giving them the chance to work in an overseas
school for a year (and get paid).

You should pay reduced tuition fees to your UK institution, or
sometimes no fees at all, and may qualify for the overseas rate of
maintenance loan.

This option would lengthen your study by a year, but should give
you some valuable experience of education and life overseas. Your
university's study-abroad office should be able to tell you more.
Third Year Abroad (www.thirdyearabroad.com) also has lots of
useful information.

Short-term study overseas

Other options for study overseas include summer schools and
short-term placements. You could spend a summer learning a
language or testing out international education, to see if you are
ready to commit to further study abroad. Check out the costs and
visa requirements well in advance of making final arrangements.

Opportunities include:

- **Study China:** a three week programme open to students studying for undergraduate, master's and Foundation degrees, PhDs, PGCEs, Nursing diplomas and HNDs, www.studychina.org.uk
- **INTO China:** Chinese language summer programmes, www.intohigher.com/china/en-gb/our-courses
- **IAESTE:** placements for full-time HE (Higher Education) science, technology, engineering and applied arts students who are in their second year of study or above. Most placements take place in the summer, but longer placement periods are also available, www.iaeste.org/students
- **pre-university summer schools at US universities such as Harvard, Stanford and John Hopkins:** www.fulbright.org.uk
- **short-term exchanges in the USA:** www.educationusa.state.gov/your-5-steps-us-study.

Talk to staff at the study-abroad office at your university to find out more.

'I want to gain a degree from an international university without leaving the UK'

There are a couple of choices on offer if you want to gain an international degree from within the UK: either distance learning; or choosing a UK-based overseas university.

Distance learning

Online and distance learning is on the increase. With thousands of international universities offering degrees by distance learning, you need not set a foot out of the house to gain an international education. Of course, you will need to be disciplined and focused, and you won't gain the experience of living in another country, but you may end up with a degree from a top university at a fraction of the cost. It is worth noting that not all universities allow you to complete a full degree by distance education; they might offer blended learning, a combination of distance and face-to-face learning.

The benefits of distance learning are affordability, convenience, flexibility, choice and support (from tutors and classmates). On the other hand, you need to be well disciplined and aware of the fact that you will lose the face-to-face interaction that you would get on campus. In addition, it can be more difficult to assess whether distance-learning providers are reliable, without a physical presence to assess them by.

How do I know that my distance-learning provider is genuine?

You need to be even more thorough when researching a distance-learning provider; see page 44 for important questions to ask of potential institutions. Remember, if it sounds too good to be true, it probably is.

There may be some warning signs to look out for when checking out a distance-learning institution's website. If the organisation only provides a PO Box address, if it has a similar name to other well-respected institutions or if you can gain a higher education qualification purely on the basis of previous experience, you might need to dig a bit deeper to ascertain whether it is genuine and accredited.

You may find it easier to be sure of the provenance of your qualifi-cations from a traditional university that happens to offer distance-learning courses. Many traditional, accredited universities across the world offer distance-learning provision, and it is particularly prevalent in the USA. If the institution claims to be accredited, double-check this with the accrediting organisation. You can find out more from the Ministry of Education of the country you hope to gain your qualification from. Check out the following websites, too.

- **International Council for Open And Distance Education (ICDE):** www.icde.org
- **Study Portals** (search for distance-learning courses worldwide): www.distancelearningportal.com
- **Distance Education Accrediting Commission Directory of Accredited Institutions (USA):** www.deac.org/Student-Center/Directory-Of-Accredited-Institutions.aspx.

Online international education is on the increase. Prestigious universities including Harvard and the Massachusetts Institute of Technology (MIT) have set up edX (www.edx.org), while Stanford, Princeton and others have founded Coursera (www.coursera.org). Both resources offer online interactive learning with no entry requirements. With the exception of professional education courses, edX is free to access, and credit is available for selected courses, depending on the institution. Coursera, meanwhile, gives subscribers the opportunity to receive a Course Certificate for a fee, which also grants users full access to additional course features for certain courses. The site also offers Specialisations, which are designed to enable students to master specific subject areas. While the courses offered on these sites are not equivalent to gaining a full degree in the USA, they could give you the chance to experience US-style teaching and develop your interest in particular subject areas.

UK-based overseas universities

Campuses for a number of overseas universities can be found
in the UK, most commonly in London. A number of these are
American universities, offering US degrees. Although these
universities recruit students from all over the world, only a
small percentage currently attend from within the UK. This may
change, with the fee hike in parts of the UK now making the fees
at these universities appear much more reasonable.

In the case of Richmond, the American International University
in London, you can gain a dual degree from the UK and the USA,
while experiencing an international university and still having
access to the UK system of loans. Another option is Regent's
American College London, which is affiliated to Regent's University
London, and offers a range of undergraduate degrees based on
the US liberal arts curriculum. However, the cost of study at these
institutions may deter some students from applying: at Richmond,
tuition fees are set at £9,000 for new UK students in 2016–2017,
with a maximum tuition fee loan of £6,000 available, while fees
for courses at Regent's American College are charged at £15,950,
although there are certain means-tested bursaries available.

International universities with a campus in the UK include the
following. You can find out more about courses, fees and how to
apply on their websites.

- **Richmond, the American International University in
  London:** www.richmond.ac.uk
- **Hult International Business School:** www.hult.edu/en/
  undergraduate/bachelor-of-business-administration/
  campuses/london
- **Azad University in Oxford (AUO):** www.auox.org.uk
- **Limkokwing University of Technology:**
  www.limkokwing.net/united_kingdom.

Student story
Katherine Taylor, Bennington
College, Vermont, USA (exchange)

'I'm studying a variety of subjects at Bennington College, Vermont, USA. I'm in my second year, which here makes me a sophomore.

'I wanted to do an exchange, because I feel that it offers a chance to be immersed in a new culture in a way that is very different to any other way of being abroad, so as my degree is in creative writing with English Literature, I asked the head of creative writing where he would recommend. As an American himself, he suggested there would be no better place to go (only semi-jokingly) than to the US, and it happened that Bath Spa had a partnership with a small liberal arts university there: Bennington College. He also told me that they would have a three-week long Easter break in which I could travel across the country (absolutely untrue – we had a five-day break halfway through April, and that was it for this term), and that they were offering to take students in the second half of term, meaning that I wouldn't have to read Samuel Richardson's *Clarissa* or do the three-hour written exam. My mind was set.

'When I arrived, there was an option to be picked up from a variety of places, although not the airport that I flew into (as it was cheaper to arrive in Boston, and get a coach up country), so I was picked up at a bus station by a taxi. There were four other new students arriving at the same time as me, so we had dinner together the first night, and a week of touring around local places and being shown around. As we were in such a small group (because we'd arrived halfway through term), we were given a lot of attention and help – I knew lots of people were looking out for me, all the students were friendly, and I felt totally comfortable asking any questions I was curious about. Being in America, I had a roommate as well, meaning that I was never alone (which had good and bad sides to it), and therefore always had someone to ask about anything I didn't understand.

'Accommodation was arranged for me by Bath Spa University – pretty much all students live on campus, so there wasn't much to be decided.

Bennington often is top of the university housing polls, and it's pretty fantastic (although also some of the most expensive housing in the country if you're not on exchange or on a scholarship) – every student fills out an extensive questionnaire and is placed in a house according to their preferences. For example, I love my quiet time, and was placed in Franklin, the silent house – I still go out to parties, but it's so nice to come home to somewhere peaceful. There are other houses that have some quiet hours, for example between 11pm and 7am, and more houses where music can always be heard pounding through the walls – I think housing here manages to fit everyone in pretty nicely, and it's not too hard to move if you're not happy with your house. Originally, Bath Spa wanted me to live on their campus from September to February, and pay for the year there, and not pay at Bennington, but as I'd already put my deposit down for a house in Bath, they allowed me to continue paying only my landlady, which saved me a lot of money.

'A lot of my classes are discussion-based, and always make room for current events. A lot of the time I'll be asked to read something and write a "response paper" to it, an informal, short essay about what I thought of it and how I felt reading it. Many of the lecturers also award marks on a participation basis, which means that students are always involved and encouraged to speak up. Bennington College is a private school, so the class sizes are very small: my dance class has about 20 students in, but one of my roommate's politics class has only two other students in! On average, I would say there's about 10–15 people in most of my classes.

'Bennington has a pretty unique course structure, called "the Plan". Any student can take any class, regardless of year or what their expected degree will be at the end. This means that although my degree at Bath Spa is Creative Writing with English Literature, here I do two poetry classes, one literature class (on artificial intelligence in literature and film), and then a class in contemporary African dance, a ceramics class, and a class on translation. It's incredible! My roommate and I often talk about how Bennington really cuts down stereotypes – no one's just a literature kid or a science "nerd", because they're also part of the farm project, or doing photography, or a silkscreen workshop as part of their curriculum.

'There are many things that have surprised me! I mostly remember the little things that surprise me still, even after two months in the US: the cars being so big, like caricatures of cars; the lights turning on in different ways; the air being different – clearer, somehow more transparent. I was surprised at how friendly every single person I met was; people I didn't know would say hello to me all the time, which is also part of being such a small institution – there are less than 700 students here. It's sort of like being in a dream: everything is how I imagined it, except I'm actually in it. Something extremely different in the US is that it's expected that you'll have a roommate – at Bennington, all first and second years are required to have one. I've gone from spending the majority of my time alone to spending almost every moment of my time with other people all around me – a change I'm not keen on, but I think is a pretty essential experience in learning about boundaries, about other people and negotiating, and about yourself, and how you can learn to adapt in an unusual situation.'

Katherine's top tips

Accommodation

'The accommodation offered is for the most part on campus, with no specific designation for international students. To graduate from Bennington, they require at least two terms of on-campus living.'

Food and drink

'Food at Bennington College is extremely expensive – it's one of the biggest downfalls of the university. Every student is required to be on the "meal plan", which is roughly $3,300 per term. Being off the meal plan is considered an accommodation, and so often students are forced to stay on it if they live on campus. In Bath, I would spend around £500 per term, so it is an incredible difference, especially as there are only certain hours that food is offered, and only two meals offered on the weekends, with no discount for vegetarians/vegans, etc. The idea of everyone eating together is supposed to reinforce community, but it's so expensive I don't know how full-time students usually cope.'

Financial support for study

'Bath Spa offered me a grant, which I very gratefully accepted, to help me pay for flights out here.'

Living and tuition costs

'As a private US college, the tuition fees, were I a full-time student with no financial aid, would be extortionate: $49,440 per year. Luckily, the college does offer a lot of merit and financial aid to many students.'

Insurance

'I took out the insurance that the college offered, which seemed like the simplest thing to do as I was rushed for time. If I'd had more time, I would have liked to have looked around, but it was all very complicated and staying with the college was the easiest option.'

Working while studying

'Bennington is great for part-time work opportunities – I work in the dining hall doing various jobs, and there are other positions all over campus, with hours ranging from one- to five-hour slots. Taking a few shorter shifts throughout the week has been great for me, as I can focus on my work and earn a little on the days when my schedule isn't so full on.'

Travel and transport

'Bennington has a bus service and also offers a "shuttle service" – essentially a free taxi affiliated with the college. The campus is pretty far away from anything else, set in the heart of some woodlands and mountains, so it's always useful to have a friend with a car (which is reasonably common as people start driving at 16 in Vermont), and there's also a Facebook liftshare site which I'm hoping to use to get back to the airport at the end of my time here.'

Bennington College is a private liberal arts college with a 440-acre campus in Bennington, Vermont. It was the first US higher education institution to include the visual and performing arts in a liberal arts education, and is the only one in the USA that requires students to spend a term every year in the workplace on an internship.

Chapter 4
Researching your options

There are so many questions to ask about yourself, your chosen country and your chosen university before you even apply. In the early stages, it is hard to even know what those questions should be. If you thought that narrowing down your UCAS choices to five was tricky, imagine trying to choose between courses and universities from across the world. If that all sounds like too much hard work, consider that somewhere out there may be the perfect course for you at the perfect price; it's got to be worth a little bit of work to find it.

Getting started

With almost the whole world to choose from, the first step should be to research the countries that you are interested in. The chapters on studying in various countries will give you an overview of the different education systems, costs and financial support, how to apply and the visa system, where appropriate. Each chapter will also feature the most useful and reliable websites where you can find out more information. This should help you start to compare what is on offer and how it fits in with your plans.

Where to study

This book focuses on opportunities taught in English, so the Republic of Ireland, USA, Canada, Australia and New Zealand are likely to have the largest choice of courses. However, many other Commonwealth countries use English, including Singapore, Malaysia and certain Caribbean, Pacific and African nations. Find out more at the Association of Commonwealth Universities, www.acu.ac.uk.

Universities in many overseas countries are now actively recruiting UK students in a way that was unheard of only ten years ago. Events such as The Student World Fair feature university exhibitors from all over the world who are keen to attract UK students; in 2016, representatives from the US, Canada, Australia, Malaysia, Turkey, Switzerland, Lithuania, the Netherlands, Italy, France, Spain, Hungary, Denmark and Ireland all took part.

Although the introduction of courses taught in English was originally aimed at international students from countries other than the UK, many UK students are starting to take advantage. Universities in the Netherlands in particular have seen a surge in the number of applications from UK students, in the wake of increased tuition fees and changes to funding in the UK.

The number of courses taught in English by accredited tertiary institutions in non-Anglophone countries is on the rise; the Academic Cooperation Association (ACA) has reported that within Europe alone, the number of English-taught programmes in non-Anglophone countries has increased by over 300% in seven years. ('English-Taught Programmes in European Higher Education: The State of Play in 2014', ACA.)

StudyPortals lists over 100,000 study programmes taught entirely in English around the world, 75% of them outside the UK. A large number of English-medium options can be found within Europe; according to their insights, in the Netherlands alone, research and applied universities offer over 1,400 English-taught degrees. In Belgium, the Catholic University of Leuven and Maastricht University both offer over 176 English-taught programmes at undergraduate level between them, while the University of Zurich in Switzerland currently offers 125 English-taught bachelor's and master's programmes combined. Outside Europe, students can also choose to study in English in main English-speaking countries, such as the United States or Australia, but also in countries such as China, Malaysia or Taiwan, which are introducing more degrees for international students.

StudyPortals tells us that a number of English-taught programmes are also available in top universities in countries such as:

- Germany
- Sweden
- Denmark
- Spain
- Finland
- Italy.

(Source: www.studyportals.com/students.)

How to choose

Many people choose a country for emotional, rather than practical, reasons. Maybe you have always longed to spend time in a particular country or you've fallen in love with a place that you've visited. Perhaps your family or friends have links with an area of the world or you have a boyfriend or girlfriend who lives overseas.

In other cases, the decisions are much more measured and logical. Some have a particular type of course in mind and their decision is driven by the availability of that course. Others have a set of requirements, in terms of prestige, entry requirements or world university rankings.

Others don't even choose a specific country, but make a shortlist of institutions that meet their particular criteria. John Magee, who studied in Norway, took a very structured approach to his search for opportunities across Europe.

> **66** Firstly, the schools had to be ranked on the *Financial Times* European Business School Rankings, so they were internationally recognisable to future employers. Secondly, the schools had to offer my desired degree, an MSc in International Business/ International Management. Thirdly, a more selfish criterion of being situated in a mountainous country that offered easy access to alpine activities. Lastly, it was preferable if the course offered an exchange semester, to help me secure the maximum amount of international experience. **99**
>
> *John Magee, BI Norwegian Business School, Norway*

In many cases, access to student financial support or scholarships is a deciding factor.

> 66 I was put off staying in the UK for postgraduate studies by the high tuition fees. The cost of studying in Germany is the same for Germans and international students alike: in most cases, there are no tuition fees, only a semester fee of around €90 (£70) that, among other things, pays for a semester-long pass for all public transport in and around the town. 99
>
> *Elizabeth Edwards, Otto-Friedrich-Universität,*
> *Bamberg, Germany*

It is also worth considering the cost of living, how welcoming the country is to international students (for example, how easy it will be to obtain a visa and whether there are opportunities to gain employment afterwards) and how well your degree will be recognised when you return to the UK.

Essentially, you need to determine what matters to you and what your priorities are. Consider some of the following factors and weigh up how important each one is to you:

- subject availability
- length of study
- professional recognition of qualifications
- university ranking
- type of institution
- size of university
- style of teaching and assessment
- specialist options (for example, internships or specialist subjects available)
- drop-out rates
- pass rates

- destinations of ex-students
- cost of tuition fees
- cost of living
- availability of loans or grants
- availability of scholarships
- opportunities to stay on and work after completion of studies
- interest in specific countries
- opportunity to learn particular languages
- lifestyle factors
- distance from home.

> **66** It can be useful to write up a list of things you want from your university experience, and use that to try and find the perfect fit. The US has over 4,500 different universities, so just because you haven't heard its name before doesn't mean it's not a respected institution. **99**
>
> *Jordan Clark, Northwestern University, USA*

What type of university will suit you best?

Whether you see yourself as an academic aiming for postgraduate study or you want a route straight to work, you're guaranteed to find a university to suit you. Many countries have polytechnics, community colleges or universities of applied sciences, where courses have a more vocational, work-related focus; these institutions share some characteristics with the post-1992 universities in the UK. If you are looking for a more traditional style of teaching from lecturers with a research background, try a research-based or research-intensive university. Make sure that you always find out which type of university you are applying to; it could have a big impact on what you get out of your university experience and which doors will be open to you when you finish.

Carefully considering what matters to you will help you to focus on essential and desirable criteria. A final list of criteria might look something like the following.

- Essential: a city-centre, research-based university in the top 200 of one of the world university league tables, offering a low cost of living and the possibility of a scholarship.
- Desirable: flight time of less than eight hours, opportunity to stay on and work.

> Terminology will differ from country to country: what we describe as a course in the UK might be called a programme or program in some countries, with course used to refer to the modules you study as part of your degree.

Researching the options

There is no wrong or right way to choose where you want to spend the next few years. Just make sure that you discover the realities of life there, not just the pictures from glossy brochures. It is not unusual to see universities overstating their position to international students, so make sure that you look for a secondary source of evidence (particularly if a university is telling you that they are among the best in the world).

Just as in the UK, courses with the same title may in fact be very diverse. You should ask about course content, course structure, how you will be assessed, and so on. You might find that the course you are looking for doesn't exist in your chosen country; there are limited history or English literature courses taught in English in continental Europe, for example. Courses where your learning relates specifically to practice in a particular country don't always travel well, so they might not be available: social work or teaching, for example. Titles may vary from country to country; whereas UK university courses often have quite broad academic titles, such as biology or mechanical engineering, vocational universities in other countries might use titles that are more specific and job-related. Look out for courses in econometrics, interaction design or human ageing.

Ask universities about additional factors, such as the ratio of students to lecturers, drop-out rates, student-success rates, library services and internet access. If you have the opportunity to visit a country or campus, take it. This can be a great chance to find out more, meet the staff and ask questions. Many students talk about the feeling they get from being on a particular campus and it is hard to 'virtually' recreate this if you have very little contact with the university before making your choices.

There are other ways of finding out more. If a visit isn't possible (and let's face it, it often isn't), try to attend recruitment events in the UK. There are a number of events that take place here in the UK: the Student World Fair, USA College Day, QS World Grad School Tour, and the Study Options Open Days. At these events, you can meet representatives from universities who are actively seeking UK students. To make best use of these events, find out the exhibitors beforehand, highlight whom you want to speak to and take your list of essential questions to ask. Note down or record any responses you get, so you can consider them later.

Don't want to restrict yourself to just one country? Can't decide between Los Angeles, Hong Kong or Milan? There are a number of options where you can study in two, three or even four different countries and even gain more than one degree. Take a look at the World Bachelor in Business partnership (http://wbb.usc.edu), SKEMA's EAI Bachelor (www.skema.edu/international/Exchange%20IN/bachelor-programme) or SP Jain's Bachelor of Business Administration (www.spjain.org/BBA), for example.

Online research

Most of the countries interested in attracting international students have their own official websites; you can find these in the 'Studying in …' chapters. For information on European opportunities, start at www.ec.europa.eu/education/study-in-europe.

All universities looking to attract international students will have their own websites with English content. Many universities have a number of other ways to engage with their potential students via social media – Facebook, Twitter, YouTube, etc. – where you can search directly for the universities you are interested in.

Following some key organisations on Facebook or Twitter when you start your research will help you to keep up to date with new developments, events and key deadlines. You can also attend virtual student fairs and web chats from the comfort of your own home. EducationUSA International Student Fairs is one example, offering a number of live virtual college fairs held each year, which should provide some useful information on study in the USA (https://educationusa.state.gov/us-higher-education-professionals/fairs-and-events). Other websites, such as the Student Room (www.thestudentroom.co.uk), have discussions on international study. Bear in mind that information from chat rooms can be useful, but isn't always reliable or up to date, so make sure to double-check any information you take from sources like this.

In 2015, UCAS announced its decision to allow universities in Europe the option of registering as UCAS providers, on condition that they meet the equivalent standards of their UK counterparts. At present, UK students can apply to two providers outside the UK through UCAS Undergraduate: the University of London Institute in Paris, which offers French studies or French studies with history; and the Amsterdam Fashion Academy, which offers fashion business and fashion with textiles design. Opportunities to apply for postgraduate courses abroad through UCAS may also be available in future.

Course search

The 'Studying in …' chapters include some of the best websites to search for courses and institutions in a specific country. If you want to search for courses before you decide on a country, try websites like Study Portals (www.studyportals.com), which allows you to search for bachelor's, master's and PhD programmes, as well as short and distance-learning courses; or EUNiCAS (www.eunicas.co.uk), which gives advice on courses overseas, and gives you the option to apply to up to eight higher education institutions. Other options include A Star Future (www.astarfuture.co.uk/what_to_study.html) or Hotcourses Abroad (www.hotcoursesabroad.com).

Is the website you need opening up in another language? Look out for the Union Jack flag or the letters EN to select the English version. If not, try a translation website like Google Translate, www.translate.google.com.

Organisations to like on Facebook

- EducationUSA
- US-UK Fulbright Commission
- The Student World
- A Star Future for Brits Studying Abroad
- Dutch Degrees
- Study in Holland
- Maastricht Students
- Study Options (for study in Australia and New Zealand)
- CUCAS-Study in China
- Campus France Paris
- Study in New Zealand
- Study in Finland
- Study in Australia
- Study in Estonia
- Study in the Czech Republic
- Study in Germany
- Study in Sweden
- Study in Norway
- Study in Denmark
- INTO China
- EUNiCAS
- Hotcourses Abroad
- Venture.

Organisations to follow on Twitter

- @TheStudentWorld
- @astarfuture
- @StudyOptions
- @CampusFrance
- @StudyInHolland
- @StudyinNorway
- @StudyinSweden
- @EdUSAupdates
- @USUKFulbright
- @studyinde
- @EduIreland
- @nzeducation
- @FutureUnlimited (for study in Australia)
- @studyinestonia
- @INTO_CHINA.

There are also plenty of study abroad blogs and diaries that are worth a read. Take a look at some of these:

- **Third Year Abroad, The Mole Diaries:** www.thirdyearabroad.com/before-you-go/the-mole-diaries.html
- **A Star Future Testimonials:** www.astarfuture.co.uk/testimonials.html
- **Fulbright Commission UK Student Blogs:** www.fulbright.org.uk/news-events/uk-student-blogs
- **The University of Southampton Study Abroad and Exchange Blog:** http://studyoverseas.soton.ac.uk/welcome-to-our-blog/
- **Durham Students Abroad:** https://durhamstudentsabroad.com.

Websites such as iAgora (www.iagora.com/studies) allow international students to rate their experiences at an institution based on categories such as housing, student life, academic, costs and so on. STeXX, the Student Experience Exchange (www.stexx.eu), allows students to review and rate their institution based on criteria such as academics, costs and funding, accommodation, social life and career perspective. Use sites like these to get a student perspective on your chosen institution.

Many schools, colleges, universities and public libraries have access to Venture (www.venture-uk.co.uk), an international careers-information database. The site features lots of useful information on studying overseas, including country profiles. Ask your UK institution for a username and password.

Students interested in postgraduate study or research should find the Prospects website useful, as it features profiles of around 30 countries offering study abroad opportunities (www.prospects.ac.uk/postgraduate-study/study-abroad).

> **"** After results day, my teacher recommended that I get in touch with A Star Future because she knew that I would be really interested in their information on clearing places at foreign universities. **"**
>
> *Clare Higgins, The Hague University of Applied Sciences, the Netherlands*

> **"** I applied through Study Options. They were fantastic and made the process so easy. They copied all my transcripts for my A level results and sent off passport, results, organised the visa, the course, everything! **"**
>
> *Kadie O'Byrne, Murdoch University, Australia*

Using an agent

Some applicants choose to use the service of an agent or an educational consultant to help them navigate the plethora of information out there. Many like the reassurance of working with an organisation that understands the education, application and visa system of particular countries. Check whether you have to pay for the service they provide and what you will get in return. Some organisations charge no fees. It is always worth asking about the affiliations of any organisation: whether they are linked to specific universities, for example.

There are a number of organisations operating in the UK, all offering different types of support and service. Some of these are listed here.

- **A Star Future:** www.astarfuture.co.uk
- **Study Options:** www.studyoptions.com
- **EUNiCAS:** www.eunicas.co.uk
- **The Student World:** http://thestudentworld.edufindme. com
- **PFL Education:** www.preparationforlife.com
- **Degrees Ahead:** www.degreesahead.co.uk
- **Mayflower Education Consultants:** www.mayflowereducation.co.uk
- **M & D Europe:** www.readmedicine.com
- **Study-International:** www.studygo.co.uk
- **PASS4 Soccer Scholarships:** www.pass4soccer.com.

Getting a different perspective

Of course, the websites listed here barely scratch the surface of the range of information available. The students featured in this book share some great ways to get a different perspective.

> **66** I did some rather intense research, checking out the university website, the city website and the online literature available. I also used more creative methods such as searching for YouTube videos of the campus and the city, listening to the local radio station online and reading the local paper online to try to get a better grip of what my future life might be like. **99**
>
> *Simon McCabe, University of Missouri, USA*

> **66** Before I came to Canada I read a couple of guide books, a number of blogs online and articles about living in Canada. These definitely gave me a couple of hints and tips, but it's really impossible to get an idea of the place before you arrive. Although it's great if you can find out a bit of information, speaking to someone who has studied abroad is probably the most useful thing to do. Otherwise, the best advice I would give is just to arrive with an open mind and be ready to embrace lots of new and different things. **99**
>
> *Laura Bowker, McGill University, Canada*

Finalising your choices

Let's recap the steps to finalising your choices.

- Consider your priorities.
- Write a list of essential and desirable criteria.
- Write a list of questions to ask each institution.
- Start to research in more detail.
- If you're struggling, write a pros-and-cons list.
- Narrow down your choices to a shortlist of five or six.

It is important to contact the university directly, talking to admissions staff, as well as course leaders or professors. When you come to apply, this can have the additional benefit of making your name known to the recruiting staff, as well as improving your understanding of what those staff are looking for.

You should clarify the application process, documentation required and the visa requirements with your prospective institution, as well as establishing a timescale for the process, so that you don't miss any important deadlines. The university should then send you the necessary paperwork or a link to the information online.

Try to apply to a number of institutions, while still considering the work required to produce a good-quality application, as well as any associated costs, and following individual deadlines and requirements. Applying to a number of institutions gives you a better chance of a selection of offers to choose from.

Student testimonial, A Star Future
Matthew Green
University: Sciences Po, France
Course: Europe-North American Undergraduate Programme at the Reims campus
Year: First year

1. Why go abroad?

For me, choosing to go abroad was only part of the greater decision to study at Sciences Po as opposed to other universities; choosing between a university in the UK and one overseas was not a conscious decision I ever made. Coming from this perspective, I was able to judge wholly what the right choice was for me.

On balance, that choice was the chance to combine Sciences Po's interdisciplinary social science course with the ability to immerse myself in a different culture and language. I felt this was a special opportunity to distinguish myself both academically and as an individual at the same time. Put simply, I felt Sciences Po could give me the most during my undergraduate studies and also that I could give the most back to Sciences Po, too. For me, my decision hinged on the possibility to study at a prestigious university but also in an intimate environment, the possibility to walk in the footsteps of the many great leaders Sciences Po has produced while having an identity and a sense of belonging at the same time.

2. How would you rate the assistance of the university before you arrived (the application process, finding accommodation, sorting out financial matters)?

While I did not receive so much of the hand-holding with my application to Sciences Po as I did from my school with UCAS, I was always able to seek help in English from the university and indeed I was able to complete the application in English. Remembering that Sciences Po recruits students from over 100 countries, the application is not as standardised as UCAS's but perseverance and getting help is the key. For me, the few extra hours I spent sorting out my application were well worth it in the end.

Once I was accepted into Sciences Po, the university provided me with a comprehensive information package that helped with finance, housing and other particulars.

3. How would you rate the assistance of the university when you arrived (orientation, etc.)?

Very good. Much of the assistance available was from students in their second year who had been asking the same questions the year before. The Reims campus of Sciences Po is very close-knit and personal due to it having a small student body, so help is never really far away.

The Sciences Po course requires all students to attend a week-long introductory week in August, which allowed me to make friends, become familiar with the course and settle into living in a different country before the real work started.

4. Did you feel prepared when you arrived and/or what surprised you?

Yes. I prepared well in anticipation of moving out, ticking all the necessary boxes, and I felt comfortable in the new environment. No surprises. It's as easy as you want to make it.

5. How would you rate the learning environment (teaching style, studying with other international students, non-native English-speaking lecturers)?

The learning environment at Sciences Po is quite intense: I have found myself under some considerable pressure at some points. Students are expected to complete readings, prepare presentations, take mid-term and final exams each semester, and be present for all classes. The most time I would spend in lessons at A2 level at school was three-and-a-half hours per day; the minimum time I spend in class per day at Sciences Po is four hours. The other side of this though is that after an intense two years of study like this, I can choose to go abroad to a partner university or to do an internship, which is an amazing opportunity to either get ahead in the world of work or to experience another country.

Each student takes a group project. I chose to be part of Sciences Econ, an economics society with the aim of getting others to start talking about economics. We print newsletters and organise debates as well as more social events.

At Sciences Po's Reims campus not much is lost in translation. Every student speaks good English and most professors do too. The very nature of the English-speaking programme in Reims attracts those most willing and most able to speak English as well as native English speakers of course.

6. Would you recommend studying abroad to a 17–18-year-old Brit who might never have thought about it before?

When I speak to anyone about this subject, I first emphasise it is not a choice between studying abroad or not – it is ultimately a choice between universities – if you're not happy at university you might become even unhappier as a result of being abroad.

There was a point when I moved from having a general notion of liking the idea of studying abroad to focusing on and applying to a course, university and city, which I had all properly researched. Those who are motivated to go through this transition will be the ones most likely to go abroad and be happy there too. I was well aware that I was doing something different to everyone else at school (even to other overseas applicants) but I was 100% certain that I was making the right choice.

7. Scholarships/Financial Aid

I was lucky enough to receive a scholarship to help finance my studies from the Sciences Po UK Alumni Charity Trust. This scholarship has relieved financial pressures, allowing me to focus on academic ones. I would highly recommend Sciences Po applicants to look into this scheme.

8. Would you recommend your course, university, city to British students?

I would recommend Sciences Po to anyone who doesn't want to limit themselves to any one subject at undergraduate level and who is looking to create a truly international profile. You have to be willing to work harder than your friends in the UK but the rewarding experience will be worth it.

*Sciences Po is the leading French university for the social
sciences and over the years they have educated most French
prime ministers and presidents as well as many global leaders.
The university has started to offer bachelor's-level education in
English recently to try to attract international students who could
benefit from their unique interdisciplinary approach. All students
are required to study a range of subjects – political science,
economics, history, law and sociology – as well as French and an
additional language. Their degrees are focused on different parts
of the world; Matthew is studying the Europe-North America
Programme, which will probably see him spend his third year at a
US or Canadian University. Other programmes available to English
speakers are the Europe-Asia Programme and Middle Eastern and
Mediterranean Programme. Students are not required to know
French at the beginning of their studies but they will be required
to learn intensively.*

*Tuition fees at Sciences Po are means-tested and based on family
income and household size. They can range from €0–€10,040 for
British students. There are scholarships available for exceptional
candidates.*

KEA – Copenhagen School of Design and Technology: Profile

Copenhagen School of Design and Technology is an Academy of Higher Education which offers over 30 different educational programmes at Bachelor degree and Academy Professional degree levels.

With a degree from KEA – Copenhagen School of Design and Technology you get a practice-oriented, higher education at Academy Professional level and/or Professional Bachelor's level, developed in close cooperation with the region's business community and educational institutions in Denmark and abroad. We are in constant dialogue with companies and industry associations to keep education programmes updated in both form and content.

This ensures that the education meets the current requirements and needs of a dynamic labour market. You are therefore well prepared when choosing a future with KEA.

We are established as an international educational institution with many exchanges both to and from KEA by both students and teachers. This gives you a wealth of international contacts that are crucial in a globalised marketplace.

KEA offers programmes at three different levels of education:

- Academy Profession Degree Programme (AP)
- Top-up Bachelor Degree Programme (BA)
- Bachelor Degree Programme (BA)

At KEA the international element is of great importance and we pride ourselves on an inter-cultural environment. Each semester, KEA welcomes a large number of international students intending to complete a full degree at KEA. In 2016, KEA offers 13 different programmes taught entirely in English and 18 taught in Danish.

All study programmes are developed in close partnership with businesses to ensure students gain an insight into real-life situations and industry needs. Tuition is project based and businesses take an active part in evaluating student skills. An internship placement (of a minimum duration of 10 weeks) is mandatory, allowing students to test their knowledge and skills in a real-world work environment.

KEA – Copenhagen School of Design and Technology: Case Study

Architectural Technology and Construction Management
Elizabeth Sonubi, from the UK.

'Coming from England alone straight after sixth form and moving to Copenhagen, while very enjoyable and worth it nonetheless, was tough because I had no connections whatever and had to start my network from scratch – a totally fresh start.

'Finding accommodation was a bit of a nightmare, but then I found out it was the same for everyone. I applied for a dorm in the April and got one in the December, so it was four months of hostel hopping. I won't lie, sometimes it got a bit much and the feeling of unsettlement made me a little homesick. However, from my crazy hostel situation came many friendships that I wouldn't trade ever. I made so many acquaintances and great friends from all over the world, some of whom I only lived with for a couple days, and some for months. All I can say is that you really aren't alone, if you end up in the same situation as I was in.

'In class we learn many things that are technical and very detailed towards a specific field. Although there is an annoying scheduling problem that still needs work, KEA has some great staff with real experience.

'We have had talks and workshops about the construction industry and from architectural firms which really gave me a great and realistic insight of the industry. KEA has a mentor programme that I also signed up for, and I was assigned a great mentor from Henning Larsens A/S; this is great because he went to KEA also so we had a common ground and could relate to each other in this. When I went to visit the firm I got to see how it really is working in the architecture industry.

'As you can see there are both good and bad points, but if you have patience and drive then apply, because there are many good opportunities you can get from the school.'

Chapter 5
Studying in Europe

Following the European Union referendum result on 24 June, 2016, arrangements for British students studying at European institutions are to be negotiated as part of wider discussions with the other Member States regarding Britain's exit from the EU. In June 2016, the Government issued a statement advising that the current arrangement will continue to apply to those currently studying in the EU and those considering beginning their studies in the next academic year. The information provided in this chapter will continue to be applicable to British students while the UK remains a member of the EU, however students are advised to keep checking government and university websites for the most up-to-date information.

This chapter focuses on EU or EEA (European Economic Area) countries where currently UK students at public universities are charged the same fees as those for home students.

UK students are lucky to have such a diverse range of countries right on their doorstep. Flights to some European cities can be as quick as a train journey within the UK. European study brings the benefit of a new cultural and linguistic experience, without having to travel too far.

One myth about studying in Europe is the need to have brilliant language skills. Increasingly, European universities are offering entire courses taught in English. Of course, living in a different country will also enable you to immerse yourself in the language, thereby developing new language skills as a bonus. Some universities will even offer you the chance to take language lessons alongside your studies.

The countries featured offer a range of courses available in English. The European countries that aren't listed in this chapter will still have opportunities for study in English (most European countries do), but you may find that some have more limited options, and that English-taught programmes are perhaps restricted to private or international institutions.

In the Times Higher Education World University Rankings 2015–2016, a listing of the top 800 universities in the world, you will find universities from many European countries in the top 200: Switzerland, France, Germany, Ireland, Sweden, Finland, the Netherlands, Italy, Belgium, Denmark, Spain, Norway, Austria and Luxembourg are all represented.

Compatibility in the education system

Although there are differences in the education systems across Europe, a system known as the Bologna process has helped to make higher education more compatible and comparable across much of the continent. With transparent, mutually recognised systems and a clear credit framework, studying across Europe is now much simpler.

The Bologna process covers the European Higher Education Area (EHEA), an area much wider than the EU or EEA. It includes some countries applying for EU membership (Montenegro and

Turkey, for example) and some post-Soviet states (such as Armenia, Ukraine and Azerbaijan).

Bachelor's degrees, master's degrees and doctorates in these countries are all comparable in level. The European Credit Transfer System (ECTS) is used to measure workload and learning achievements of a course, and allows comparison between degrees in different countries. This makes it fairly straightforward to study a first degree in one European country and a postgraduate degree in another; some students even move part-way through their studies. Credit can be awarded for academic study, relevant placements and research, as long as they are part of the programme of study. Sixty credits equate to one full-time academic year. You may see bachelor's degrees of 180 or 240 credits, for example. The process of studying for an entire degree abroad is sometimes known as 'diploma mobility'.

Another benefit of the coordinated system is the diploma supplement, a detailed transcript used across Europe and the EHEA which outlines any studies you complete and gives full details of the level, nature, context, content and status of your achievements. It is particularly helpful if you intend to work or study in another country, as it provides a recognisable context for any accomplishments.

The coordination of quality assurance standards means that higher education across all these countries has to meet minimum requirements. It is important to note that this doesn't remove the need for thorough research into the tuition you will receive at a European university. You will find a range of different types of opportunity on offer: just as in the UK, universities across Europe vary in their prestige, quality of research, teaching and facilities.

Ensuring that you find a good match to your needs should form a key part of any research that you undertake.

It is important to note that most bachelor's degrees outside the UK are not typically classed as honours degrees; extra study is normally required to gain an honours degree.

Finding a course and institution

Both A Star Future (www.astarfuture.co.uk/what_to_study.html) and EUNiCAS (www.eunicas.co.uk) feature course listings for undergraduate courses taught in English. Another option is to use the Study Portal websites: www.bachelorsportal.eu, www.mastersportal.eu and www.phdportal.eu, but make sure that you select English as the language of instruction. You can use also PLOTEUS (Portal on Learning Opportunities throughout the European Space) at www.ec.europa.eu/ploteus/en, while EURAXESS has a database of research opportunities across Europe (www.ec.europa.eu/euraxess).

Individual websites often bring up a different range of courses, so it is worth searching more than one website. Although these websites are a good starting point, the information on application deadlines and fees is not always correct or up to date, so you should turn to the institutions for the latest information; you will be able to clarify any details with them.

ENIC-NARIC (European Network of Information Centres – National Academic Recognition Information Centres) has information on the education system of 55 countries, within Europe and beyond. The website also lists higher education institutions for each country, so you can be sure that your chosen institution is recognised (www.enic-naric.net).

Entry requirements

Entry requirements vary between countries and individual institutions. Many European countries ask that you have completed A level study or equivalent, without asking for specific grades; they are often more concerned with your performance once you start at university than your previous achievements, so some students may lose their place after the first year if they cannot cope with the academic demands of the course. Some European countries expect a wider range of subjects than UK students would normally take. It is standard practice in certain countries to ask for a qualification in maths or a foreign language at A level standard, even for non-related courses. If you haven't studied these subjects, look closely at the entry requirements to be sure that you will be considered for a place. If knowledge of the language is a prerequisite for entry on to a particular course, you may also be required to sit a language test as part of the admissions process.

Certain courses in some countries are subject to selective recruitment; look out for the terms *numerus clausus* or *numerus fixus*, which might indicate a competitive system for restricted places.

What is your UK qualification equivalent to?

Unless you have taken an internationally recognised qualification, such as the International Baccalaureate, it is possible that your UK qualifications will need to be compared to the qualifications in the country where you wish to study. A levels and the International Baccalaureate tend to be understood overseas, but many other UK qualifications will require further evaluation. Each country has its own system for ensuring the adequate comparison of academic qualifications. Your chosen institution will be able to advise you further on any information that they require, so it is best to speak to them initially. You may later need to contact the ENIC-NARIC organisation in your host country for a formal comparison of your qualifications (www.enic-naric.net). There will be a fee for this service.

Applying

Each European country has its own system and timescale for application. In order to make the application procedure as smooth as possible, it is important to check the following before you apply:

- entry requirements for the course, including language requirements (though this is usually only applicable if the programme is taught in a language other than English)
- application procedures: countries such as Denmark and the Netherlands operate a centralised application system similar to UCAS, while for other countries, including Italy and Switzerland, you will need to apply directly to your chosen institution
- deadlines for receiving applications
- details of any supporting documentation required by your university
- information on any admissions tests or interviews
- accommodation options on offer.

Country-specific information on these points is covered in the individual country profiles in this chapter.

Registering your stay

Currently, British citizens are entitled to live and work in the EU or EEA, and the guidance provided in this section and the subsequent one is still applicable to British students while the UK remains a member of the EU. The terms of the rights of British citizens within the EU or EEA after the UK exits the EU are to be determined as part of the UK's formal negotiations with the other EU Member States.

Although you won't have to apply for a visa if you are studying in the EU or the EEA, you may need to register your stay if you are going to be in the country for longer than three months. It is advisable to do this as early as possible, as in some countries you will have to report your presence upon your arrival. To register your stay, you will need to visit the relevant local authority (usually the local police station or immigration department), after which you will be issued with a registration certificate proving your right to live in your host country. To obtain a registration certificate, you will need to bring supporting documents with you when you register your stay, which are likely to include:

- a valid passport
- evidence of enrolment at an approved educational institution
- evidence of comprehensive medical insurance
- proof that you have adequate resources to fund your stay without recourse to income support.

Your university's international office will be able to advise whether it is necessary for you to register your stay and should assist you with the process, if required.

Costs and help with finances

For course fees, UK nationals studying at public universities in other EU countries are treated in the same way as home students from that particular country. That means that currently UK students pay the same fees as those for home students.

While England's tuition fees are now the highest in Europe, many countries charge no tuition fees to full-time EU students, including:

- Austria
- Denmark
- Finland
- Germany
- Norway
- Sweden.

Tuition fee loans may also be available to EU students, in countries where they are offered to home students. There is no requirement to offer maintenance grants or loans to EU students, although some countries choose to do so. Your university should be able to tell you more about the possibility of a loan or grant and any conditions you might need to meet in order to be eligible to receive funding.

The Netherlands is one of the few countries offering maintenance and tuition fee loans to EU students, although you will need to meet certain requirements. For more details, see the country profile for the Netherlands on page 168. In Denmark, EU students who work a minimum of 10 to 12 hours per week may be eligible for financial aid from the Danish government (SU). For more information on studying in Denmark, see page 127. For further details on funding opportunities in Europe, use some of the websites listed in the country profiles, or get in touch with staff in the international office of your chosen university.

There are public and private universities across the EU and EEA. Public universities are more likely to have a standardised system of tuition fees. In France, for example, courses at public universities tend to cost the same, regardless of the subject. In other countries, different courses or universities can charge varying amounts. Private institutions will charge a broader range of fees, often based on what they believe the market (i.e. the student) is prepared to pay. On the other hand, private institutions may well have additional opportunities for scholarships and favourable financial support, so it is worth investigating further to see what type of funding is available.

Cultural differences

Although you may be familiar with some of the European countries on the UK's doorstep, there will still be cultural differences to come to terms with. Different countries and their inhabitants have their own distinctive characteristics that you will need to get used to if you are to adjust properly. Although the language barrier may not impact on your ability to study (where courses are taught in English), it may make you feel isolated outside the university environment. Taking advantage of language classes can be an important factor when trying to settle in.

In some countries, many students stay in their local area and part-time study is common, while elsewhere students traditionally go to university when they are older; all this will impact on your university experience, so it is important to look into this before you decide on your venue for study.

Talk to your university's international office or try to make contact with other UK students to prepare yourself for the cultural differences you will face.

> **❝** It's a wonderfully chilled and relaxed lifestyle, the people are friendly and their English is great. They have many celebrations at points of the year where one can become a part of their culture and tradition. **❞**
>
> *Simran Gill, Fontys University of Applied Sciences,*
> *the Netherlands*

Working while studying

The following guidance will continue to apply to British citizens while the UK remains a member of the EU. The rights of British citizens to live and work within the EU or EEA after the UK exits the EU are to be determined as part of the UK's wider discussions with the EU. The opportunities to work will vary from country to country, and are often based on the number of local job opportunities for those with skills in English. In some countries, your opportunities will be limited so, to be on the safe side, you should plan your finances with the expectation that you will not find work.

If you need to work to get access to student grants and loans, as in Denmark, it may be worth moving to your new country a little earlier to begin the search. Alternatively, you can search for job opportunities through the European Job Mobility Portal (EURES) at https://ec.europa.eu/eures/public/homepage. Your university may also have job shops advertising student-job vacancies.

If you hope to work in Europe, either during or after your studies, it may be useful to prepare a Europass CV, which comprises a standard CV template used widely across Europe; it should make your educational background and work experience more easily understood. Find out more at www.europass.cedefop.europa.eu.

> **❝** I have a job at the university proofreading English and posting on the university's Facebook page in English. If you're a native English speaker, it's not too hard to get a part-time job or two. Your first port of call could always be the university in seeking work. **❞**
>
> *Hannah Burrows, University of Southern Denmark*

Staying on after study

Currently, while the UK remains a member of the European Union, staying on after study should not be restricted by legislation, although it may be limited by local opportunities. Competence in the local language, economic issues and local job opportunities may determine whether you choose to stay on for further study or work. Even if they don't remain in their university town or country, most students talk about the realisation that there is a whole world of opportunities out there for them.

Country-specific information

Note

Following the UK's decision to leave the EU, arrangements for British students studying at European institutions are to be negotiated as part of formal discussions with the EU. In June 2016, the Government issued a statement advising that the current arrangement will continue to apply to those currently studying in the EU and those considering beginning their studies in the next academic year. The country-specific information provided in the rest of the chapter will continue to be applicable to British students while the UK remains a member of the EU, however students are advised to keep checking national and university websites for the most up-to-date information.

While the number of English-taught programmes on offer in Europe is increasing, opportunities to study English-taught programmes at European institutions are much more widely available at postgraduate level than for undergraduate study. Several European countries offer a fairly limited number of under-graduate courses taught in English at public institutions: the list includes Austria, Belgium, France, Iceland, Italy and Norway.

However, private providers and international universities in these countries do offer a range of undergraduate degrees taught in English; they will be more expensive than the public institutions, but could still be cheaper than their UK counterparts, due to a more generous package of scholarships or financial support.

Belgium

In 2013, there were 242 UK students enrolled in higher education in Belgium, according to a study published by the UNESCO Institute for Statistics (UIS). (Global Flow of Tertiary-Level Students, UNESCO Institute for Statistics (UIS), 2013, www.uis. unesco.org/datacentre.)

Higher education in Belgium

The Flemish and French communities each have their own education systems. The higher education system in the Flemish community is split into universities and university colleges: universities offer academic degrees up to doctorate level, while university colleges award associate degrees and bachelor's degrees with a more professional focus.

Higher education in the French community is comprised of universities, or *hautes écoles*; and arts colleges, or *écoles supérieures des arts*. The French-language universities offer three-year bachelor's, two-year master's (with the exception of medicine and veterinary medicine) and doctorates requiring at least three years' study, while the *hautes écoles* are somewhat comparable to the Flemish university colleges, offering courses in scientific and technical fields. The *écoles supérieures*, meanwhile, offer program-mes in subjects such as art, design, music and performing arts.

Most higher education opportunities in Belgium require Dutch- or French-language skills, but there are some courses taught in English available, particularly in Brussels. There are often more opportunities to study in English at postgraduate level, with quite limited options for undergraduate study.

> **❝** I decided to study in Belgium due to the opportunities to intern in Brussels alongside studying. KU Leuven fitted the bill perfectly; it has the best reputation both in Belgium and within EU institutions. **❞**
>
> *Tom Aitchison, KU Leuven, Belgium*

Applying

Application dates vary, although a number of institutions require applications by 1 June. Check the deadline with your chosen university before applying.

Costs

Tuition fees will vary according to whether the course is offered by a university in the French-, Flemish- or German-speaking community; see the 'You could study ...' section on page 123 for examples of current course fees. The cost of living in Belgium is comparable to that in France and Sweden, which makes it slightly less expensive than the UK. It is ranked at number 18 out of 122 countries on the Numbeo 2016 Cost of Living Index at www.numbeo.com/cost-of-living/rankings_by_country.jsp.

Accommodation

Some universities offer students the opportunity to live in halls (known as *kot*), which cost around €400 (£310) per month on average, according to Study in Belgium (www.studyinbelgium. be). Places are often limited, so it is important to contact your institution's accommodation office early, to give yourself the best chance of securing a room. Study in Belgium suggests that average accommodation costs in the private sector range from €400–€650 (£310–£465) per month.

Four of Belgium's universities can be found in the top 200 of the Times Higher Education World University Rankings 2015–2016, with one institution featured in the top 50.

You could study ...

Philosophy BA
KU Leuven, Brussels campus
Three years
Apply by 1 June
Annual fees €890 (£690)
Monthly living costs €750 (£581)

MSc Physics
University of Antwerp
Two years
Apply by 30 April
Annual fees €1,550 (£1,201)
Monthly living costs €800 (£620)

Master in Management
Université catholique de Louvain
Two years
Apply by 31 August
Annual fees €835 (£651)
Annual living costs €9,500 (£7,410); allow a minimum of €2,500 (£1,950) for the first month to cover start-up costs

Useful websites

www.highereducation.be (Flemish community)
www.studyinbelgium.be (French community)

Also worth considering ...

Luxembourg could provide an alternative venue to
Belgium, although any opportunities taught in English
are likely to require additional skills in French, German or
Luxembourgish. The only public university is the University
of Luxembourg (wwwen.uni.lu), although there are a couple
of international campuses there too. Find out more at
ENIC-NARIC's Luxembourg page, www.enic-naric.net/
luxembourg.aspx.

Czech Republic

The Czech Republic has a long tradition of higher education and is
home to the oldest university in central Europe. It offers a range of
courses in English and low living costs. According to a 2016 study
by UNESCO Institute for Statistics (UIS), 443 UK students were
studying in the Czech Republic in 2013 (Global Flow of Tertiary-
Level Students, UNESCO Institute for Statistics (UIS), 2013, www.
uis.unesco.org/datacentre).

Higher education in the Czech Republic

Courses in the Czech Republic are based at public and private
universities and private colleges, some of which are international.
They run a two-semester system, with courses starting in mid-
September or mid-February. There are usually exams at the end of
each semester, followed by a break.

Undergraduate studies tend to take three to four years. Master's
degrees take one to three years if they follow on from bachelor's

degrees, or they may be full programmes, lasting four to six years. Doctorates last from three years.

There are opportunities to study for competitive courses such as medicine, dentistry and veterinary science in the Czech Republic and in other countries in eastern Europe.

Certain Czech institutions also are part of the Erasmus+ Joint Master Degree programme, which currently provides EU-funded scholarships for joint study programmes in at least two European countries. Czech universities participating in the scheme include the Czech Technical University in Prague, Charles University in Prague and the University of South Bohemia. For information, visit www.britishcouncil.org/study-work-create/opportunity/study-abroad/erasmus-joint-masters-degree.

Applying

Applications are made directly to your chosen university. Deadlines will vary from institution to institution, but applications usually have to be submitted between February and April. You will normally be required to submit an online application form on the university website, and you may have to pay an application fee. In addition, it is likely that you need to obtain an official document formally recognising your qualifications; the recognition procedure is known as *nostrification*, and your university will be able to advise on what is needed. Additional requirements might include academic transcripts and certificates, a letter of motivation, an admissions test and interview. Your university's international office will provide further and more detailed information on all aspects of the application process.

You can search for courses taught in English through EducationCZ (www.education.cz) and Study in the Czech Republic (www.studyin.cz).

Costs

Although courses taught in Czech are free regardless of your nationality, you will be charged tuition fees for courses taught in English. The universities set their own tuition fees for such courses and there is no maximum limit.

Fees usually start at around €1,500 (£1,163) but can be as much as €13,000 (£10,076) for a degree in medicine or dentistry. Scholarships may be available; you can find out more at the Ministry of Education, Youth and Sports (www.msmt.cz) or from your university.

For its cost of living in 2016, the Czech Republic is ranked 79 out of 122 countries, according to Numbeo (www.numbeo.com/cost-of-living/rankings_by_country.jsp), which is considerably lower than much of western Europe and the Nordic countries. Study in the Czech Republic (www.studyin.cz) suggests allowing for living costs of around US$350–US$750 (£240–£515) per month, though prices are likely to be higher in cities such as Prague.

Accommodation

Most universities offer students accommodation in shared dormitories, with an average monthly rent of €120 (£93), according to Study in the Czech Republic. Private accommodation costs around €250 (£194) per month, and will require the payment of a deposit.

You could study ...

Bachelor Computer Science

Charles University, Prague
Three years
Apply by 31 May
Annual fees CZK140,000 (£4,009)
Monthly living costs €400–€600 (£310–£465)

MA Architecture and Construction
VŠB – Technical University of Ostrava
Two years
Apply by 30 April
Annual fees €4,000 (£3,096)
Monthly living costs €250–€300 (£194–£232)

PhD Visual Arts: Multimedia and Design
Thomas Bata University in Zlín
Three years
Apply by 30 June
Annual fees €2,500 (£1,035)
Monthly living costs CZK5,000–CZK6,000 (£143–£172)

Useful websites
www.studyin.cz
www.education.cz

Also worth considering ...

If you're interested in opportunities in eastern Europe, have you considered Bulgaria, Croatia, Hungary, Poland, Romania, Slovakia or Slovenia? Find out more at:

- **ENIC-NARIC country page for Bulgaria:** www.enic-naric.net/bulgaria.aspx
- **Study in Croatia:** www.studyincroatia.hr
- **Study Hungary:** www.studyhungary.hu
- **Study in Poland:** www.studyinpoland.pl
- **ENIC-NARIC country page for Romania:** www.enic-naric.net/romania.aspx
- **Study in Slovakia:** www.studyin.sk
- **Slovenia:** www.slovenia.si/en/study.

Denmark

According to the UNESCO Institute for Statistics (UIS), 653 UK students chose to study in Denmark in 2013 (Global Flow of Tertiary-Level Students, UNESCO Institute for Statistics (UIS), 2013, www.uis.unesco.org/datacentre). Education in Denmark centres on problem-based learning and requires active participation, which will develop your ability to present creative solutions to complex problems. Alternatively, there are more vocational courses on offer at Danish university colleges and academies of professional higher education. The country has a strong tradition of public universities and at PhD level there are even fully funded, salaried opportunities in English.

Higher education in Denmark

Denmark offers over 700 higher education programmes taught in English. You can study at research universities (*universitet*) at undergraduate and postgraduate level; it takes at least three years to complete a bachelor's degree, two years for a master's, and three or four for a doctorate. Currently, certain Danish institutions, including the Technical University of Denmark and Aalborg University, offer programmes as part of the Erasmus+ Joint Master Degree scheme.

The University of Copenhagen (ranked 82), Aarhus University (106) and the Technical University of Denmark (167) are in the Times Higher Education World University Rankings 2015–2016 top 200. UK universities with comparable rankings are the University of Warwick (80), the University of Southampton (110) and the University of Leicester (which is tied with the Technical University of Denmark, the University of California, Riverside in the USA, Belgium's Université catholique de Louvain and the National Taiwan University).

Programmes at university colleges (*professionshøjskole*) are more professional in nature, leading to three- to four-year professional undergraduate degrees in areas such as engineering, teaching or business. Academies of professional higher education (*erhvervsakademier*) offer academy profession (AP) degree programmes, which normally last two years. An AP offers the opportunity to complete work placements in Danish or overseas companies; for some courses, this can be topped up to a professional bachelor's degree with further study.

The academic year runs from September to June, with the possibility of February intake too. Some courses are competitive and have additional requirements beyond the completion of A level-standard qualifications. Courses in Denmark are assessed by oral, written or practical exams.

> **❝❝** The university I chose is the biggest in Denmark, and the course gave me the best opportunities of all of those I looked at. It's entirely in English and I study a full-time two-year programme to get a broad base of topics. I also get the opportunity to do internships and study abroad as part of the programme. I can have a part-time English-speaking student job alongside studying. The university offers accommodation for the full length of my degree, and all my teachers are recognised experts on America. The teaching style is more like seminars than lectures, with a discussion by all students and teacher together. You have a lot of group work in class, and sometimes homework can be preparing a Powerpoint presentation with two other students. **❞❞**
>
> *Hannah Burrows, University of Southern Denmark*

Applying

At undergraduate level, applications for programmes taught in English are made through the Danish Co-ordinated Application System (KOT) at www.optagelse.dk/admission/index.html. Applications for undergraduate courses starting in August or September open on 1 February and close on 15 March at 12pm (CET). Applications are made online, but you will also need to send a signed signature page to every institution that you apply to, as your choices will only be able to download your application from KOT once they have received the signature page. Most Danish universities will accept the signature page via email.

You can choose up to eight courses through KOT; if you apply for more than one course, you will be required to list your courses in order of preference before submitting your application, with the option of changing the order up until 12pm (CET) on 5 July. Unlike UCAS, where you can receive up to five offers for undergraduate applications, you can only receive one offer through KOT. So, if you apply to eight courses and receive an offer from the fourth choice on your list, this means that your applications to your first three choices have been unsuccessful, and you will not receive any communication from your lower-placed choices. Each institution has its own means of communicating its decision, so it is important to check this information on individual university websites.

Students applying through KOT also have the option to be put on standby, which means being added to a waiting list if you are not admitted initially. Applying for a standby place does not hinder your chances of being admitted directly to the course of your choice; should you be rejected, you will be assessed for a standby position at the same institution. However, receiving a standby place does not necessarily guarantee you a place in the year you apply; places are likely to be limited, as they will be dependent on the number of cancellations received by the institution, so you may have to wait until the following year before starting your course.

Direct application is required at postgraduate level, with deadlines varying; your chosen university will be able to advise you further.

Costs

Currently, Danish students are eligible for State Educational Support (SU): a grant of up to DKK5,941 (£619) per month and access to a loan of DKK3,040 (£317) per month. Students from other EU or EEA countries may qualify for this support, provided that they work 10 to 12 hours per week in Denmark. Make sure you check on the Ministry of Education website, www.su.dk/english/su-as-a-foreign-citizen/equal-status-according-to-eu-law/you-work-in-denmark, at the time of applying. Some scholarships may also be available; see Study in Denmark's scholarship page (http://studyindenmark.dk/study-options/tuition-fees-scholarships) for details.

Denmark is an expensive country to live in. It comes in at number six in Numbeo's cost-of-living rankings for 2016 (www.numbeo.com/cost-of-living/rankings_by_country.jsp), making it the third most expensive country in Europe. With wages of around €10–€12 (£7.75–£9.30) per hour for students, it is still possible to have a reasonable standard of living. Students with no Danish-language skills may be able to find jobs in English-speaking bars and cafés, for example.

Accommodation

Study in Denmark (www.studyindenmark.dk) suggests that you can expect to pay €240–€460 (£186–£357) per month for a room in a halls of residence, and between €270–€600 (£209–£465) per month for a room in a privately rented flat. Your university should be able to assist you with finding accommodation, and you can find more information and advice at http://studyindenmark.dk/live-in-denmark/housing-1/how-to-find-housing.

You could study ...

BSc Chemical Engineering and Biotechnology

Aalborg University, Esbjerg campus

Three years

Apply through www.optagelse.dk by 15 March

Tuition fees DKK0

Monthly living costs DKK3,500–DKK5,500 (£364–£572)

MSc Economics

University of Copenhagen

One year

Apply by 1 April (autumn semester) or 1 November (spring semester)

Tuition fees DKK0

Monthly living costs DKK7,000–DKK9,000 (£729–£937)

PhD History, Archaeology and Classical Studies

Aarhus University

Three years

Apply by 15 March

Tuition fees DKK0

Monthly living costs DKK5,000 (£520)

Useful websites

www.studyindenmark.dk

Estonia

Estonia offers good value for money and a vibrant student life. As many as 89% of international students say that Estonia is a good place to study (International Student Barometer™ 2014) but, so far, there aren't many UK students based there. It is also one of the safest countries in the world to live in, according to a 2016 study conducted by the Statistic Brain Research Institute. ('Safest Countries to Live in the World – Statistic Brain.' Statistic Brain Research Institute, publishing as Statistic Brain. Accessed 29 April 2016. www.statisticbrain.com/safest-countries-to-live-in-the-world.)

Higher education in Estonia

The country is keen to attract international students and is expanding its courses taught in English; it currently offers more than 100 recognised English-taught degrees. These programmes are accredited and are available at the following institutions:

- **Estonian Academy of Arts:** www.artun.ee
- **Estonian Academy of Music and Theatre:** www.ema.edu.ee
- **Estonian University of Life Sciences:** www.emu.ee
- **Tallinn University:** www.tlu.ee
- **Tallinn University of Technology:** www.ttu.ee/en
- **University of Tartu:** www.ut.ee
- **Estonian Business School:** www.ebs.ee
- **The Estonian Information Technology College:** www.itcollege.ee/en
- **Estonian Entrepreneurship University of Applied Sciences:** www.euas.eu
- **Euroacademy:** http://euroakadeemia.ee/en/euroacademy/.

Some higher education institutions offer alternative options taught in English, including modules for exchange students or short courses; e.g., Tallinn University offers a three-week international programme in summer and winter, and the University of Tartu holds two- to four-week courses during the summer.

Education in Estonia takes place in public universities, private universities and professional higher education institutions. The academic year starts in September and is divided into two semesters. Generally, you would be looking at a three- to four-year academic bachelor's degree, a one- to two-year master's qualification, and a three- to four-year doctorate. Programmes in medicine, dentistry, pharmacy, veterinary science, architecture and civil engineering take five to six years.

All courses include written and/or oral exams, which take place at the end of each semester. Depending on the course, students either sit the *arvestus*, which is a straight pass/fail assessment, or the *eksam*, which is a graded examination. Grades for the *eksam* are standardised, ranging from A (or 5) to E (or 1). Grade F (or 0) means that the assessment has not been passed.

Applying

You can search and apply for many courses online through Dream Apply (https://estonia.dreamapply.com). If you are applying through Dream Apply, you can select up to two programmes per university, and up to five universities with a single application, giving a maximum of ten choices. Deadlines are set by the individual institutions and usually range from January to July for English-taught courses starting in September. Some universities will charge an application fee.

Costs

According to Study in Estonia, fees for bachelor's and master's degrees range from no fees to €5,000 (£3,875) per year. Fees for veterinary medicine and medicine courses are higher, and can be as much as €11,000 (£8,526) per year. Free tuition fees are more common at postgraduate level.

Estonia is one of the countries offering some form of financial support to EU students (which currently includes the UK). The government offers a need-based study allowance: students with an average monthly income of below €358 (£277) per family member may be entitled to a monthly allowance of €75–€220 (£58–£171).

The Estonian government offers additional financial support through its National Scholarship Programme. The scholarship is paid in monthly instalments for twelve calendar months until the final year of study, at which point payments are made over the course of ten months. At bachelor's and master's level, successful applicants receive €350 (£271) per month, while PhD students receive €422 (£327) per month. For undergraduate study, you must be studying a course relating to Estonian language and culture in order to be eligible for the scholarship. In addition to filling in the application form, you will need to submit various supporting documents with your application, including a CV, study plan, an academic transcript and a letter from your chosen institution, confirming your place and explaining their reasons for accepting you. For more details on how to apply, visit http://adm. archimedes.ee/stipendiumid/en/valisriikide-stipendiumid.

Other scholarships are available, primarily for postgraduate study; ask your university for more information, or visit the scholarships section of the Study in Estonia website at www.studyinestonia.ee/scholarships-degree-studies.

Living costs in Estonia are reasonable. On average, Study in Estonia suggests you should allow €300–€500 (£233–£388) per month for living costs. In addition, public transport in Estonia is often free or subsidised for students: students studying in Tallinn benefit from free public transport, while students in Tartu can get a discounted a monthly season ticket. Estonia is ranked at number 58 out of 122 countries on the cost-of-living rankings for 2016; this is considerably lower than the UK and much of western Europe.

Accommodation
Some universities offer student dormitories, which can be single, double or triple rooms in a shared apartment, and range from

€80–€150 (£62–£116), according to Study in Estonia. Prices will vary considerably for private accommodation, but you can expect to pay up to €450 per month (£349) for a private flat, and you will normally be required to pay a deposit, which is usually the equivalent of three months' rent.

You could study ...

BA Crossmedia in Film and Television

Tallinn University
Three years
Apply through Dream Apply by 1 June
Annual fees €2,800 (£2,168)
Monthly living costs excluding accommodation €300–€500 (£232–£387)

MSc Engineering Physics

Tallinn University of Technology
Two years
Apply directly by 1 May
Annual fees €0
Monthly living costs for food and on-campus accommodation €370–€420 (£287–£325)

PhD Management

Estonian Business School, Tallinn
Four years
Apply through Dream Apply by 1 August
Fees €50 (£39) per credit (core and special subjects), supervising fee €750 (£585)
Monthly living costs for food and other basic expenses, excluding accommodation €250–€300 (£193–£232)

Useful websites

www.studyinestonia.ee

Study in Estonia has put together a *Survival Guide for International Students*, which includes an Estonian phrasebook, bucket list and student event calendar. Students receive a printed copy when they start their studies; however, if you want to take a look at what's on offer before you get there, the guide is available to download as an app from the Apple App Store and Google Play.

Also worth considering ...

If you're interested in opportunities in the Baltic states, have you considered Latvia and Lithuania? Find out more at Study in Latvia, www.studyinlatvia.lv and Study in Lithuania, www.lietuva.lt/en/education_sience/study_lithuania.

Finland

Finland is considered to be a safe and forward-looking nation with a high-quality education system. Temperatures can range from +30°C to –20°C and the sun never sets in parts of the country in June and early July. The academic year runs from August to the end of May; it is usually split into two semesters, August to December, and January to May. Most students start in August, with limited opportunities to join in January.

The latest figures from the UNESCO Institute for Statistics (UIS) show us that 220 UK students were studying in Finland in 2013 (Global Flow of Tertiary-Level Students, UNESCO Institute for Statistics (UIS), 2013, www.uis.unesco.org/datacentre).

Higher education in Finland

Higher education in Finland takes places in research-based universities and vocationally focused polytechnics (or universities of applied sciences – UAS). In the universities, few programmes are taught in English at undergraduate level, although master's and doctoral degrees are more widely available. It is the opposite in the polytechnics, where there are plenty of programmes taught in English at undergraduate level, with a smaller number of English-taught master's programmes. (Doctoral qualifications are not available in the polytechnics, only in the universities.) To access a UAS master's programme, you will need three years of relevant experience, in addition to any academic requirements. To search for programmes, go to the Study in Finland database at www. studyinfinland.fi/study_options/study_programmes_ database.

The degrees vary in length as follows:

Universities
- **Bachelor's degree:** three years
- **Master's degree:** two years
- **Doctoral degree:** four years.

Polytechnic/university of applied sciences
- **Bachelor's degree:** three-and-a-half to four-and-a-half years
- **Master's degree:** one to one-and-a-half years (after at least three years of relevant experience)
- **Doctoral degrees:** not available.

Applying

Applications tend to be online, although the application process and timescale differ between the universities and polytechnics.

At universities, applications to English-taught undergraduate and master's programmes can be made directly or via www.studyinfo. fi, the study portal for University Admissions Finland (UAF); ask your university which way to proceed.

If you are applying for an undergraduate university programme through www.studyinfo.fi, you can make a 'joint application', which allows you to apply to up to six programmes with one application, while applications for master's courses tend to be made individually; applications can be made directly to the institution, or via www.studyinfo.fi. If you are applying through a joint application, you will need to list your choices in order of preference; this order cannot be changed once the application period has ended (usually the end of January for degree programmes taught in English).

Doctoral programmes require direct application; the application timescale varies between institutions: some accept applications at any time, while others have specific timescales in which to apply. Speak to the international office or the relevant faculty at your chosen university.

At polytechnics, undergraduate applications should be made in January via www.studyinfo.fi. Some UAS undergraduate courses may offer the option of a spring term intake, and prospective students wishing to enter in the spring should usually apply in September. If you are applying for a UAS master's degree, you should apply directly to the polytechnic or via www.studyinfo.fi. at the time they specify, usually between January and April. However, some institutions may set their own separate admissions period; you can find out more on your chosen institution's website.

Undergraduate admissions procedures normally require an entrance exam. This tends to be a written test, but may be an audition or portfolio for certain art, drama or music programmes. Most university tests are taken in Finland, but some polytechnic entrance tests can be taken outside the country; see www.jamk.fi/en/Education/finnips/further-information for more information.

Make sure that you prepare fully, following any instructions provided by the institution.

> As the academic year in Finland begins in August, shortly after A level results are released, there is normally insufficient time to confirm a place, so you might need to consider a gap year.

Costs

Higher education in Finland is free to EU students (which currently includes the UK) at all levels of higher education. However, unless you have lived in Finland for a minimum of two years prior to starting your course, you are not entitled to receive state grants or loans.

Scholarship opportunities are very limited for bachelor's and master's programmes in Finland, and tend to be more widely available at doctoral level. Finland also runs a number of Erasmus+ Joint Master's programmes, for which there are certain awards available. For more details of current scholarships on offer, speak to your institution, or see the 'Scholarships' section at Study in Finland, www.studyinfinland.fi/tuition_and_scholarships.

Overall, Finland is ranked at number 20 in Numbeo's cost-of-living rankings for 2016 (www.numbeo.com/cost-of-living/rankings_by_country.jsp), making it slightly cheaper than the UK, and comparable to living in France or Belgium. The average monthly living costs are €700–€900 (£543–£698), according to Study in Finland; expect to pay more in Helsinki than in smaller towns and cities. EU citizens have the right to work in Finland, although language issues and a fairly heavy workload at university mean that it may be difficult to find time to accommodate both study and work in your schedule. If you are staying in the country for longer than three months, you will need to register your residence, either at a local police station or through the Enter Finland e-service: https://enterfinland.fi/eServices/info/europeanpermits.

Accommodation

Most student accommodation in Finland is organised through student housing foundations; for a full list of accredited organisations, see www.soa.fi. Student housing is reasonably priced; Study in Finland indicates that students can expect to pay between €160–€340 (£124–£264) per month for a single room in a shared flat, and your university should support you in finding accommodation. Private accommodation is likely to be considerably more expensive.

> 66 The housing is very cheap (cheaper than the UK) and relatively decent. The only thing that costs a lot is the food and the alcohol, but as long as you are aware of money, then it should work out! 99
>
> *Fiona Higgins, HAAGA-HELIA,*
> *University of Applied Sciences, Finland*

You could study ...
Bachelor Physiotherapy, Bachelor of Health Care
Satakunta University of Applied Sciences, Pori
Three-and-a-half years
Apply by 27 January
Tuition fees €0
Monthly living costs €500–€700 (£387–£542)

Master Global and Transnational Studies
University of Tampere
Two years
Apply by 27 January
Tuition fees €0
Monthly living costs €700–€900 (£543–£698)

PhD Commercial Law
Hanken School of Economics, Helsinki
Four years
Apply by 1 April for August start, 30 September for January start
Tuition fees €0
Monthly living costs €780–€1,180 (£605–£915)

Useful websites
www.studyinfinland.fi

Also worth considering ...

If you're interested in the Nordic countries, perhaps you would be interested in studying in Iceland. To find out more, go to Study in Iceland at www.studyiniceland.is and the ENIC-NARIC country page for Iceland at www.enic-naric.net/iceland.aspx.

France
France is the UK's closest continental neighbour, offering good-quality education with a strong international reputation. According to the UNESCO Institute for Statistics (UIS), in 2013, the country attracted 6% of all international students at university level, with 2,013 UK students opting to study there (Global Flow of Tertiary-Level Students, UNESCO Institute for Statistics (UIS),

2013, www.uis.unesco.org/datacentre). On the downside, it has
limited English-medium options at undergraduate level in its
public universities, though some courses are taught partially in
English. This may well change, as the rules preventing teaching
in English at public universities have been relaxed.

France has five universities in the Times Higher Education
World University Rankings 2015–2016 top 200 universities,
including the École Normale Supérieure, which appears
above the University of Manchester in the current rankings.

Higher education in France

There are three main types of higher education institution in
France: teaching takes place in public universities, *grandes écoles*
(which include French business and engineering schools), and
schools of art & design and architecture. In addition, France has
a large number of public and private specialised schools offering
training in vocational courses such as nursing, journalism and
hotel management.

Universities offer three-year bachelor's degrees (*licence*), two-year
master's and three-year doctorates. Admissions to undergraduate
degrees require the baccalauréat (A levels) or equivalent, although
for courses such as medicine or dentistry, students will often
have to sit competitive exams at the end of the first year of study
for a restricted number of places in the second year. The master's
degree you choose depends on your future plans: you can opt for
the research master's (*master recherche*), which typically leads to
a doctorate, or the professional master's (*master professionnel*),
which is usually taken by those intending to start their career
straight after graduation.

The *grandes écoles* tend to focus on political science, engineering, business and management courses. The standard qualification conferred by the *grandes écoles* is equivalent to a master's degree, and usually lasts for three years. Many of these institutions require a competitive exam for entry, the *prépa*, which students may spend two years working towards (after achieving A level-standard qualifications). There may be some opportunities for the best international students at these institutions; you are advised to contact them directly to discuss their requirements, though it is likely that you will need a high level of proficiency in French if you wish to be considered for admission.

France has over 100 public schools of fine and applied arts, or *écoles supérieures*, offering diplomas taken over three to five years of study. Higher education at the French schools of architecture follows a similar structure to the public universities: first-cycle diplomas are awarded after three years of study and are equivalent to a bachelor's degree, after which students can proceed to a second-cycle diploma, which lasts two years and is equivalent to a master's qualification. At PhD level, an additional three years of study is required to obtain a third-cycle diploma.

The academic year starts in September or October and ends in May or June, much as in the UK.

> ❝ The class size is around 30–40 students, and there is an emphasis on group work. Furthermore, the professors are always willing to help students individually, and often give up their spare time in order to ensure that each student is on the same level. ❞
>
> *Alican Spafford, Rouen Business School, France*

Applying

Applications for courses taught in English should usually be made through the international office of your chosen institution, and you can normally make direct applications from around November. Application deadlines vary between spring and summer, but do apply as early as you are able. Some institutions have a rolling programme of application and recruitment throughout the year.

In addition to submitting an application form and paying the application fee, you may need to include the following documents:

- academic transcript
- certificates
- personal statement, to include motivation for studying and future career goals
- letters of recommendation (normally two)
- research proposal (for postgraduate research)
- copy of passport.

There is a centralised application process known as APB or *Admission Post Bac*, which is compulsory for a number of courses; for a full list, see www.admission-postbac.fr/site/guide_2016/ Guide_du_candidat_euro_2016.pdf. Applications are made via the APB website at www.admission-postbac.fr, where you will be asked to create your student 'file' by filling in a form online with your personal information and details of your education to date.

The application window is the same for domestic and international students: applications open from 20 January and close at 6pm on 20 March for courses starting in September. You can apply to up to twelve courses through APB, and will be asked to list your choices in order of preference, though it is possible to change the order up until 31 May.

Admission to the *grandes écoles* is highly competitive, and is usually made on the basis of the test score that students achieve in the *prépa* after two years of preparatory study in the *classes préparatoires aux grandes écoles* (CPGE); applications for these preparatory classes are made through APB. Some *grandes écoles* offer international students the opportunity to transfer on to one of their courses after a year of initial study at another university, on the basis of their academic record and their performance in admissions tests. However, each school will have its own admissions procedures, so you should check with your chosen institution before applying.

Applications to the *écoles supérieures* (art schools) should be made online through Campus Art, www.campusart.org/home/apply-online. Admissions procedures for *écoles supérieures* are selective, and you may be asked to attend an interview. Students wishing to enter one of the national schools of architecture should apply via APB.

Costs

France spends approximately €10,000 (£7,750) per student per year on higher education. One result of this is the low price for degrees awarded at public universities, which are often under €500 (£387) per year for undergraduate and postgraduate study. Students will usually be required to pay administration fees, which are set by individual institutions, although the total cost of study is still much lower than studying at a comparable institution in the UK. Fees at public universities are set by law, while private institutions are more expensive, ranging from €3,000–€10,000 (£2,325–£7,750) or more per year, though some establishments will offer scholarships to help fund study.

The fees listed below are those set for 2015–2016.

- **Bachelor's degree or *licence*:** three years, annual tuition fees of €184 (£143).
- **Master's degree:** two years, annual tuition fees of €256 (£198).
- **Doctoral degree or doctorate:** three years, annual tuition fees of €391 (£303).

France is a fairly expensive place to live, ranked number 19 of 122 countries in Numbeo's cost-of-living index (www.numbeo.com/cost-of-living/rankings_by_country.jsp), a few places below the UK. Campus France suggests that students would need around €600–€800 (£465–£620) per month to cover housing, transportation and food. Costs in Paris are considerably higher: etudiantdeparis.fr recommends that students in Paris should budget for at least €900–€1,000 (£697–£775) per month for living expenses.

Grants may be available to some international students through the French Ministry of Foreign and European Affairs, while Entente Cordiale scholarships are awarded for postgraduate-level study. Information on these and other scholarships can be found at CampusBourses (http://campusbourses.campusfrance.org/fria/bourse/#/catalog). Note that application deadlines for funding may fall earlier than course application deadlines.

Accommodation

University accommodation is managed by regional student-service agencies, known as CROUS, though places are limited. According to Campus France, the average monthly rent for public university accommodation tends to range from €120 (£94) for a single room to €350 (£274) for a studio apartment. Some of the *grandes écoles* and other private institutions have their own halls of residence, with costs ranging from €250–€350 (£196–£274) a month. Renting in the private sector will be considerably more expensive, and accommodation costs in Paris are likely to be high. Campus

France has compiled a directory of reliable accommodation agencies, which are listed according to the maximum length of stay permitted, location and rates offered. The directory can be downloaded at http://ressources.campusfrance.org/guides_etab/logement/fr/adresses_logement_fr.pdf (available in French only).

You may be eligible to receive a government housing allowance (ALS) to subsidise your rent, which is paid in monthly instalments through CAF (*Caisses d'Allocations Familiales*). Applications can be made online at www.caf.fr and must be submitted within three months of moving in to your place of residence. You will need to open a French bank account and provide supporting documentation when you apply, including a copy of your passport and a document proving your tenancy in France. Assistance is granted from the month after you move in to your accommodation, so if you move in on 1 September, you will be eligible to receive your first payment from 1 October, though it may take longer than this to process your application. For more information, see www.campusfrance.org/en/page/housing-assistance-students.

You could study ...

Bachelor Marketing & Business

Burgundy School of Business (private)

Three years

Apply by 10 June

Annual fees €7,000 (£5,436)

Monthly living costs €770–€800 (£598–£621)

Master of Civil Engineering

École Centrale de Nantes (public *grande école*)

Two years

Apply by 25 May

Annual fees €500 (£388)

Monthly living costs approximately €660 (£512)

PhD Neuroscience and Cognition

Université de Lyon (public)

Three years

Rolling applications; applicants are required to find a thesis
director and secure financial aid before applying

Annual fees €391 (£303)

Monthly living costs not provided; thesis allowances available

Useful websites

www.campusfrance.org/en

Germany

Germany is the largest economy in Europe and offers a world-
class education, with the added benefit of no tuition fees for
undergraduate study and a number of master's courses at public
universities. In 2013, 1,499 UK students opted to study there,
according to the latest data from the UNESCO Institute for
Statistics (UIS) (Global Flow of Tertiary-Level Students, UNESCO
Institute for Statistics (UIS), 2013, www.uis.unesco.org/datacentre).

> Germany has improved upon last year's strong performance
> in the Times Higher Education World University Rankings,
> with 20 of its universities featuring in the top 200 for
> 2015–2016, retaining its position of third place, behind the
> USA and the UK.

Higher education in Germany

In Germany, higher education is run by each of the 16 states,
rather than by one central Ministry of Education. You can choose
between universities, universities of applied sciences and specialist
colleges of art, film or music. Universities offer the more academic
options up to doctoral level, with universities of applied sciences

taking a more practical approach, but only to master's level. Colleges of art, film and music offer creative or design-based courses and often have additional entry requirements to determine artistic skill or musical aptitude. It should be noted that most courses at these specialist colleges are taught in German only. You can search for courses in English at www.study-in.de/en/plan-your-studies/find-programme-and-university.

Most institutions are publicly funded, with a smaller number financed by the Church or privately funded. The majority of German students study at public institutions; they are cheaper and the standard of education is comparable to that in the UK, although they can suffer from overcrowding. At HochschulKompass (www.hochschulkompass.de), you can search for institutions by the way they are funded or by the category of institution.

> **❝** Studying is much more independent here; I choose how much work to put into my classes, and no-one chases students up if they don't hand in homework or come unprepared to a class. This can be very freeing, since the atmosphere is very unpressured and I put effort into my studies because I want to, not because I have to. However, the flip-side of this is that I have to motivate myself to work and use my time productively of my own accord, which has taken some getting used to.**❞**
>
> *Elizabeth Edwards, Otto-Friedrich-Universität,*
> *Bamberg, Germany*

The academic year begins in September, with classes starting in September or October. *Wintersemester* teaching runs until mid-February or March, while *Sommersemester* commences in March or April and ends in early July. Some courses are also available to start in the *Sommersemester*; to search for courses by start date, go to www.study-in.de. The semester dates vary slightly between universities and universities of applied science.

If you want to study in Germany, you'll need a *Hochschulzugangs-berechtigung*, or university entrance qualification. You can check whether your qualifications are comparable at the German Academic Exchange Service (DAAD) online admissions database, www.daad.de.

Applying

Application processes vary between different universities and even between different courses at the same institution. Some will opt for a central application service, such as those listed below, while others require direct application. The best advice is to check with the international office at your university.

Where you submit your application depends initially on the subject for which you apply. Before you begin the application process, you should check with your institution whether your chosen subject is with central *numerus clausus* (NC), local NC, or no NC at all. If you are applying to study a subject with local NC or no NC at all, you should check whether your university is a member of uni-assist (the university application service for international students, most often used when applicants have qualifications from outside Germany; a full list of member institutions is available on the website, www.uni-assist.de).

Applications via uni-assist are made online, though some universities may require you to supply additional forms or documentation as part of your application, and each university has its own deadlines. The application fee is €75 (£58) for applications to a single university; applications for courses starting in the same semester cost an additional €15 (£12) per university. If your institution is not a member of uni-assist, you should apply directly to the university and follow their admissions procedures carefully.

What is *numerus clausus*? This phrase relates to courses that have far more applicants than there are places. Some courses, including medicine, dentistry, veterinary medicine and pharmacy, have a nationwide *numerus clausus* (central NC), while other courses may be restricted only at a particular university (local NC). If your chosen course is classed as *numerus clausus*, pay careful attention to any additional entry requirements and check how applicants are chosen.

If you are applying for a subject with a central NC, such as medicine or dentistry, you should send your university application to the Trust for admission to higher education (Stiftung für Hochschulzulassung). Applications are made via their website, www.hochschulstart.de, and you can apply for up to 12 courses. No application fee is required. Regardless of the system you use, you may need to provide additional information or evidence, including:

- certificates of qualifications achieved (your university will tell you how to get an authenticated copy)
- CV
- essay
- academic reference
- educational transcript
- SAT or ACT (American College Test) scores (see College Board for further details, https://collegereadiness. collegeboard.org/sat)
- research proposal (for postgraduate applications).

Some German universities prefer students to have studied maths at A level, even for courses without mathematical content. A language A level, not necessarily German, is also a common requirement.

Most application processes are open between October and June or July (for an autumn start), although you should check individual deadlines and apply in good time.

Costs

There are no fees for undergraduate-level study at public institutions. However, higher education institutions across the country make a charge for semester contributions; this covers certain administration charges and may entitle you to student discounts and free public transport. The cost varies between institutions; you should budget for around €250 (£194) per semester.

Many master's degrees at public universities are free if they follow on directly from a related bachelor's programme obtained in Germany. Where fees are charged for postgraduate study, they range from around €500 (£387) to as much as €10,000 (£7,750) per semester. You can expect to pay higher fees at private universities and colleges, at both undergraduate and postgraduate level, in some cases as much as €30,000 (£23,238) per year. Tuition fees for doctoral degrees in public universities are free for the first six semesters (equivalent to three years of study), although PhD students are still required to pay a semester contribution.

If you're lucky enough to get a scholarship, it is unlikely to cover all costs. Scholarships are particularly limited for undergraduate study. Search on the DAAD Scholarship Database, www.daad.de/deutschland/en, and ask your university about their opportunities.

Living costs vary depending on where you study and the type of lifestyle you enjoy. According to the Study in Germany website (www.study-in.de), students should allow around €800 (£620) per month on average. Cities such as Dresden and Aachen offer a more reasonable cost of living, with Munich, Hamburg, Heidelberg and Frankfurt among the most expensive cities.

Germany is ranked number 29 of 122 countries on a 2016 cost-of-living ranking (www.numbeo.com/cost-of-living/rankings_by_country.jsp), so living there should be not only cheaper than the UK, New Zealand, the Netherlands and Singapore.

Accommodation

Most universities offer halls of residence, though student demand is often high, so it is important to apply as early as possible upon receiving confirmation of your place. Most applications for university halls are processed by *Studentenwerk*, the Student Services Organisation; applications can be made via their website at www.studentenwerke.de/en. You can search for halls of residence on the Study in Germany website at www.study-in.de/en/plan-your-stay/accommodation/dormitoryfinder. For accommodation in the private rental sector, you can start your search at www.wg-gesucht.de/en.

> **66** Many students choose to rent a room in a student flat (*Wohngemeinschaft*, WG), which often costs the same or less than student halls. There tend to be good websites and social media groups where free rooms or flats are advertised, so it might be useful to look into that before arriving to avoid having to couch-surf on arrival. **99**
>
> *Elizabeth Edwards, Otto-Friedrich-Universität,*
> *Bamberg, Germany*

You could study ...

BA Art History

University of Leipzig

Three years

Apply via uni-assist by 1 September (for winter semester) or
1 March (for summer semester)

Tuition fees €0

Monthly living costs €650 (£505)

MA Aviation Management

Technical University of Applied Sciences Wildau

Two years

Apply via uni-assist by 15 June

Tuition fees €9,300 (£7,225) for the two-year programme

Monthly living costs €700 (£544)

PhD Sociology

Graduate School of Economics and Social Sciences, University of
Mannheim

Three years

Direct application by 31 March

Tuition fees €0

Monthly living costs €600–€700 (£467–£544)

Useful websites

www.study-in.de/en

www.daad.de/deutschland/en

www.uni-assist.de

> **Also worth considering ...**
>
> Alternatives to Germany could be Austria or Liechtenstein. Research education in Austria at www.studyinaustria.at/ study_in_austria, and opportunities in Liechtenstein through ENIC-NARIC, www.enic-naric.net/liechtenstein.aspx.

Republic of Ireland

The Republic of Ireland is close to home and English-speaking, with a higher education system that has much in common with the UK system. It is therefore a popular choice among UK students, with 2,106 UK students based there in 2013 (Global Flow of Tertiary-Level Students, UNESCO Institute for Statistics (UIS), 2013, www.uis.unesco.org/datacentre).

Higher education in Republic of Ireland

Higher education is split into the university sector, institutes of technology, colleges of education and independent private colleges. There are seven universities in Ireland, which offer degree programmes at bachelor's, master's and doctorate level. Institutes of technology provide education and training programmes in areas such as engineering and business at certificate, diploma and degree level. Colleges of education, meanwhile, offer specialised training for primary school teachers, and award 18-month postgraduate diplomas and three-year Bachelor of Education degrees.

In addition, several independent private colleges provide courses in professional training and business. Some colleges are affiliated to universities or professional associations, and award qualifications that are validated by foreign universities or the QQI (Quality Qualifications Ireland, the awarding body for the Irish National Framework of Qualifications).

Trinity College Dublin and University College Dublin both feature in the top 200 of the Times Higher Education World University Rankings 2015–2016.

For a full list of higher education institutions in Ireland, see www.educationinireland.com/en/Where-can-I-study, and for general information on the country's higher education system, go to the Irish Council for International Students website, www.icosirl.ie.

The qualifications on offer differ slightly from those in England, Wales and Northern Ireland in that a three-year ordinary degree is available, as well as a three- or four-year honours degree (Scotland offers a similar choice). The grading system (first, upper second, lower second and so on) echoes the UK. Taught and research master's degrees should take one to two years, with doctorates taking a minimum of three years' research.

You can search for undergraduate and postgraduate courses through the Qualifax Course Finder (www.qualifax.ie). Postgraduate options can also be found through Postgrad Ireland (www.postgradireland.com).

Entry requirements

The A level requirements for most degrees (or matriculation requirements, as they are sometimes known in Ireland), contrasts with many other European countries, where the completion of A level-standard qualifications is sufficient for admission at undergraduate level, and specific grades aren't always necessary. Irish universities tend to be looking for academic subjects that echo those taken at school in Ireland. If you are applying with different qualifications, you should speak to the university's international office or admissions office in advance; they may need to evaluate your qualifications before you apply.

Most degree-level programmes ask for three Cs at A level or equivalent as a minimum requirement. At universities, associated colleges and the Dublin Institute of Technology, your best four A levels (or three, plus an AS in a different subject) will be considered up to a maximum of 600 points (or 625 points, for applicants with a grade E or above in A level mathematics, further mathematics or pure mathematics). The Central Applications Office (CAO) in Ireland has its own point allocation system for secondary school qualifications, much like the Tariff points system used by UCAS. Under the CAO system, the following points are awarded for each of the first three A levels:

- grade A* = 180 points
- grade A = 150 points
- grade B = 130 points
- grade C = 100 points
- grade D = 65 points
- grade E = 45 points.

If a fourth A level is offered, points are assigned as follows:

- grade A* = 60 points
- grade A = 50 points
- grade B = 45 points
- grade C = 35 points
- grade D = 20 points
- grade E = 15 points.

Applicants with an AS are assigned points accordingly:

- grade A = 30 points
- grade B = 25 points
- grade C = 20 points
- grade D = 15 points
- grade E = 10 points.

With the exception of the Dublin Institute of Technology, institutes of technology operate on a slightly different points system. For full details, see the Central Applications Office website at www.cao.ie/index.php?page=scoring&s=gce.

For the more competitive courses, such as medicine, the need for particularly high grades can make four A levels a necessity.

Entry to medicine

For entry to medicine, applicants must have at least 480 points (which can be obtained from three Bs and one C at A level, for example), plus any minimum requirements from their university. Applicants will also be required to sit the HPAT (Health Professions Admissions Test), a written, multiple-choice assessment that is divided into three sections: Logical Reasoning and Problem Solving, Interpersonal Understanding and Non-Verbal Reasoning. The test lasts two-and-a-half hours. For full details, visit www.hpat-ireland.acer.edu.au. Both exam results and HPAT scores will be considered when offering a place. See the Undergraduate Entry to Medicine brochure for more details (www2.cao.ie/downloads/documents/2016/UGMedEntry2016.pdf).

> The Health Professions Admission Test (HPAT, www.hpat-ireland.acer.edu.au) is required for undergraduate entry to medicine, while the Graduate Medical School Admissions Test (GAMSAT, www.gamsat.acer.edu.au/gamsat-ireland) is needed for applications to postgraduate medicine. Application dates are often early and test dates may be restricted to a single day.

Applying

While the academic year is in line with the UK (September to June), the application system has its differences. Undergraduate applications are based on actual grades (and an admissions test, in some cases) and little else, so offers aren't made until the Irish Leaving Certificate results are announced, which is usually in mid-August, around the same time that A level results are released.

You can apply online or on paper from 5 November through the CAO at www.cao.ie. Most applications should be made by 1 February or earlier, particularly for restricted-entry courses such as medicine, which have early assessment procedures that can start as early as February. You can apply for up to ten courses; course choices can be changed up until 31 January free of charge, after which you will have to pay a processing fee if you wish to make any further amendments to your list of courses. There is also a later closing date of 1 May for certain courses. In most cases, there is no need for references or a personal statement. Application fees vary, depending on when you apply; for full details, see www.cao.ie/handbook.php?page=4.

Postgraduate applications

Postgraduate applications can be made directly to your chosen university, often via the international office. Some institutions use the Postgraduate Applications Centre (PAC) at www.pac.ie. Closing dates vary, even within a single institution. In most cases, a minimum of a 2:2 grade in an undergraduate honours degree is required for a taught master's degree. For entry on to a research master's degree, you will normally need at least a 2:1 grade, particularly if you are seeking funding to help cover the cost of your studies.

In addition to the application form and fee, you may need to include an academic transcript, references, a CV, a research proposal (where relevant) and a statement of interest, explaining your motivation, commitment and what you hope to achieve. You may also be asked to attend an interview.

Costs

Currently, UK students on their first full-time undergraduate degree should not have to pay tuition fees. However, you will be required to pay a student contribution or registration fee, which covers non-tuition services such as entry fees and support for student services, societies and clubs. For 2016–2017, the student contribution charge is set at €3,000 (£2,324), but be sure to check university websites at the time of applying for the latest fee information. Fees for private institutions are set by the individual establishments and will be considerably more.

According to Postgrad Ireland, you can expect postgraduate fees of over €4,000 (£3,124) for research degrees, with taught programmes ranging from under €4,000 (£3,099) to as much as €29,500 (£22,857) for an MBA. For information on options for postgraduate funding, visit http://postgradireland.com/advice-and-funding/funding/postgraduate-funding-there-any-still-out-there.

At number 15 out of 122 countries on a 2016 cost-of-living ranking, Ireland is slightly cheaper than the UK (see www.numbeo.com/cost-of-living/rankings_by_country.jsp for more details). Education in Ireland estimates that, on average, a student can expect to spend €6,000–€11,000 (£4,649–£8,523) per year; of course, this will depend on where you live and the lifestyle you choose. Dublin is the most expensive place to live, with the Irish Council for International Students reporting living costs of around €10,000–€15,000 (£7,750–£11,621) per year.

Accommodation

All universities have halls of residence for first-year students, which are often apartments for four to eight students. On-campus accommodation is paid in two instalments (September and February), and a month's rent is usually required in advance for the deposit. Private accommodation is available for a lease of either nine or twelve months; start your search on www.daft.ie/student-accommodation/?s[search_type]=rental and www.myhome.ie.

You could study ...

BA Music

Trinity College Dublin

Four years

Apply through CAO by 1 February

Registration fee €3,000 (£2,333)

Monthly living costs €670 (£521), excluding accommodation

MFA Fine Art

National College of Art and Design, Dublin

Two years

Apply directly by 29 April

Annual fees €5,400 (£4,201)

PhD Speech and Language Therapy

NUI Galway

Four years

Apply as early as possible through PAC

Annual fees €4,529 (£3,525)

Monthly living costs from €1,000 (£778)

Useful websites

www.educationireland.ie

www.citizensinformation.ie

www.icosirl.ie

Italy

Few public universities in Italy teach their courses in English. The latest figures recorded 300 UK students studying in the country (Global Flow of Tertiary-Level Students, UNESCO Institute for Statistics (UIS), 2013, www.uis.unesco.org/datacentre). Italy remains a popular destination for exchange students.

Three Italian universities feature in the top 200 of the Times Higher Education World University Rankings 2015–2016.

Higher education in Italy

The majority of universities in Italy are state-funded, although there is a range of alternative provision, including non-state universities, universities for foreigners (focusing on Italian language, literature and culture), specialist postgraduate schools, technical institutes and telematic (or distance learning) universities. Most programmes are taught in Italian; English-medium opportunities in Italy are most often found at private universities and colleges.

There are a number of options to study medicine in English at Italian universities; tuition fees are partially income-assessed, and so are often much more reasonable than those in the UK:

- **University of Bari:** www.uniba.it/offerta-formativa/english-medical-curriculum
- **University of Milan:** www.imschool.it
- **University of Pavia:** http://nfs.unipv.it/medeng/od/frame.html
- **Sapienza University of Rome:** http://en.uniroma1.it/node/12831
- **Tor Vergata University of Rome:** web.uniroma2.it/module/name/Content/newlang/english/
- **Second University of Naples:** www.dipcardiotoracicherespiratorie.unina2.it/it/il-corso-di-studio
- **University of Naples Federico II:** http://dmcc.dip.unina.it/
- **Humanitas University:** www.hunimed.eu/courses/medicine/courses-and-exams.

Competition can be intense and you will need to learn Italian to cope with patient contact as the course progresses. The IMAT test often forms a key part of the selection process. The IMAT is a 100-minute written assessment, divided into four sections. Section 1 (General Knowledge and Logical Reasoning) is composed of 22 multiple-choice questions, and is designed to test applicants' skills in problem-solving, data analysis, inference and understanding argument. Sections 2, 3 and 4 (Scientific Knowledge) comprise 38 multiple-choice questions, which focus on candidates' ability to apply scientific knowledge from school biology, physics, chemistry and mathematics. You can find out more at Admissions Testing Service (www. admissionstestingservice.org).

The academic year runs from September or October until July. The qualifications on offer are a three-year *laurea*, which is the Italian bachelor's degree, the two-year *laurea magistrale*, which is comparable to a master's degree, and the *dottorato di ricerca*, which is comparable to a doctorate and lasts from three years.

Much of the assessment in Italian higher education takes the form of oral exams, though there are written exams for certain subjects. Exams at undergraduate and master's level are graded on a scale of 0 to 30, with a pass mark of 18. All exam results count towards the final degree mark, which ranges from 0 to 110, with 66 as the pass mark. The final result is based on exam results and the presentation of a project or dissertation. Doctoral students are required to submit a research project in their final year, written in both Italian and English. The project is assessed by external professors and, if the assessment is successful, the student is then invited to debate their work in front of a commission, who must approve the work in order for the doctorate to be granted.

The Politecnico di Milano now delivers many of its postgraduate degree courses in English.

Applying

Provided that you meet the general entry requirements for higher education in the UK and have completed at least 12 years of education, you can be considered for undergraduate study in Italy. If you have a bachelor's degree, you can be considered for a master's degree, and if you have a master's degree, you can consider applying for a doctorate. For admissions to PhD programmes, you may be required to pass a competitive exam in Italian, which is specific to each university. You should apply directly to individual institutions, which will each have their own deadlines and may set their own additional entry requirements.

You will also need to submit a pre-application request form via the Italian consulate or embassy in your home country, together with certain supporting documentation, for which you will need to obtain an official Italian translation by an approved translator.

Once you have supplied the appropriate documentation and completed the application form, the consulate will issue a *dichiarazione di valore*, which is a letter acknowledging the value of the qualifications you have completed to date, within the context of your home educational system. You may have to pay a processing fee for this service. The consulate will then send the supporting documents to your chosen institution, who will communicate their decision directly to you.

The type of form and documentation required varies depending on whether you are applying for undergraduate or postgraduate study, but will usually include copies of your certificates, an academic transcript and proof of identification, in addition to any further documentation or forms required by your university. For more information, contact your university's international office or your nearest Italian consulate or embassy. If you have taken your first degree in the UK or another EU country, you may be able to substitute the *dichiarazione di valore* with a diploma supplement (see page 112). Discuss the process and timescale with your university's international office before you apply.

Costs

Fees are set by the individual institutions and are partially means-tested. According to Study in Italy (www.study-in-italy.it), you should expect to pay €850–€1,000 (£659–£775) per year for undergraduate study in public institutions, although some institutions will charge more for courses taught entirely in English. Fees at private institutions are higher again, although these might still end up costing less than many of the courses in the UK, particularly as fees tend to be reduced for those with a low family income. Postgraduate fees start at around €2,000 (£1,550) per year. Doctoral students may have the opportunity to apply for a grant from their university to cover the cost of tuition fees.

EU students (which currently includes the UK) should be entitled to the same student financial support as Italian students. This includes student loans and housing assistance. You'll find out more at your chosen university's *Diritto allo studio universitario*, or DSU. For living costs, Italy is somewhat cheaper than the UK. It is ranked 25th (to the UK's 12th) in Numbeo's cost-of-living rankings for 2016 at www.numbeo.com/cost-of-living/rankings_by_country.jsp.

Accommodation

Very few Italian universities offer halls of residence, though their accommodation office should be able to offer advice on student housing. According to Study in Italy, private accommodation can range from €300–€1,000 (£232–£775) per month. As is the case with a lot of private accommodation, you should never sign a contract without viewing the property first, and indeed it is much easier to find accommodation once you are in the country. This means that you may need to organise short-term accommodation for the first few weeks of your stay, although a good place to start is www.uniplaces.com/accommodation.

You could study ...

Bsc International Politics and Government
Università Commerciale Luigi Bocconi, Milan
Three years
Apply by 20 January (winter session) or 19 April (summer session)
Annual fees €5,196–€11,621 (£4,042–£9,039) depending on family income
Monthly living costs €600–€800 (£443–£591)

MSc Mechanical Engineering
Sapienza University of Rome
Two years
Apply by 1 September
Annual fees €2,924 (£2,274)
Monthly living costs of up to €1,000 (£777)

PhD Science and Management of Climate Change
Ca' Foscari University of Venice
Three years
Apply by 21 April
Maximum annual fees €1,896 (£1,484)
Monthly living costs from €750 (£583)

Useful websites
www.study-in-italy.it

Also worth considering ...

If you're looking for higher education near Italy, then how about Malta? The island attracts a number of UK students every year. Find out more at the ENIC–NARIC country page for Malta: www.enic-naric.net/malta.aspx. Malta only has one public university; the website for the University of Malta is at www.um.edu.mt.

Greece could also provide an alternative to Italy, although few international students choose Greece for their studies. You can find out more at the Greek Ministry of Education (www.minedu.gov.gr).

> 66 I can't say I was ever one of these people who had a burning desire to move abroad, but looking back on the last four years I've spent in Malta, I'm so glad I did. In terms of studying, don't let the laid-back Mediterranean lifestyle fool you – the Maltese students are generally extremely hard-working and competitive in their studies. 99
>
> *Catherine Foreshaw, University of Malta*

The Netherlands

Interest in the Netherlands as a study venue has been growing steadily, with its cheaper fees and hundreds of programmes taught entirely in English. The Netherlands is the second-best country for English proficiency (EF English Proficiency Index, Education First, www.ef.se/epi). Dutch universities are keen to attract international students and have been actively recruiting in the UK by visiting schools and attending education fairs. In 2012, 888 UK students were studying in Dutch universities (Global Flow of Tertiary-Level Students, UNESCO Institute for Statistics (UIS), 2012, www.uis.unesco.org/datacentre).

The Netherlands has an impressive 12 universities in the Times Higher Education World University Rankings 2015–2016 top 200. The country has the fourth highest number of institutions in the top 200 for the second year running, after the US, UK and Germany.

Higher education in the Netherlands

The style of teaching in the Netherlands is interactive and student-centred, with tutorials and seminars taking place in smaller groups than you would expect in many UK institutions. The academic year runs from early September to late June.

You can opt to study at a research-based university (WO) or a university of applied sciences (HBO), which offers more vocational options. An academic or research-oriented bachelor's degree (WO) takes three years, while the applied alternative (HBO) would take four years, with the chance of a work placement and often a study-abroad opportunity. HBOS also offer associate degrees, which take two years to complete, with the option to then move on to an applied bachelor's degree in the arts or sciences.

If you are not ready to specialise in a single subject, a number of institutions in the Netherlands offer liberal arts programmes, where you can select from several subject options before deciding on a final major subject.

> **"** We're taught in a classroom. There are no lectures. The classes are very practical and laid back. I find the teaching style very personal as there are only up to 30 people in a class. We're really aided and guided. **"**
>
> *Rebecca Jackson, Stenden University of Applied Sciences,*
> *the Netherlands*

> **"** I had to get used to a more concise way of writing, but it was more the workload that presented the real challenge for me. I did far more in my first few months in comparison to my friends at UK-based universities. I guess you are eased into it in the beginning but by the second month you are expected to be up to speed. Now that I'm in the second year, I would say that the course has now become more focused, whereas last year it was rather generalised. **"**
>
> *Simran Gill, Fontys University of Applied Sciences,*
> *the Netherlands*

At master's level, you again have the choice of either a research-based degree (WO) or the applied route (HBO), both of which take one to two years. In contrast, doctorates are only available through the research universities (WO), and take from three years.

To find a course, you can use Study in Holland's database at www.studyinholland.co.uk/what_to_study.html.

Applying

In most cases, two or three A levels, or equivalent, should be sufficient to meet the requirements for most bachelor's degrees. If you studied an alternative qualification, you should discuss it with your chosen university. At postgraduate level, you will need a bachelor's degree to progress to a master's. It is likely that any offer you receive will require you to pass your courses, rather than achieve specific grades. Although getting a place at university may seem easier than in the UK, the university will need you to prove your capability in the first year. Students who can't cope academically will be asked to leave the course.

In popular subjects, such as medicine or law, places may be restricted through a scheme known as *numerus fixus*. For these courses, the allocation of places is decided through a complicated lottery system, which can vary according to the requirements of the university. According to Study in Holland, if you're applying to courses such as medicine, psychology, economics, physiotherapy or law then you may be affected by *numerus fixus*. In addition, some universities set their own restrictive quotas for certain courses, which may include entrance exams, selection days or interviews. Talk to your chosen institution to gain an understanding of how to give yourself the best chance of success.

As A level results are published after the qualification confirmation deadline for Dutch institutions, you should be asked to complete a late submission form. Your university will be able to tell you how and when to complete this.

Studielink

You can apply to most public institutions at undergraduate and postgraduate level through Studielink (http://info.studielink. nl/en/studenten/Pages/Default.aspx), though it is recommended that you inform your university that you are intending to apply prior to submitting your application. Applications open from

September or October onwards. You can choose up to four options, including one *numerus fixus* course. Requirements for supporting documentation vary, but could include:

- certificates
- academic transcript
- personal statement or letter of motivation indicating why you are applying
- copy of passport
- CV
- two letters of recommendation
- research proposal (where relevant).

For some postgraduate study, an admissions test such as the GRE revised General Test (www.ets.org/gre) or Graduate Management Admission Test (GMAT; visit www.mba.com/global) will be needed. In all cases, your institution will be able to tell you whether they require application through Studielink and any supporting information they need.

Most courses have an application deadline of the beginning of May, although *numerus fixus* courses require an earlier application. You can find a helpful guide to Studielink at the Study in Holland website, www.studyinholland.co.uk/studielink.html. Some courses will require direct application instead.

Costs

In the public universities, the standard annual fees were set at €1,951 (£1,512) for 2015–2016 at undergraduate and master's level; the fees for most courses have been agreed at €1,984 (£1,537) for 2016–2017. Universities will normally give you the option of either paying the fee upfront or through a monthly instalment system. Fees at universities of applied sciences and private institutions are higher, and range from €8,500–€10,500 (£6,585–£8,135) per year, according to Study in Holland.

EU undergraduate and postgraduate students can apply for a loan from the Dutch government (*collegegeldkrediet*) to cover the full cost of tuition fees, once they have a confirmed offer of a place from their chosen institution. The *collegegeldkrediet* is open to EU students who are under the age of 55 at the start of their course. For 2016–2017, the typical amount available for statutory fees is €1,984 (£1,537). Be sure to check the information when you apply.

You will be able to borrow more if you are applying to an institution that charges higher fees, such as the universities of applied sciences. In order to receive the loan, you will first need to open a Dutch bank account, and you will also need a Dutch citizen service number (*burgerservicenummer*), which will be given to you once you have a permanent address in the Netherlands. You only have to start paying back the loan two years after you graduate; however, unlike in the UK, the loan must be repaid in full over a maximum of 15 years.

You may also be eligible to receive a maintenance loan (*studiefinanciering*), provided you are working part time for at least 56 hours per month in a registered Dutch job. More information on student finance can be found at www. studyinholland.co.uk/loans_and_grants.html. Some scholarships are also available; you can search for scholarships at www.studyinholland.nl/scholarships/find-a-scholarship.

At number 23 out of 122 countries on the 2016 Numbeo (www. numbeo.com/cost-of-living/rankings_by_country.jsp) cost-of-living ranking, studying in the Netherlands is comparable to living in Italy, and you should find it slightly better value for money than in the UK. According to www.studyinholland.nl, you should budget for between €800–€1,100 (£620–£852) per month.

> **"** Living costs are relatively cheap. There are low price supermarkets which offer a wide variety of products at good prices. Food is pretty much the same here as it is in the UK. Supermarkets are tremendously accessible; I live above one. I'd recommend setting a budget and making food in bulk, if necessary. Going out to party is not too expensive, as drinks are cheap in Venlo and I rarely spend over €80 (£63) a week. **"**
>
> *Simran Gill, Fontys University of Applied Sciences,*
> *the Netherlands*

Accommodation

Dutch universities can assist you with finding a room; however, provision of student halls of residence varies considerably from institution to institution, so it is advisable to get in touch with your university's accommodation office in good time, preferably by May for a September start. According to Study in Holland, many universities also rent blocks of rooms from private landlords, which they then sublet to students; your institution's accommodation office will be able to advise on whether they offer this type of agreement. The accommodation office will often charge a fee to use their service, but you are much more likely to secure a room if you apply for accommodation through them. Costs for shared student housing are typically €300–€450 (£232–£349) per month.

You could study ...
Bachelor Artificial Intelligence
Radboud University
Three years

Apply by 1 May

Annual fees €1,984 (£1,543)

Annual living costs €8,800 (£6,846)

MA Global Criminology

Utrecht University

One year

Apply by 1 May

Annual fees €1,984 (£1,543)

Monthly living costs €800–€1,000 (£622–£775)

PhD Medical Education

Maastricht University

Four years

Apply by 1 March (autumn start) or 1 October (spring start)

Annual fees €2,660 (£2,080)

Monthly living costs €840 (£654)

Useful websites

www.studyinholland.nl

www.studyinholland.co.uk

Norway

With around 9,200 students from overseas (Global Flow of Tertiary-Level Students, UNESCO Institute for Statistics (UIS), 2013, www.uis.unesco.org/datacentre), and no fees at public universities, studying in Norway is certainly a worthwhile option. Norway offers a handful of undergraduate courses in English, and has many more available at postgraduate level. Norway has high costs but one of the best standards of living in the world: it has achieved first place in the UN Human Development Index no less than 12 times. It can be cold, but has a great outdoor lifestyle.

> ❝ Within the first month of arriving here, I'd been on fishing trips, hiking trips, whizzing around in a little rib boat on the Saltstraumen, swimming in some of the most beautiful lakes which are a 15-minute walk from the university, and even met the Norwegian Prime Minister. It's been quite something! ❞
>
> *Megan Doxford, University of Nordland, Norway*

Higher education in Norway

Higher education takes place at universities, specialised university institutions and university colleges (which includes two public colleges of the arts). Universities have a research focus, while university colleges focus on professional studies. It is possible to gain a master's degree and sometimes even a doctorate at a university college. Most higher education institutions in Norway are state-funded, with some private university colleges. In Norway, you would generally study a three-year bachelor's degree, a two-year master's (which includes the completion of a thesis), and a three-year doctorate. At undergraduate and master's level, teaching is normally delivered via lectures and seminars, but project work is also important. The academic year runs from mid-August to mid-June. It is common for students in Norway to take a gap year before university, so they may be a little older.

You can search for study opportunities through Study in Norway at www.studyinnorway.no.

Norway has two universities in the top 200 of the Times Higher Education World University Rankings 2015–2016.

You will need to register your stay no later than three months after arriving in Norway; registration is free and you can book an appointment through the Norwegian Directorate of Immigration (UDI) website at https://selfservice.udi.no/en-gb/UserRegistration. You will need to take your passport, confirmation letter from your university, EHIC card or private health insurance card, and evidence that you have sufficient funds to support yourself during your stay, after which you will be granted a student residence permit.

Applying

According to the GSU list (the list of minimum requirements for admission to Norwegian higher education), you will need a minimum of three A levels for undergraduate study. Students from Scotland will need to pass five Highers or Advanced Highers. Some subjects will have additional requirements. You can find the GSU list at the Norwegian Agency for Quality Assurance in HE (NOKUT) website, www.nokut.no/en/facts-and-statistics/surveys-and-databases/gsu-list. Successful completion of a bachelor's degree is needed to progress to master's level.

You should apply directly to your chosen institution sometime between December and March for courses starting in August. Application deadlines vary; your institution can advise on specific dates and any supplementary information needed, such as:

- academic transcript
- copies of certificates, for qualifications already gained
- CV
- research proposal, where necessary.

Costs

Whether you are studying at undergraduate or postgraduate level, you are unlikely to have to pay fees at a state-funded university or university college, regardless of your nationality. However, as is the case in Germany, there is a small semester fee of NOK300–

NOK600 (£25–£50), which entitles you to a student discount card, along with membership of student welfare associations, access to campus health services, sports facilities and so on. Private institutions charge fees, although these should still be lower than those charged by universities in the UK, perhaps with the exception of some MBAs.

There are some scholarships available for study in Norway; see www.studyinnorway.no/Study-in-Norway/Scholarships for details.

Living costs in Norway are high; in fact, it ranks number four out of 122 countries in a 2016 cost-of-living index; see www.numbeo.com/cost-of-living/rankings_by_country.jsp. You should expect to have at the very least NOK8,900 (£748) per month for living expenses; this can rise to NOK10,000 (£841) in cities like Oslo.

You could study ...

BSc International Environment and Development Studies
Norwegian University of Life Sciences, Ås
Three years
Apply by 1 December
Tuition fees NOK0
Monthly living expenses NOK9,080 (£767)

Master Product Design
Oslo and Akershus University College of Applied Sciences
Two years
Apply by 1 March
Tuition fees NOK0
Monthly living expenses NOK10,000 (£841)

PhD Literacy Studies
University of Stavanger
Three years

Rolling applications

Tuition fees NOK0

Monthly living expenses NOK8,565 (£724)

Useful websites

www.studyinnorway.no

Spain

Although the option to study in Spain on an exchange programme is a popular one for UK students, opportunities to study a full degree taught in English are limited. Most options at public institutions are taught in Spanish, though there are opportunities in private institutions, which make up around a third of the higher education institutions in Spain. Nonetheless, the number of courses taught in English is on the increase as a direct result of the Spanish government's interest in recruiting more international students; for example, for 2016–2017, the University of Barcelona is now offering over 70 bachelor's degrees in English.

> Spain has three universities listed in the top 200 of the Times Higher Education World University Rankings 2015–2016.

Higher education in Spain

You can find information on studying in Spain and search for courses at Study in Spain (www.studyinspain.info/es/index.html). To search for courses taught in English, try Study Portals (www. studyportals.eu), EUNiCAS (www.eunicas.co.uk) and A Star Future (www.astarfuture.co.uk).

Undergraduate degrees take three to four years, master's degrees last one or two years, while doctorates take a maximum of three years of full-time study. Some of the private universities offer accelerated programmes to reduce the length of study. The academic year runs from October to June.

> **❝** It is a young university that is keen to keep growing with student participation; I was excited to influence and to be part of a new and growing institution. **❞**
>
> *Tudor Etchells, IE University, Spain*

Applying

Application deadlines tend to fall between May and early July for courses starting in October, but it is worth applying well in advance of this date, as there are often more applicants than places. Some courses also offer a February intake.

As long as you have the general qualifications to access higher education (HE) in the UK, you should meet the general requirements for HE in Spain. Talk directly to your chosen university about their application procedures. You will need to register with UNED at www.uned.es for an evaluation of your qualifications, or *credencial de acceso*, which is valid for two years and requires a fee. You will then need to print out the application form from the UNED website and post it to UNED, along with the following supporting documentation:

- photocopy of your passport
- certified copies of your qualifications containing the general entrance requirements under the UK's higher education system
- photocopy of your GCSE and A level certificates
- bank receipt for payment of the application fee.

Completion of a bachelor's degree in the UK or the European Higher Education Area will satisfy the general requirements of a master's degree. At least 300 ECTS credits (which includes 60 ECTS credits from a master's degree programme) are required to progress to research at doctoral level.

> ❝ The university application process explored your whole range of interest and motivations. It was personal and comprehensive, wanting to derive the best aspects from their applicants. ❞
>
> *Esme Alexander, IE University, Spain*

Costs

Tuition fees for a bachelor's degree or *grado* at a public university are set by the autonomous communities and range between €750–€3,700 on average (£590–£2,909) per year. At private universities, fees start at around €5,000 (£3,930), but can be considerably higher than this, although these institutions often have generous schemes of financial support.

Master's (*master*) and doctoral (*doctorado*) degrees at public universities are calculated on a pay-per-credit system, with the cost of each credit ranging from €17–€65 (£13–£50). Master's degrees generally have 60 to 120 credits in total, with doctoral degrees worth 180 credits.

There are certain scholarships are available, which can be found through the Study in Spain website at www.studyinspain.info/en/reportajes/propuestas/How-to-obtain-a-grant-to-study-in-Spain. You can also ask the international office of your chosen university.

Living costs are lower than in a number of the European countries mentioned in this chapter. Spain is ranked number 40 out of 122 countries in a cost-of-living survey for 2016 (see www.numbeo. com/cost-of-living/rankings_by_country.jsp), comparing favourably to the UK at number 12. Prices in the major cities, such as Madrid or Barcelona, can be much higher.

Accommodation

You can search for student halls at RESA (www.resa.es/en), which offers accommodation in 30 Spanish universities, with starting prices ranging from €229–€930 (£180–733) per month; for a full list of participating institutions, see www.resa.es/en/our-partners. For shared private rented accommodation, a good place to start is www.idealista.com, which allows you to filter your search according a number of different preferences, including price range and male or female flatmates.

You could study ...

BSc Philosophy, Politics and Economics
Pompeu Fabra University, Barcelona (public)
Four years
Apply by 1 July
Annual fees €1,657 (£1,291)
Monthly living costs €1,000 (£775)

Master European Studies and Human Rights
UCAM Catholic University of Murcia (private)
One year
Rolling applications
Annual fees €5,800 (£4,522)
Monthly living costs €450–€550 (£351–£429)

PhD Cognitive Science and Language
University Rovira I Virgili, Tarragona (public)

Apply by 1 March

Annual fees €548 (£427)

Monthly living costs €550 (£429)

Useful websites

www.universidad.es/en

www.studyinspain.info/?/=en

Also worth considering ...

Interested in studying in Portugal? Nearly all courses are in Portuguese, but you can find out more at www. studyinportugal.edu.pt or DGES (General Directorate for Higher Education) at www.dges.mctes.pt/DGES.

Sweden

According to the most recent data, as many as 25,400 international students chose Sweden for their studies, with 327 of them from the UK (Global Flow of Tertiary-Level Students, UNESCO Institute for Statistics (UIS), 2013, www.uis.unesco. org/datacentre). Sweden offers an attractive proposition for UK students, as it was ranked as the top country in the world for English proficiency in 2015 (EF English Proficiency Index, Education First, www.ef.se/epi). In addition, with its strong focus on innovation and a forward-thinking, student-centred academic environment, Swedish higher education has much to offer.

Five Swedish institutions are in the Times Higher Education World University Rankings 2015–2016 top 200, with one institution ranked in the top 50.

Higher education in Sweden

The academic year runs from late August to early June and is divided into two semesters. Three-year bachelor's degrees or *kandidatexamen* are the norm. A master's degree or *masterexamen* will take one to two years, while doctoral research or *doktorsexamen* takes at least four years.

Higher education takes place in universities and university colleges, with universities the only institutions with the automatic right to issue doctoral degrees. University colleges can apply for authorisation to award doctoral degrees through the Swedish Higher Education Authority. Local collaboration is widespread, so many institutions offer options reflecting the needs of local industries and businesses.

Teaching is delivered via a combination of lectures, seminars and laboratory work, where appropriate. Students are expected to contribute actively to class discussions, as well as undertaking extensive independent study. Degree programmes are split into individual courses (modules), with examinations set at the end of each course. Assessments typically take the form of written and oral tests, laboratory or group work, and special projects.

You can search for study options at www.universityadmissions.se.

The name of the institution will not always reveal whether it is a university or university college; most university colleges will call themselves universities, while some universities are called *högskola* (or university college) in Swedish. Degrees awarded by both types of institution are equivalent to one another.

Applying

Any qualification that gives you access to HE in the UK should
do the same for undergraduate studies in Sweden. Individual
institutions then set their own procedures for selecting applicants;
this might include grade requirements, assessment of samples
of work, interviews, admissions tests or work experience. Your
institution's international office will be able to advise further about
any special requirements.

For bachelor's and master's degrees, applications are made online
through University Admissions at www.universityadmissions.
se. You can apply to a maximum of four bachelor's or master's
courses. Deadlines are generally mid-January for an August start
and mid-August for any courses starting in spring. In addition
to completing the application form, you will also need to upload
certain supporting documents as part of your application.

At doctoral level, applications are made directly to the institution
and often to a specific department, accompanied by copies of
certificates, academic transcripts and letters of recommendation.
Check any deadlines with your academic department.

The minimum requirement for a bachelor's degree is a total of
five subjects, of which two must be A level or equivalent, while
a bachelor's degree (or equivalent) from an internationally
recognised university is a prerequisite for entry on to a master's
degree. The minimum entry requirement for a PhD is a bachelor's
level degree (or equivalent) in a relevant subject although, in most
instances, a master's degree is required. Your university will be
able to advise on any specific requirements.

As the Swedish academic year begins in August, shortly after A level results come out, there may be insufficient time to confirm a place for the same academic year; applicants might need to consider a gap year.

Costs

In most cases, university courses in Sweden are free of tuition charges, although student-union membership fees are payable at SEK50–SEK350 (£4.23–£29.69) per semester. A range of scholarships are available at Study in Sweden (www.studyinsweden.se/Scholarships). Ask your institution about any scholarships that they administer.

An average monthly budget for a student is around SEK8,000 (£676). Sweden is ranked number 17 out of 122 countries in Numbeo's 2016 cost-of-living table at www.numbeo.com/cost-of-living/rankings_by_country.jsp, which makes it cheaper than the UK, Australia, Ireland and New Zealand.

Accommodation

Student accommodation is usually managed by external companies, rather than the universities. However, your university should be able to provide information on local student housing organisations; many of these operate on a queue system, whereby accommodation is allocated based on your place in the queue, so it is important to sign up as early as possible in order to give yourself the best chance of securing a room. For a room in a student hall or flat, the average monthly rent is SEK,2500–SEK6,500 (£214–£556), according to Study in Sweden. Accommodation in the private rental sector is managed by central housing systems and is likely to be considerably more and, as with student accommodation, most flats are allocated via a queue system.

You could study ...

BSc Physical Geography and Ecosystem Analysis

Lund University

Three years

Apply via www.universityadmissions.se by 15 January

Tuition fees SEK0

Monthly living costs SEK7,974–SEK9,000 (£679–£766)

MA Fashion Studies

Stockholm University

Two years

Apply via www.universityadmissions.se by 15 January

Tuition fees SEK0

Monthly living costs from SEK8,010 (£682)

Useful websites

www.studyinsweden.se

Switzerland

If you choose Switzerland for your studies, you'll be in good company: Albert Einstein studied and carried out research at the country's universities at the turn of the last century. More recently, 455 UK students chose Switzerland for their higher education in 2013 (Global Flow of Tertiary-Level Students, UNESCO Institute for Statistics (UIS), 2013, www.uis.unesco.org/datacentre). Switzerland offers world-class programmes in science and technology, but it is also a good country for budding linguists. There are four national languages: German, French, Italian and Romansh. Most higher education courses are offered in German and French, though there is a growing number of English-taught programmes, particularly at postgraduate level.

Seven Swiss institutions feature in the Times Higher Education World University Rankings 2015–2016 top 200, with the ETH Zurich – Swiss Federal Institute of Technology ranked an impressive ninth place, making it the first non-Anglo-American university to make the top ten in the rankings for a decade.

Higher education in Switzerland

The academic year runs from September to June and is split into two semesters. A bachelor's degree tends to take three years to complete. A master's degree will take one-and-a-half to two years, while doctoral research takes from three to five years.

Higher education takes place in cantonal universities, federal institutes of technology and universities of applied sciences. If you're looking for traditional, research-based learning, the universities offer the best choice. The two federal institutes of technology are world-class centres of education and research in technology and the sciences. The universities and federal institutes of technology both offer education up to doctoral level.

The universities of applied sciences focus on technical or vocational learning; many of these institutions include some form of work experience. You may well have heard of the Swiss hotel management schools. They are known all over the world, although you will pay a premium in tuition fees for their quality and prestige.

You can find links to the Swiss institutions at Swiss University, www.studyinginswitzerland.ch.

Applying

Entry to a bachelor's degree in Switzerland is possible with A levels or equivalent qualifications. There is a competitive entry process known as *numerus clausus* for some courses including medicine, dentistry and veterinary medicine, which may involve sitting an aptitude test. However, it is important to note that, due to a restricted number of places, universities do not normally accept international applicants on to their medical programmes, except in certain special cases. The international office at your university will be able to advise you on the university's admissions policy when you apply. Entry to a master's degree or PhD is possible after a bachelor's degree or master's degree respectively.

Applications should be made directly to your chosen institution, with research university deadlines generally set around April for admissions in September, although an earlier February deadline will apply to certain courses, such as medicine and sports science. Deadlines for universities of applied sciences vary considerably, so you should refer to individual institution websites for the most up-to-date information. Some universities of applied science will also accept admissions in the spring semester.

Many public universities ask for an A level or equivalent qualification in maths or a natural science; you may struggle to get a place if you do not hold a qualification in one of these subjects, even for unrelated courses. University-specific admissions information for UK applicants can be found on the Swiss Universities website at www.swissuniversities.ch/en/services/admission-to-universities/countries/great-britain-1. The private universities might be a bit more flexible. In addition, at some institutions, you'll be required to sit an entrance exam.

Costs

For undergraduate-level study at a public institution, tuition fees start at around CHF500 (£352) per semester, rising to around CHF2,000 (£1,408). You can expect to pay considerably more in private institutions, including the schools of hotel management.

Universities can provide details of any scholarships they offer. Swiss University provides some information on application processes for funding at www.studyinginswitzerland.ch/grants-scholarship-fees.htm.

Switzerland is not a cheap country to live in. In fact, it appears in second place in Numbeo's 2016 cost-of-living table (www.numbeo.com/cost-of-living/rankings_by_country.jsp). Studying in Switzerland estimates that you should budget between CHF18,000–CHF28,000 (£12,669–£19,706) per year for living expenses.

Accommodation

Subsidised halls of residence are available in some universities; in any case, your university should be able to assist you in finding accommodation. The Complete University Guide (www.thecompleteuniversityguide.co.uk) suggests students should budget for around €500 (£387) per month for private rented accommodation. For more information on accommodation, visit the Swiss Universities website at www.swissuniversities.ch/en/higher-education-area/studying/studying-in-switzerland/apartments.

You could study ...

BSc Life Sciences and Technology

École Polytechnique Fédérale de Lausanne

Three years

Apply to university by 30 April

Annual tuition fees CHF1,266 (£890)

Monthly living costs CHF1,950 (£1,386)

MA World Literature

University of Bern

Two years

Apply to university by 30 April (autumn start) or 15 December (spring start)

Tuition fees per semester CHF750 (£533)

Monthly living costs from CHF1,500 (£1,066)

PhD Cinema Studies

University of Zurich

Three years

Apply to university by 31 July (autumn start) or 31 January (spring start)

Tuition fees per semester CHF250 (£178)

Monthly living costs CHF1,870 (£1,328)

Useful websites

www.studyinginswitzerland.ch

Pros and cons of study in Europe

Pros

- Relatively close to home.
- Rising number of English-taught programme options, particularly at postgraduate level.
- Opportunity to gain new cultural and educational experiences that will enhance your CV.

Cons

- Language issues.
- Some countries have high costs of living.
- Pressure to do well in first year to remain on the course.

Student story
Elizabeth Edwards, Otto-Friedrich-Universität, Bamberg (University of Bamberg), Germany

'I am currently studying a master's at the Otto-Friedrich-Universität in Bamberg, Germany. Most master's courses on the continent last two years, which are divided into four semesters (the European equivalent of a British "term"). Semesters in Germany run from early October to early February, and early April to early July. The master's programme comprises three semesters of classes and a final fourth semester, which is set aside for students to write their master's theses.

'Although I am in the second semester of my master's course in Bamberg, this is not my first year living here: as part of my bachelor's degree in Modern Languages, I spent my year abroad here too, studying music (a particular hobby of mine). This means that settling into life in Bamberg and Germany was pretty easy this time round. In fact, I settled in very quickly on my year abroad too, which is largely thanks to the very competent and helpful international office at the university. Among other things, they sorted out accommodation for me in one of the private student halls. There is usually quite a long waiting list for the various student halls in the town, so I am very grateful for their help. Many students choose to rent a room in a student flat (*Wohngemeinschaft*, WG), which often costs the same or less than student halls. There tend to be good websites and social media groups where free rooms or flats are advertised, so it might be useful to look into that before arriving to avoid having to couch-surf while settling in to a foreign country and looking for a place to live.

'I decided to return to Germany for a master's because I felt that one year was insufficient to hone my language skills and understanding of German culture and the German mindset. Having decided to return to Germany, the choice of Bamberg was fairly self-evident. The town itself is beautiful (Bamberg is one of few German cities to be listed as a UNESCO World

Heritage Site) and the amount of music going on is surprisingly great for such a small city. I was put off staying in the UK for postgraduate studies by the high tuition fees. The cost of studying in Germany is the same for Germans and international students alike: in most cases there are no tuition fees, only a semester fee of around €90 (£70) that, among other things, pays for a semester-long pass for all public transport in and around the town.

'My course is taught in German and has the rather long-winded title of "German Studies: Linguistics with an emphasis on German as a foreign language"; in other words, I am studying German linguistics from the point of view of someone who intends to utilise their degree by teaching German as a foreign language. Indeed, once I have completed my degree I will be qualified to teach German as a foreign language (*Deutsch als Fremdsprache* or "DaF") in Germany. I am by no means the only international student on the course; the subject matter makes it appealing to Germans and internationals alike, and in some of my classes half the students are non-natives, so I never feel like the odd one out!

'The majority of the work that I do for my course is for seminars. These generally take place once a week and each lasts for one semester. I am required to attend six seminars in linguistics, which works out as two per semester for the first three semesters. During term-time, it is expected that students come prepared for seminars by doing any necessary reading, and in most seminars students are also required to give a presentation on a subject relevant to the class. I have found that presentations like these are generally much more popular in Germany than in Britain, (I only had to give one presentation during my bachelor's), so I do feel rather lacking in experience compared to German students. I have found these presentations to be the hardest part of my course, simply because it can be difficult to stand up in front of a class of Germans and talk to them in their language about their language! However, having to do presentations can be really useful; I pay much more attention to my spoken language when speaking in front of a class, and this is often very beneficial for my spoken language skills. The presentation topic can also serve as the basis of the paper that is written for the seminar. One paper is written per seminar, and usually this is done in the holidays when there is more time. For my course, papers tend to be between 15 and 20 pages long and can be on a subject of your choosing.

'It has taken me a while to get used to the structure of my course and the relationship between student and teacher. Teachers are always addressed by their surnames and generally keep a distance from their students, tending not to treat them as equals. I am used to a more informal relationship with my teachers, so this is something that I have had to become accustomed to. The pace of my course is slower than I am used to: as an undergraduate I was expected to get to grips with fairly complicated linguistic topics within a couple of weeks before moving on to the next; here one of these topics might be the basis for a semester-long seminar or lecture series. Studying is also much more independent here; I choose how much work to put into my classes, and no-one chases students up if they don't hand in homework or come unprepared to a class. This can be very freeing, since the atmosphere is very unpressured and I put effort into my studies because I want to, not because I have to. However, the flip-side of this is that I have to motivate myself to work and use my time productively of my own accord, which has taken some getting used to.

'Overall my experience of life abroad has been very positive. There have always been friends around who are happy to help where needed (and correct my German!), and living abroad generally helps you to be more tolerant and respectful of other cultures and attitudes. However, I think it would be fair to say that most, if not all, internationals have moments of loneliness or homesickness, or having to drag themselves out of their front door to go out and meet people, especially at first. This becomes easier with time and persistence, and with an open and positive attitude to getting to know new cultures and people. Difficulties aside, the positive aspects of living abroad far outweigh the negative in terms of what internationals gain in experience and open-mindedness, and the rich multicultural friendships that they make along the way.'

Elizabeth's top tips

Travel and transport

'Travel within Bamberg is very easy. Most students have bicycles, but the buses are frequent, reliable, and free with a Bamberg university student card. Having a bike is especially useful for students who live just outside the city centre in the larger student halls. However, even without a bike, the town is small enough that most journeys on foot take 20 minutes or less.'

Application

'When I applied for my master's, I was required to send copies of documents with my application. The university should supply a list of necessary documents. These copies must be officially approved by taking them with the original to the German Embassy to be stamped. There is a fee of around £8 for each set of documents. Since I needed to send copies of documents that I did not yet have (such as my bachelor's degree certificate), I ended up having to take more than one trip to London to get documents stamped. This can get tedious (and expensive), so be as organised as you can and get all your documents stamped in one go if possible.'

Living and tuition costs

'Living costs in Germany are less than in the UK. I usually spend less than €30 per week on groceries. In terms of accommodation, you can expect to find a perfectly reasonable place to live for €300– €350 a month. Of course, this will vary depending on the town. If you're planning on renting privately, make sure you know whether or not an advertised rent includes utilities (with utilities, "*warm*"). Sometimes the advertised rent excludes the cost of utilities ("*kalt*"). Also, be aware that there are two types of *Wohngemeinschaft* (WG): *Zwangs-WGs* (compulsory shared flats) are apartments that are shared purely for financial reasons. This usually means that flatmates will not be interested in interacting with one another, so if that doesn't appeal to you, make sure to find a room in a flat that is a voluntary shared flat ("*keine Zwangs-WG*").'

Lifestyle and culture

'It is a cliché to speak of British politeness, but living in Bavarian Germany has made me realise that the stereotype is relatively accurate. Bavarians do not go out of their way to be polite and inoffensive to the same extent as Brits. However, this should in most cases not be taken as insulting; it is often simply one sign of a different mindset. It is important to bear in mind that local behaviour when living abroad will probably differ from your norm, and not to take offence too easily. In some situations I still find it hard to tell whether I am being treated rudely or not; in these cases I find it helpful to ask German friends for their opinion.'

Otto-Friedrich-Universität (University of Bamberg) is one of the oldest universities in Bavaria, and specialises in the humanities; social sciences; economics and business administration; and applied computer science. It has a large international focus, offering 300 programmes in collaboration with partner institutions in 60 countries worldwide.

HAN University of Applied Sciences: Profile

Inspiring environment. Innovative and skilled professional staff. International student body. At HAN University of Applied Sciences, we make it our business to offer higher education of an outstanding quality to students across the globe.

HAN University of Applied Sciences is one of the largest providers of education in the Netherlands, with more than 31,000 students and almost 3,100 staff members spread over two campuses. With more than 3,000 international students, HAN excels at putting theory into practice in an international context throughout all years of study. Spread over the cities of Arnhem and Nijmegen close to the German border, HAN has modern buildings, state-of-the art multimedia centres, world-class laboratories and wireless internet access.

By following a course at HAN University of Applied Sciences, students obtain a degree that will be an asset to any employee anywhere in the world. Fully accredited by the Dutch Ministry of Education and internationally recognised, the HAN degree is the starting point of graduates' successful careers and further studies in international postgraduate programs.

The starting point of the education offered at HAN is the integration of theory and practice. Our students tackle concrete problems and opportunities facing the workplace today using the latest theoretical insights. Professionals from the industry and the business world contribute to curriculum development at HAN, ensuring the courses are up to date and relevant. By tailoring the courses to industry requirements, students have a clear edge in the career market.

At HAN University of Applied Sciences students benefit from the experience and knowledge of foreign lecturers and international companies. Independence is stimulated and initiative rewarded by providing students with the opportunity to spend part of their education in more than one country. Students attend lectures in the Netherlands, do their work placement abroad, study at partner universities anywhere in the world and do their graduation assignment for an international company.

To maximise the learning process, classes are held only in English and in small groups of maximum 30 students, facilitating individual contact with teachers and fellow students. At HAN, personal development is just as important as professional education, therefore student guidance is offered throughout all years of study. Joining the international student body means merging education with social and professional networks. In the dynamic HAN community students are the heart of a multitude of activities: city trips, parties, thematic weeks, etc.

Bachelor courses taught in English:

- Automotive Engineering
- Communication
- Electrical and Electronic Engineering
- Finance and Control
- International Business and Management Studies
- Logistics Management (Economics)
- Life Sciences

www.han.nl/english

HAN University of Applied Sciences: Case study

Automotive Engineering
Ben Pyman, from the UK

'This world is at a constant state of change, evolving and changing towards a brighter future. Increased internationalism and the feeling of a smaller world is one important aspect of the future of the planet. HAN University of Applied Sciences is already a part of this international future. It's a place where you'll find people from all across the globe; from Australia to Canada and everywhere in-between! The differences in cultures can be interesting, entertaining or scary, but will always manage to enlighten you further and better your perspective of the world.

A well balanced course gives you both academic and practical skills essential to excelling in a professional environment. The learning environment itself is also great; with small class sizes and flexible teachers willing to spend extra time if you need the extra help. Smaller groups are also created for the purpose of set group projects which teach you great teamwork and leadership skills as you rotate through different assignments in the group.

Not only is the class internationally focused, but so is this course itself; with opportunities to do six months' study abroad, along with six months' internship abroad during your final two years, which make for great life and professional experiences. These international experiences, along with the practically focused parts of the course are certain to make you more appealing and interesting towards prospective employers; it definitely gives you some good stories to tell!'

STUDYING ABROAD

Liam Gerlin, from the UK

'I originally decided to study abroad due to the rising tuition fees in the UK and my desire to experience living in another country and integrating into a foreign society. It was always my intention to study engineering and among other universities which I considered, the HAN was the one which stood out as the best.

It has certainly been an experience deciding to study outside of the UK. It is a different mindset at a European university. The studies take number one priority and the emphasis really is on the fact that we are here to get a degree. Although the program is full-on and sometimes stressful, the institution is great and there is also good preparation and guidance for a future career which is of course, the reason we are here. It feels like it will certainly be worth it at the end of the four years. The opportunity to leave university with a top quality degree is there but one has to put the hours in. The language or culture has never been a barrier for me or anyone I have spoken to and it really is a great way to meet people from all over the world, I only have a handful of British friends here in the Netherlands.

Overall it has been a great experience and I would recommend studying abroad to anyone. When I step back and look at the bigger picture, think of the friends I have made and the travelling I have done as a result of being here, I believe leaving your home country to study is well worth it.'

University of Twente: Profile

University of boundary crossers

Ready to get an academic degree and busy scanning the globe for a university offering you the perfect programme and environment? Allow us to introduce an exciting option. The University of Twente offers a wide range of high-quality, internationally oriented bachelor's and master's programmes. Studying with us will give you excellent international experience and good job opportunities. Our innovative research programmes enjoy worldwide renown. We are strong in connecting technology to real-world issues. Our distinct entrepreneurial spirit ensures that the knowledge developed on our beautiful, park-like campus is put to use in commercially viable activities. Welcome to the University of Twente!

High Tech, Human Touch

The University of Twente, while relatively small-scale, is one of the world's leading universities. Our tagline, 'High Tech, Human Touch', reflects how our students and faculty members engage not only in developing pioneering technologies, but also in combining them with behavioural research, social sciences and economics. This interdisciplinary approach is one factor that makes us stand out from other universities – and makes our graduates the problem-solvers of the future. We like students and staff who have the ambition to make a difference in the real world, using technological insight to tackle the challenges people and societies are facing today. As a student, our university will encourage you to break through existing academic boundaries. The interaction between new technologies and society is an exciting field of research – and we are at its forefront.

Develop yourself on three fronts

We are based in a country that enjoys international acclaim for its problem-based learning methods and for training students to analyse and solve practical problems independently, through self-study and self-discipline.

Our 'High Tech, Human Touch' approach to education is highly innovative. We've structured our programmes to help you develop three complementary profiles: that of a researcher, a designer and an organiser. As a researcher, you will grow in critically assessing existing scientific knowledge and adding to the development of new knowledge. As a designer, you will become skilled in integrating scientific knowledge with the systematic development of new solutions to complex problems. And as an organiser, you will become an expert in combining knowledge from various scientific fields with the aim of implementing new solutions in a complex societal environment.

Campus vibes

One of our greatest assets is our campus. All of our education and research buildings are grouped together here, along with all the facilities needed for some 10,000 students and 2,000 staff to live, work and study together – from lecture halls, libraries and labs to shops, restaurants and sports facilities. Located on 146 hectares of beautifully landscaped and sustainably managed parkland just 15 minutes' cycling from downtown Enschede, it offers you the perfect setting for engaging in your studies, sports, arts, culture, fun and challenging student events. It is a place where exploration meets inspiration. Where professional and personal growth merge.

CuriousU: summer school meets summer festival

CuriousU is a great way to get to know our university and to pick up some valuable knowledge and skills. A festival-style summer school of one week, it offers you a range of high-tech courses and a taste of living and working on the only American-style campus in the Netherlands. The first edition of CuriousU took place in 2015, featuring numerous well-known speakers and top-notch entertainers. The 2016 edition will offer lectures and workshops on key research topics, such as health, serious gaming, design and entrepreneurship – and at all levels, from beginner's to advanced. The evenings are reserved for fun social activities: music, science, movies and much, much more. Keep an eye on www.utwente.nl/curiousu for programme details.

The Dutch touch
The Netherlands is known for its capital city, Amsterdam, as much as for its bikes and tolerance. But what is it really like to study in this small country in north-west Europe? And what secrets are there to discover in our university city, Enschede?

University life, Dutch style
As many international students will tell you, one of the great benefits of studying in the Netherlands is that it can help you develop an open mind and a more international perspective. We have many thousands of internationals studying and working here and the Dutch education system is interactive with an exceptional focus on teamwork and independent, proactive thinking.

International student associations
All Dutch universities have their own network of student-run associations that bring students together for academic activities, sports and recreation. Three of the larger international ones are active at the University of Twente: AIESEC, AEGEE and the Erasmus Student Network (ESN). UniTe is our own student platform for internationalisation and integration. These associations will assist you with everyday situations and help you settle in and make friends.

Most Dutch people understand English
The Netherlands is a small country and home to almost 17 million people. Many European capitals are within easy reach: Brussels is two hours away by train and a short flight from Amsterdam will take you to London, Paris, Madrid or Berlin. Most Dutch people speak, or understand, English. Public transport is well-organised and safe. To travel the Dutch way, of course, get a bicycle (we actually have more bikes than people in the Netherlands).

Enschede, a typical student city
The city of Enschede, located in the east of the Netherlands near the German border, has a population of 158,000 – one third of whom are students. The city boasts colourful weekly markets, bustling shopping streets and well-tended parks – in fact, it is one of the greenest cities in the Netherlands, with a 52-kilometre walking and cycling route winding right

through its green belt. But its student population gives the city its unique flair. Every day, you'll see students biking to their classes, reading on the banks of Rutbeek Lake or making merry in the Old Market pubs. Enschede is home to three higher education institutions: the University of Twente, Saxion University of Applied Sciences and the ArtEZ Institute of the Arts. The centre of student life is undoubtedly the University of Twente's unique campus.

Did you know that the University of Twente ...

- is set on a beautiful park-like campus – the only true, American-style campus in the Netherlands?
- is one of 14 Dutch universities recognised and funded by the government of the Netherlands?
- provides an internet connection of 1 gigabit per second and a campus-wide wifi network?
- lies in the east of the Netherlands, close to the German border and in the heart of Europe?
- is home to MESA+, one of the world's largest nanotechnology research institutes?
- is the most entrepreneurial university in the Netherlands, according to ScienceWorks and Elsevier, the world's leading provider of science and health information?
- is a founding member of the European Consortium of Innovative Universities (ECIU, www.eciu.org)?
- has strong ties with universities in Germany, Sweden, Poland, China, Indonesia, India and numerous other countries?
- is the finish line of the biggest relay race in the world, the 'Batavierenrace', which is followed annually by Europe's most massive all-night student party?

Ready for an international academic experience in The Netherlands? See www.utwente.nl/en/education.

Chapter 6
Studying in the USA

The USA is a consistently attractive destination for UK students; last year, over 10,700 UK students chose to study in the USA, according to the UK-US Fulbright Commission. The majority opted for undergraduate-level study, followed by postgraduate education, with the rest on non-degree programmes or post-study work schemes.

An increasing number of students seem drawn to the appeal of the American higher education system: a system with a choice of over 4,500 universities and a broader, more flexible approach to university studies than that of the UK. Quality of education in the USA is unsurpassed; 63 of the top 200 universities featured in the Times Higher Education World University Rankings 2015–2016 are from the USA, with the California Institute of Technology taking first place for the fifth year in a row. Some students are turning down places at the leading universities in the UK to take advantage of the breadth and quality of education on offer stateside.

The academic year in the USA is normally split into two semesters and runs from mid-August or early September to late May or early June. Some institutions also have a summer semester; however, most university students opt not to attend classes during the third semester, and instead choose to pursue holiday or work opportunities.

The education system

In the States, the terms 'university' and 'college' are generally used interchangeably. However, community colleges are different; they can only offer two-year associate degrees, rather than four-year bachelor's degrees.

Choosing where to study

When deciding where to apply, you need to consider which type of institution is right for you.

- **Public universities** are funded by the state and tend to have more students and lower fees. International students will end up paying more than state residents.
- **Private universities** tend to be campus-based, with better facilities and fewer students. They are funded by private donations, grants and tuition fees. Fees are higher, but the same fees are charged for all. More scholarships tend to be available.
- **Community colleges** offer associate degrees over two years (see page 210), with the possibility of transferring to a university to top up to a full bachelor's degree. They are often cheaper and less competitive.

The Ivy League is made up of eight prestigious private universities and colleges in the north-east of the USA. It started out as a sports league, rather than any kind of elite group or ranking system. For this reason, many top universities from across the country are not in the Ivy League, including Berkeley, which is a public university, and Stanford, which is on the west coast.

Keep an eye out for the public Ivy League, which includes the universities of Michigan and California; these institutions offer a quality education without such extortionate fees.

Also of note is the Association of American Universities (AAU), an organisation composed of leading research universities in the USA and Canada, which is somewhat comparable to the Russell Group in terms of standing and prestige. There are currently 62 member universities; universities are usually invited for membership based on the quality of their research, scholarship and education programmes. The most recent members include Georgia Institute of Technology and Boston University, and there are currently two Canadian member institutions: McGill University and the University of Toronto.

American degrees offer a much wider choice of subjects to study than you would expect in the UK. They are made up of a range of types of courses.

- **Core** (or general education), providing the compulsory foundation for university study. Students will often be required to select from a broad range of courses (modules), including sciences, history, maths, English composition and literature, and so on.
- **Major**, your main subject area; choose from options such as English, engineering or history. Most students will choose their main subject at the end of their sophomore (second) year; this is known as 'declaring' a major. A major accounts for one third to one half of the total number of courses needed to complete a degree. It is also possible to opt to study a double major, which is akin to the joint honours system in the UK.

- **Minor**, taken in a secondary subject or allowing you to specialise within your main subject area. You could minor in a foreign language or consider adding a computer science minor to a maths major. However, you cannot do a minor in place of completing a major.
- **Electives**, courses chosen from any department other than your major. Electives allow you the freedom to explore other topics of interest, and contribute towards the total number of credits needed to graduate.
- **Academic track**, a group of courses focused on a specific topic within a major; a student majoring in computer science could select a track in computer systems, for example.

Some universities offer co-operative education programmes, which incorporate paid work experience, rather like sandwich courses in the UK. In other cases, unpaid internships may offer degree credit.

> " Studying abroad was something that always interested me, but I was drawn to the US in particular by the flexibility of a liberal arts education. Unlike my peers in the UK, I'm not bound to studying one specific subject. Instead, I take classes in a wide array of disciplines, from French to chemistry, while pursuing two major fields of study in computer science and radio, television and film. "
>
> *Jordan Clark, Northwestern University, USA*

Finding a course

You can use College Board (undergraduate), www.collegeboard.
org, or College Navigator (undergraduate and postgraduate),
www.nces.ed.gov/collegenavigator, to search for courses at public,
private or community colleges. Before you begin your search, the
EducationUSA website features advice on how best to research your
options: see www.educationusa.state.gov/your-5-steps-us-study.

The US system means it is essential to find somewhere that is the
best match for you and what you have to offer. With this in mind
and with so many institutions to choose from, it might help to
start by writing a list of essential and desirable criteria relating to
your preferred US state, size of institution, funding or activities on
offer; whatever most matters to you. Use the information to filter
your search at College Board or Peterson's (www.petersons.com).
If you're looking for a student perspective on specific courses and
colleges, you'll find some useful information at Princeton Review
(www.princetonreview.com).

Transfers

It is possible to transfer from a UK institution to a US institution,
as well as between different universities in the USA, without losing
all your previous academic credit. Transfers would normally take
place after one year of study. As you need a minimum of two years
at a US university to graduate, transferring any later than after
your second year could prove difficult.

The Sutton Trust runs a US Summer School Programme
to encourage talented young people from low-income
backgrounds to consider university in the USA. You can find
out more at www.us.suttontrust.com.

Associate degrees

Associate degrees, such as Associate of Arts (AA) or Associate
of Science (AS), are two-year programmes of general studies,
together with foundation courses in a chosen subject (a major
or field of concentration). The AA and AS are tailored to allow
students to acquire the required skills and knowledge to transfer
to a US bachelor's degree for an additional two years of study in a
two+two format, or to prepare them for employment.

Associate of Applied Science (AAS) degrees are more practical
in content, and are designed to prepare students for the
workplace, or to help those already in employment top up their
existing skills.

Students who are only applying with GCSE qualifications could
apply for an associate degree. Certain vocational qualifications
might be accepted by community colleges, but not by the more
competitive universities.

American college year names

Year 1 Freshman Year
Year 2 Sophomore Year
Year 3 Junior Year
Year 4 Senior Year

Bachelor's degrees

Bachelor's degrees generally take four years to complete, although
there are some five-year courses in architecture, sciences and
engineering. A US bachelor's degree is comparable in level to a
British bachelor's degree. Unlike in the UK, where you choose

your subject before you apply, you can apply for an undecided major, and decide on your chosen subject at the end of sophomore (or second) year. This has more in common with the Scottish education system than with the rest of the UK. Much of the first year, and some of the second year, is spent on a range of introductory courses. Some of this core curriculum will relate to subjects you may wish to make your main subject choice (or major). For example, if you are considering majoring in psychology, you might opt for maths and quantitative reasoning, and social and behavioural sciences as your core subjects.

> **❝** I have had one-to-one support from the international student adviser who was fantastic in setting up my schedule and what I was going to study. **❞**
> *Stuart Bramley, Scottsdale Community College, USA*

Entry requirements vary, but most would require a minimum of five passes at GCSE or National 5, including maths and English. You would need to show that you are completing advanced-level study; the universities will be able to check your attainment from your academic transcript and any admissions tests you sit. Competitive universities will be looking for three A levels or equivalent. Less competitive universities may consider vocational qualifications, such as a BTEC National Diploma, a vocational course broadly equivalent to three A levels. For more information on applying, see the following section.

Honours degrees

Gaining an honours degree in the USA tends to indicate that the student has defended an undergraduate thesis (or piece of original research), known in the UK as a dissertation. Confusingly, a degree with honours can also mean that someone has achieved particular academic merit, although this is more usually known in the USA as *Cum laude* (with honour), *Magna cum laude* (with great honour) or *Summa cum laude* (with highest honour).

Graduate school

What we know as postgraduate education in the UK is described as graduate education or grad school in the USA. Master's degrees and PhDs gained in the USA are comparable to British master's degrees and PhDs. Certain subjects that you could start at undergraduate level in the UK can only be taken at graduate level in the USA; these include medicine and law. Pre-med and pre-law programmes are available at undergraduate level, although these programmes aren't mandatory for medical or law school.

At master's level, students can take an academic master's degree (also known as a research master's degree). This usually takes two years to complete, and normally involves the completion of a thesis. There is also the option of taking a professional master's degree, which is available in more vocational subjects, such as architecture and social work, and typically requires two years of study. Doctoral degrees are four to six years in length, and usually involve two years of coursework, culminating in qualifying written and oral exams; PhD students must pass these exams in order to be admitted to doctoral candidacy, after which they begin research for their dissertation.

Applying

The application process for undergraduate and postgraduate courses has some similarities to the UK system, although there are certain key differences. For the most part, applications are made directly to the chosen institution, although a number of

Hogeschool van Arnhem en Nijmegen
HAN University of Applied Sciences

Our international degree is an asset to any employer anywhere in the world.

Bachelors in English
- Automotive Engineering
- Communication
- Electrical and Electronic Engineering *NEW!!*
- Finance and Control
- International Business and Management Studies
- Logistics Management (Economics)
- Life Sciences

Masters in English
- Automotive Systems
- Control Systems Engineering
- International Business
- Molecular Life Sciences

★ THE NETHERLANDS ★ (ELSEVIER)
NO.1
THE NETHERLANDS ★ CATEGORY LARGE UAS 2013 & 2014

THE WORLD IS YOURS... GO INTERNATIONAL!

HAN www.han.nl/international

DO YOU WANT TO HELP CHANGE THE WORLD WITH TECHNOLOGY AND DESIGN?

PROGRAMMES

AP DEGREES
AP IN COMPUTER SCIENCE
AP IN DESIGN, TECHNOLOGY AND BUSINESS
AP IN IT TECHNOLOGY
AP IN MULTIMEDIA DESIGN AND COMMUNICATION
AP IN PRODUCTION TECHNOLOGY

BA DEGREES
BA IN ARCHITECTURAL TECH. AND CONSTR. MANAGEMENT
BA IN BUSINESS ECONOMICS AND IT
BA IN JEWELLERY, TECHNOLOGY AND BUSINESS

AP TOP-UP DEGREES
BA IN DESIGN & BUSINESS
BA IN DIGITAL CONCEPT DEVELOPMENT
BA IN SOFTWARE DEVELOPMENT
BA IN WEB DEVELOPMENT
BA IN PRODUCT DEVELOPMENT AND INTEGRATIVE TECHNOLOGY

CHALLENGE THE ORDINARY |  kea
KØBENHAVNS ERHVERVSAKADEMI

DIGITAL   BUILD   DESIGN   TECH   KEA.DK/

The definitive guide to teaching English as a foreign language

16th Edition

Are you looking for an exciting opportunity to travel and work abroad?

Covering over 600 language schools in over 100 countries worldwide, *Teaching English Abroad* will give you all the vital information you need to find job opportunities abroad, including:

- A country-by-country guide to English-language teaching opportunities

- A directory of language schools worldwide, including contact details

- Real-life accounts of teaching English as a second language

- Essential advice and tips on how to apply

- Advice for preparing and overcoming any problems

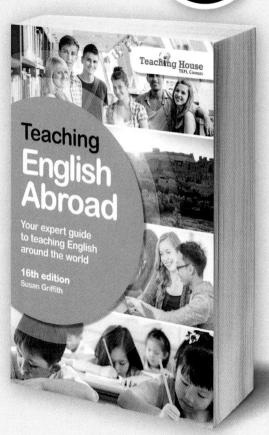

Teaching House
TEFL Courses

Teaching English Abroad

Your expert guide to teaching English around the world

16th edition
Susan Griffith

'We consider this to be our Bible!'

Managing Director, TEFL Worldwide, Prague

Get 10% off online!
Enter 'StudyAb' at checkout

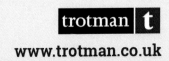

www.trotman.co.uk

Travel the world
Funding your trip as you go

17th Edition

For jobs abroad, including volunteering and summer jobs, *Work Your Way Around the World* is the number one guide for the self-funded world traveller, providing all the information you need to successfully find work abroad.

This book reveals the best places to find work, how to get the necessary permits, tips for travelling safely and much more, including:

- Hundreds of job opportunities across the globe
- Insightful case studies from travellers who have been there and done it
- Advice on applying for and securing jobs abroad
- Culture and lifestyle information by country

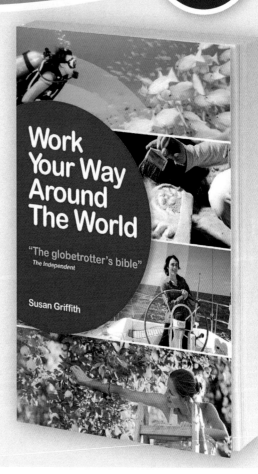

Work Your Way Around The World

"The globetrotter's bible"
The Independent

Susan Griffith

'The Globetrotter's bible'
The Independent

Get 10% off online!
Enter 'StudyAb' at checkout

trotman **t**

www.trotman.co.uk

universities now use the Common Application for undergraduate programmes; see page 214 for more information.

As part of the application process, you will be required to send detailed academic records and official course information for qualifications you have completed. You may need to submit your academic documents to an organisation that can convert your qualifications to a comparable level of study in the USA. Your university will give you further details of which organisation to use or, for a list of approved agencies, try the National Association of Credential Evaluation Services (NACES), www.naces.org.

Undergraduate applications

The timescale for applications is similar to that of UCAS, although there is a separate system if you are applying for a sports scholarship.

After Christmas in your first year at sixth form or college (Y13 in Northern Ireland or S5 in Scotland), you will need to start researching degree programmes and universities. It is suggested that you narrow down your choices to between three and seven universities, due to the time and costs involved.

The process of application is likely to include some or all of the following:

- application form
- admissions test scores
- a few essays (of around 500 to 750 words)
- transcript (details of your academic performance)
- two or three recommendation letters
- financial statement
- possibility of an interview.

You should expect to pay an application fee of around $50–$100 (£34–£68) per university.

You will be applying to the university as a whole, so you will need to demonstrate why the university should consider you. Admissions staff will decide your fate, rather than academic staff from your chosen department. They will be looking at more than just success at A level; GCSEs, your passion for learning, your love for your subject (if you have decided on a major), your extra-curricular activities and you as a person will all be considered. You'll need to demonstrate a match between what you have to offer and the type of institution you are applying to, so thorough research is essential.

> **"** The application process for US colleges is very different to the system in the UK. The process is a lot more holistic – they consider you more as a rounded individual and not just grades on paper. **"**
> *Jordan Clark, Northwestern University, USA*

Although you can apply for an undecided major, you will normally apply to a particular school within the university, for example, the School of Arts, School of Engineering or School of Management.

Application forms

If you are applying for undergraduate study in the USA, you may now be able to apply through the Common Application at www.commonapp.org, which is used by more than 600 universities;

for a full list, see www.commonapp.org/member-institutions.
Applications for the Common Application open on 1 August, and
the system operates in a similar way to UCAS, as it allows you to
apply to several universities with one application, although the
Fulbright Commission recommends that you narrow down your
choices to between six and eight universities.

You will be able to search by college, state, college type (public or
private), and additional criteria (co-ed or single sex education).
Each university involved still retains its own deadlines,
administration fees and additional requirements, which is likely
to involve submitting two to three essays and sitting entrance
tests, such as the SAT or ACT (for more information on these tests,
see page 217). You will be able to track each of your university's
requirements and deadlines through your student dashboard.

In addition, you will need to write a Common Application Essay,
which should be between 250 and 650 words in length, and is
submitted to every university to which you apply. The Common
Application Essay differs considerably from the UCAS personal
statement, as the former focuses less on your academic potential,
and instead invites you to reflect on your own personal experience,
and how this has shaped you as a person. Every year, the Common
Application releases a number of essay prompts, and students
must respond to one of these prompts in their essay. To see the
essay prompts for 2016–2017, go to www.commonapp.org/whats-
appening/application-updates/common-application-announces-
2016-2017-essay-prompts.

You will also need to select representatives from your school, two
teachers and one guidance counsellor, to support your application
to each university that you apply for. The teachers should each
submit letters of recommendation detailing your academic and
extra-curricular promise, while the guidance counsellor will be

required to submit a school profile and comment on your overall school performance. If you have undertaken work experience or any extra-curricular activities, it is also possible to submit extra reference letters. More information on how to apply can be found on the Common Application website or at www.fulbright. org.uk/study-in-the-usa/undergraduate-study/applying/common-application/tips-and-hints.

All other universities require direct applications, so you may have a number of forms to complete. Even if you're not using the Common Application, most applications are similar, so you will not have to start completely from scratch with each one. There tend to be more sections to complete and more space available than on the UCAS application, so it can result in quite a lot of work. You will be able to copy and paste information, as long as you remember to amend and target it each time.

Universities tend to offer separate deadlines for early decision and early action applications, usually sometime in November. The benefit of applying early is that you are being considered before the majority of applicants and competing with fewer students, so you might have a better chance of an offer. On the downside, you'll need to sit any admissions tests early. Most institutions offer either early decision or early action; some offer neither.

The main difference between the two is that early decision is binding, whereas early action gives you the security of knowing you have an offer, but allows you to keep your options open. You can only apply to one university as early decision; this university will need to be your first choice worldwide, and you are therefore committing yourself to that university if they offer you a place. This demonstration of commitment can have its benefits for consideration by the university and for scholarships. You might choose early decision if you have your heart set on one specific university, but it could be risky if the level of scholarship or financial aid you are offered will play a part in deciding where you study.

Regular admissions deadlines fall a little later, often in December or January. Check individual institutions for full details.

Undergraduate admissions tests

You will need to check whether an admissions test is necessary. Many universities will be looking for both good grades and strong admissions-test scores; this is particularly so if you are applying for academic merit-based scholarships (see Help with finances on page 231). Where an admissions test is required, the amount of importance placed upon the test scores varies between universities.

Most universities ask for the American College Test (ACT) or the Scholastic Assessment Test (SAT) for undergraduate-level study; both tests are designed to assess academic potential. If the university accepts both, you will be able to choose which test to sit. Although the tests are both well recognised and essentially achieve the same objective, the tests themselves are different and you may find that one will suit you more than the other. The SAT originally set out to measure aptitude, while the ACT was achievement-based, although both have changed since their inception; indeed, a new SAT test has been introduced for applicants taking the test from May 2016. If your institution accepts both tests, and you are unsure which to choose, The Princeton Review has a useful infographic on its website that allows you to compare the test features side-by-side; see www.princetonreview.com/college/sat-act.

The ACT has 215 multiple-choice questions, which are divided into four sections: English, reading, science and maths, and which applicants have 2 hours and 55 minutes to complete. The ACT comprises a single test, which includes a short break. For the more competitive universities, you are likely to have to complete a supplementary writing test, which is a 40-minute essay, and is taken as part of the same test. The ACT costs $39.50 (£27) or $56.50 (£39) including the written section.

The ACT is only available in limited locations in the UK. Outside the USA, there are a number of different test dates, each of which has its own corresponding registration deadline, though not all centres will be available on every testing date. The test is usually taken between September and June, with registration deadlines falling roughly a month before each test. If you miss the registration deadline, you will have to pay a late fee.

In March 2016, College Board launched a new SAT test, with first testing for international applicants from May 2016. It now comprises a single test of 154 questions, taken over three hours. The SAT is split into three sections: reading, writing & language, and maths. All questions in the reading and writing & language sections are multiple choice. Most questions in the maths test are also multiple choice; however, some questions, known as 'grid-ins', will require you to solve mathematical problems and fill in answer grids provided on the answer booklet. There is also a 50-minute SAT essay, though this is not required by every university.

You can search for UK test centres on the SAT website at https://collegereadiness.collegeboard.org/sat/register/find-test-centers. The SAT is available to take outside the USA sometime between October and June.

The SAT costs $43 (£29) or S54.50 (£37) if you are also taking the essay. In addition, you will be required to pay a non-U.S. regional fee of $38 (£26).

It is essential to be prepared for these tests. Take a look at www.fulbright.org.uk/study-in-the-usa/undergraduate-study/

admissions-tests and https://collegereadiness.collegeboard.org/sat to help you prepare.

Some universities may also require you to sit a SAT subject test in addition to the SAT or ACT. For example, some use subject tests to help place you on a course once you have arrived on campus, as the tests provide a good indication of your academic interests. The subject tests are available in five main subject areas: maths, science, English, history, and languages; more information is available on the SAT website at https://collegereadiness. collegeboard.org/sat-subject-tests, and your university will be able to advise you on whether to sit the additional test.

Sitting a test in early autumn of year 13 in England and Wales, Y14 in Northern Ireland or S6 in Scotland, is ideal, as it gives you time to resit, if necessary. Some candidates choose to take their first test as early as the previous spring. Candidates need to register sometime between spring and mid-September. It is worth registering early, as places can quickly fill up. You can register and find a testing centre through the ACT website, www.act.org, and the SAT website, www.sat.collegeboard.org.

Essays

You will be required to respond to two to three essay questions per application. Essays are likely to be based on your response to specific questions set by the university; make sure that you answer the questions fully and directly. They may want to find out about your skills and personality traits; why you want to study at this university; what are your goals; and what inspires you. Although you might choose to write on a subject related to your area of interest, you do not normally have to do so. The Fulbright Commission (www.fulbright.org.uk/study-in-the-usa/ undergraduate-study/applying/essays) has examples, video tips and useful handouts on this subject.

Below are examples of essay questions from University of Florida.

- Tell a story from your life, describing an experience that either demonstrates your character or helped to shape it.
- Has there been a time when you've had a long-cherished or accepted belief challenged? How did you respond? How did the challenge affect your beliefs?
- What is the hardest part of being a teenager now? What's the best part? What advice would you give a younger sibling or friend (assuming they would listen to you)?

(Source: www.admissions.ufl.edu/ugrad/personalessay.html.) *University of Florida has been consistently ranked among the top 5 best value public colleges by Forbes and Kiplinger Reports. It is a top 200 university in the Times Higher Education World University Rankings 2015-2016.*

Transcripts

The transcript should include predicted grades from your current qualifications, but also your progress from year 10 (Y11 in Northern Ireland or S3 in Scotland) onwards. It could include GCSE or National 5s, details of any exams taken since then (AS grades and so on), results of mock exams or other internal assessments and any academic honours achieved. Where relevant, ask your school or college to include explanations for any anomalies in your academic record. Qualifications may also need to be explained and details of the institution incorporated.

The format of the transcript is generally chronological. It should be around a page in length and produced on official headed paper. In addition, it will need to be signed by a school official and stamped with a school seal of certification. You will need to provide original transcripts for each institution to which you apply. It is important that you work with your school or college to help them prepare this, directing them to sample transcripts, such as those on the Fulbright Commission website (www.fulbright.org.uk).

On the application form, you'll be asked for your Grade Point Average (GPA). The GPA cannot be officially converted from UK qualifications, so you should leave this section blank.

Recommendations

You will need to arrange two or three letters of reference or recommendation from staff who know you well; follow your chosen university's guidelines on whom to ask. The restrained and often modest tone taken in a UCAS reference might not be enough for a US university. Recommendations from US schools tend to be far more detailed and far more positive, so you will need to prepare your referee to really sell you. Refer potential referees to the Fulbright Commission website for tips and sample letters, www. fulbright.org.uk/study-in-the-usa/undergraduate-study/applying/ reference-letters.

The EducationUSA website explains why you might choose to waive your right to see a copy of the recommendation.

> **❝❝** A recommendation form may include a waiver where you can relinquish your right to see what is written about you. If this option is offered, most admissions officers prefer you to waive your right so that recommenders may feel more comfortable when writing their evaluations. Admissions officers usually interpret waived recommendations as more honest. **❞❞**
>
> *Source: http://www.4uth.gov.ua/usa/english/educ/edusa/*
> *undergra/admissio/applicat/complete.htm*

Financial statement

How will you fund your studies in the USA? Your university will want to know, so you will need to complete any requests for evidence. You can use the evidence again when applying for a visa. You will need to show that you can at least cover the first year's costs, maybe even the costs for the full duration of the course. If you need financial assistance, you should include how much will be required. In most cases, a 'need-blind' admissions system means that your application will not be affected by this evidence.

Interview

Interviews will usually take place over the phone or on Skype. You may be surprised to find yourself being interviewed by an ex-student. Alternatively, the interview may be with a member of admissions staff. They may come to the UK or may ask you to go to the States, in which case you could enquire about help with travel expenses.

Potential interview questions may include why you have chosen this university, how you will contribute and why you intend to study in the USA. They will want to know about your subject interests, whether you have any ideas about your major or what your strengths and weaknesses are.

To prepare, you should look over the research you did when choosing this university. You can read over the essays you sent and look at how you can expand upon what was written. You should prepare questions to ask of the interviewer, but make sure that any questions aren't already answered in the university's prospectus or on their website. It might also be worth arranging a few mock interviews with your teachers or school careers adviser.

Offers

Early action and early decision applicants will usually receive admissions decisions by the end of December, while regular applicants will typically hear back from prospective universities by 1 April. The response could be one of three options: accepted, wait list, or not accepted. Those accepted can choose to accept, decline or defer. (Deferring is rare, so you should always check the process with your university. Even if your university agrees, any offers for funding might not also be deferred.) A deposit of around $500 (£342) will secure your place.

If you are placed on a wait list, there is still a possibility that you will be offered a place; follow any instructions you receive about the wait-list process and keep your fingers crossed. If you are placed on a wait list for your first-choice university, the Fulbright Commission suggests that you might wish to send the university an email to confirm that you will take up your place, should you be offered one, as universities may be more likely to accept applicants who have shown that they are committed to attending their particular institution.

Your offer won't be conditional, but it is still important to work hard and do well. You may gain university credit or advanced standing from good UK qualifications.

Applying for graduate school

As with undergraduate admissions, students apply directly to their chosen universities. The Fulbright Commission suggests restricting applications to between four and six institutions.

The details of closing dates, entry requirements and application fees will vary, although most will require some of the following:

- application form
- admissions test scores
- personal statement (approximately two typed pages)
- writing sample
- research statement
- CV listing your professional and extra-curricular achievements
- transcript (details of your academic performance)
- two or three recommendation letters
- possibility of an interview.

There will be an application fee to pay of around $50 to $100 (£34–£68) per university.

Each application may be different but, rather like a job application, you should be able to adapt the information you provide, rather than starting from scratch each time.

Most universities will be looking for at least a 2:2 from UK undergraduate study, with the more competitive universities asking for considerably more. They will be looking at your all-round offer, not just academic achievements, but also the way you demonstrate a good understanding of your chosen university and how this matches you as an individual. US universities are also keen to know about your involvement in extra-curricular activities. Contact the universities directly to discuss their requirements.

Much of the information in the previous section on applying for undergraduate study will also apply to postgraduate applications (see page 213). Notable differences include the research statement, personal statement and the admissions tests.

Research statement

The research statement allows you to outline your areas of interest, specialism and plans for how and why you intend to complete your research. Here are some of the key points that you need to consider when writing a research statement.

- Sum up your current plans for research, understanding that they may well change as you refine your ideas or as other developments occur.
- Relate your plans to your chosen university department and professors.
- Pinpoint shortcomings in any relevant literature that you have read, and set out objectives that you intend to address.
- Outline why you want to conduct your research at this particular university.
- Demonstrate your intellectual skills, but without alienating the admissions staff who may be considering your application.

Personal statement

This is the most important component of any graduate school application that you make, as it is your chance to make your application stand out and convince admissions staff that you are particularly worthy of consideration as a candidate.

There is no set structure or formula for the personal statement; according to the Fulbright Commission, often, universities will simply indicate the word count or number of pages required. However, you should treat it as an opportunity to really sell yourself to admissions staff, as the personal statement gives you the space to show your personality, in addition to illustrating your motivations for pursuing your field of study, and any academic or professional objectives you may have. For tips on writing a personal statement and sample statements, visit the Fulbright Commission's Personal Statement page at www.fulbright.org.uk/ study-in-the-usa/postgraduate-study/applying/personal-statement.

Graduate admissions tests

Most postgraduate options require an admissions test and there are a number of different tests to consider:

- **Dental Admissions Test (DAT):** www.ada.org/dat.aspx
- **Graduate Management Admissions Test (GMAT):** www.mba.com
- **Graduate Record Exam (GRE) revised General Test:** www.ets.org/gre
- **Law School Admissions Test (LSAT):** www.lsac.org
- **Medical College Admission Test (MCAT):** www.aamc.org/students/applying/mcat.

The cost of these tests can be quite substantial, with the GMAT costing $250 (£171) and the MCAT costing from $400 (£273). Some tests are available across the country, with others restricted to London, and the DAT currently only being tested in North America.

How the tests are used also varies, with some tests being a central factor in a successful application, while other tests are considered along with a variety of different aspects. In some cases, looking at how your scores compare to last year's averages can help to indicate your chances of success.

Preparation is vital, as the system tends to rely quite heavily on multiple-choice testing. Remember that you will be competing with US students who are used to this style of testing, so you need to know what to expect. See the individual test websites for sample papers or use the Fulbright Commission's 'Preparing for Admission Exams' page at www.fulbright.org.uk/study-in-the-usa/postgraduate-study/admissions-tests/preparation.

You could study ...

BA Linguistics

University of Pennsylvania (private)

Four years

Apply by 1 October

Annual fees $7,771 (£5,047); need-based financial aid available

Annual living costs $17,876 (£12,283)

Master of Music

University of Michigan (public)

Four years

Apply by 1 December

Annual fees $42,016 (£28,866); need and merit scholarships available

Annual living costs $20,130 (£13,822)

PhD in Microbiology

Massachusetts Institute of Technology, Cambridge (private)

Two years before admission to a PhD candidacy

Apply by 1 December

Annual fees $40,665 (£26,410); financial aid available

Annual living costs (room and board) $16,460 (£11,351)

Visas

If you plan to study in the USA and you aren't a US citizen or a permanent resident in the USA, you will need to obtain a visa before leaving the UK. If you live in England, Wales or Scotland, you should make your application to the US Embassy in London, while students in Northern Ireland should apply through the Consulate General in Belfast (https://uk.usembassy.gov/embassy-consulates/belfast). You can find out about the rules and procedures on the embassy website at https://uk.usembassy.gov.

There are two visa categories, F-1 Student Visa and J-1 Exchange Visitor Visa. F-1 is for students undertaking a full-time programme in the USA at an educational institution that is a Student And Exchange Visitor Program (SEVP) certified school; you can search for certified institutions on the Study in the States website at https://studyinthestates.dhs.gov/school-search. J-1, meanwhile, applies to those who are sponsored to study by the US government, the UK government or an international organisation; for example, many students studying on short-term study-abroad programmes or exchanges will travel on the J-1 visa. Your university will tell you which one you should apply for. There are differences in restrictions on these two visas: whether you can work, for example (see page 234).

> **❝** After you receive your visa you will need it upon entry to the USA and then again for opening accounts, etc. After this you should store it carefully. Be aware of things that may impact on it, for example, if you decide to travel or get a job. **❞**
>
> *Simon McCabe, University of Missouri, USA*

Once you have been offered a place at a university and provided evidence as to how you will fund the first year of your studies, your institution will prepare a Form I-20 (F-1 visa) or Form DS-2019 (J-1 visa); you will need this to apply for your visa. The visa process will usually involve the following steps.

- **Scheduling an appointment** at the US Embassy in London or the US Consulate in Belfast. This should be done as soon as possible once you have received your Form I-20 or Form DS-2019 and paid the 1-901 SEVIS fee (see below).
- **Payment of the Student and Exchange Visitor (SEVIS) 1-901 fee,** which costs $200 (£137) for F-1 students, and $180 (£123) for J-1 students. The SEVIS fee should be paid online at www.FMJFee.com, and no later than three days before your visa interview. It is important to keep a copy of the fee receipt, as you will need to provide this when applying for your visa.
- **Payment of the non-immigrant MRV $160 (£109) visa application fee.** You should pay the MRV when you schedule your visa interview.
- **Completion of the online visa application form, or DS-160,** at https://ceac.state.gov/genniv. You will need to print the confirmation page and bring this to your visa interview.

If your application is successful, you will normally be admitted for the duration of your student status. You should check any visa restrictions and follow them to the letter, as breach of these conditions is an offence.

Costs and help with finances

Tuition fees in the USA can be considerably higher than across the rest of the world. However, weigh this up against a strong tradition of financial aid and things might not always be as expensive as first anticipated. One-third of international undergraduate students in the USA have a scholarship as their main source of funding, while two-thirds of undergraduate students receive some form of financial support.

When considering the cost of tuition, it is important to make the distinction between the 'sticker price' and the 'net price'. Sticker price refers to the university's published tuition fees, while net price is the university's sticker price minus any grants and scholarships that you are eligible to receive, and there can often be a significant difference between the two. Net price is the real price you will pay for tuition, and will vary depending on your personal circumstances and the level of financial aid available at your chosen institution. Most universities will have a net price calculator on their website that you can use to estimate the overall contribution that you will have to make towards tuition fees.

Costs

According to the College Board (www.collegeboard.org), the average annual tuition fees are as follows:

- **four-year, public institutions (out-of-state students):** $22,958 (£15,772)
- **four-year, private institutions:** $31,231 (£21,458).

Fees for out-of-state students at two-year community college should be around $8,000 (£5,497) per year.

If you are looking at ways to make US education more affordable, you could consider taking a year or two at a community college before transferring to a university.

You should allow in the region of $10,000–$12,000 (£6,835–£8,202) per year for accommodation, food, books and materials, travel and so on. Costs could be higher than this, as they will vary depending on where you live and your lifestyle. Universities will provide an idea of local living costs on their websites.

The USA comes in at number 21 of 122 countries on a cost-of-living ranking from Numbeo (www.numbeo.com/cost-of-living/rankings_by_country.jsp). This suggests that its living costs are more reasonable than the UK, Australia, New Zealand and much of northern Europe.

Help with finances

According to the US-UK Fulbright Commission, over 600 universities support their international students by offering scholarships of over $20,000 (£13,672) per year for undergraduate study, with many institutions offering considerably more than this amount.

While you cannot access UK student loans for full-time overseas study, there may be some alternative options available. You should be researching universities and investigating funding concurrently, since your choice of university will impact on your options for certain scholarships or financial aid. Start early and consider that support will often come from a number of sources:

- scholarships from universities
- scholarships from external bodies
- sports scholarships
- savings or personal loans from the UK
- financial aid.

Much of the additional funding you may be applying for is provided by US universities. Scholarships are allocated based on a range of criteria: merit, financial need or personal qualities set out by the university or an individual sponsor or donor (for example, country of origin, ethnicity or talents). Use the admissions or financial aid pages on the university's website to find out which institutions offer scholarships to UK students. Keep in mind that even if you are lucky enough to get a scholarship it is unlikely to cover all your costs.

The amount of financial aid varies between colleges. For example, if you have the brains to get into Harvard or Yale and your family income is under $65,000 (£44,435) per year, then you would not have to pay anything. The threshold is $75,000 (£51,272) at MIT (Massachusetts Institute of Technology). Further financial aid is awarded on a sliding scale for family income over these amounts up to around $200,000 (£136,747).

> You might be able to speed up your studies, and thereby reduce some of your costs, by taking additional courses each semester or gaining credit over the summer break.

Sports scholarships are a highly competitive option and you will need to start the process even earlier than you would for a mainstream application. Applicants must meet and maintain academic standards, while also having the sporting talent to participate at varsity (inter-university) level. Scholarships are awarded for a range of sports, with opportunities for UK students in soccer, golf, athletics or swimming, for example.

Certain sporting associations will require scores over a particular level on SATs or ACTs. You can make contact with university coaches directly or use the services of an agent, who will often charge a fee. Both EducationUSA and the Fulbright Commission have handouts on their websites taking you through each option.

There are a range of external bodies that offer scholarships, each with their own specifications and deadlines. Try this web page for more details of organisations you might want to contact: www. fulbright.org.uk/study-in-the-usa/undergraduate-study/funding/ external-funding-bodies.

The following websites will help you get started on your search for funding:

- www.educationusa.info
- www.edupass.org/finaid/databases.phtml
- www.iefa.org
- www.internationalscholarships.com.

Cultural differences

If you have watched enough Hollywood films, you may feel that you already know what life in the USA is like. You may have heard of Thanksgiving and Spring Break and you probably have some ideas about campus life. Therefore, you might not expect to experience culture shock when leaving for this Western, English-speaking country. Although the changes won't necessarily be too extreme, it may still take a little while to adjust and feelings of homesickness and uncertainty are normal.

Meeting new people and making friends are important to help you start to feel at home. It may be tempting to stick with other international students, but if you want to get to know the real America, you will need to meet some Americans. As a nation, they are much more open than the Brits, so introduce yourself to hall mates and classmates or get involved with activities.

Drinking is less of a way of life than in the UK. The legal age is 21 and many university events, and even whole campuses, are dry.

> **❝** Yale is, obviously, a top-class institution, but what drew me to it was the sense of community that I found there. Yale splits its students into colleges, akin to the ones at Oxbridge, which fosters a collaborative atmosphere for social and academic activities. **❞**
>
> *Stephanie Addenbrooke, Yale University, USA*

Working while studying

It may be possible for you to work while you are studying in the USA, but it is essential to follow the rules to the letter. Remember that breaking employment law could lead to deportation. The information here should provide some of the basic details to get you started. For the latest rules and regulations, talk to your university's international office. You should check with them before taking on any work or voluntary commitments.

Full-time students on a Student Visa (F-1) can work up to 20 hours per week on campus when the university is in session, and full time on campus when the university is not in session, or during the annual summer vacation. If you're on an Exchange Visitor Visa (J-1), you may request permission from your international office to work for up to 20 hours per week on campus, but this is not guaranteed. Whichever visa you hold, you must have all the appropriate paperwork, including your Form I-20 or DS-2019 (as appropriate), a valid passport and Social Security Card; speak to your university for more information. Campus jobs might include library, cafeteria or office work. It makes sense to wait until you have had time to adjust to your new country before you start looking for work.

If you are on an F-1 visa, opportunities to work off-campus might be offered as part of your degree, after the first year of study. The work must be related to your area of study and is subject to prior authorisation by the United States Citizenship and Immigration Services (USCIS). Alternatively, Optional Practical Training (OPT) offers the option to work for up to 12 months during or after university. Under new regulations that came into effect in March 2016, students studying for science, technology, engineering or mathematics (STEM) degrees may apply for an additional 24 months of OPT, making a total 36 months' employment.

Students on a J-1 visa may be eligible for Academic Training, which can be completed during or after study. Academic Training is employment that your academic department considers integral or important to your degree. The duration of the training is directly proportional to the length of time you have been enrolled as a student, up to a maximum period of 18 months.

Staying on after study

Once your course has finished, unless you have further study or Optional Practical Training lined up, it will be time to return to the UK. You normally get 30 (if you have a J-1 visa) or 60 (if you have a F-1 visa) days' grace at the end of your studies, which you could spend tying up your affairs or exploring what this vast country has to offer. If you have any queries about when you should leave, try your university's international office.

Occasionally, some students get job offers, which means that they can stay on and eventually apply for a green card, giving the right of permanent residence. Alternatively, if close family are permanent residents of the USA, they may be able to sponsor you to stay on permanently. Don't go to the States banking on the chance to stay; these opportunities are the exception, rather than the rule. You can find out more at the website for the US Citizenship and Immigration Services, www.uscis.gov.

Pros and cons of study in the USA

Pros

- Some of the most highly rated universities in the world.
- More international students choose the USA than anywhere else.
- Opportunities for financial aid or scholarships for international students.
- Great facilities and campuses.
- English-speaking country.

Cons

- Few opportunities to stay on permanently.
- High university tuition fees.

Student story
Jordan Clark, Northwestern University, USA

'I'm currently a freshman at Northwestern University. One of the reasons why I chose Northwestern in particular is because of its location – the campus is situated on the shores of Lake Michigan in Evanston, Illinois. It boasts two on-campus beaches in its leafy suburban setting, yet it's only 30 minutes away from downtown Chicago. Additionally, Northwestern had several scholarship programmes I was eligible for. This means they cover all the costs of my attendance with grants, allowing me to graduate debt free.

'Studying abroad was something that always interested me, but I was drawn to the US in particular by the flexibility of a liberal arts education. Unlike my peers in the UK, I'm not bound to studying one specific subject. Instead, I take classes in a wide array of disciplines, from French to chemistry, while pursuing two major fields of study in computer science and radio, television and film. There's also a strong focus on extra-curricular activities and getting involved in things outside the classroom here, which further appealed to me.

'Academically, it's very rigorous and fast-paced. Instead of sitting one final exam at the end of the course, I'm constantly taking quizzes and mid-term exams. This, along with participation, attendance and homework, can all count towards your final grade depending on the class, which can often help to relieve some pressure.

'Moving to the other side of the world can seem incredibly daunting, but Northwestern offers lots of support to incoming international students. Before the 10-day orientation program that all first year students go through, there was an additional 3 days prior to this just for international students. We were assigned a current international student as a peer advisor, who offered great support and advice as they understood what we were going through. They also helped us with practical issues like setting up a bank account or getting a phone contract.

'One of the biggest differences I've encountered is the food. Portion sizes are huge, and it's really easy to miss your mum's home-cooked Sunday dinner. Also, believe it or not, there is an acute language barrier. Words like "chips" and "pants" have very different meanings and it's easy to forget this at times.

'Something else I found surprising was how much school spirit is valued. Everyone takes pride in being a Northwestern student, which is shown by people wearing the school colours or attending sporting events and cheering on the Wildcats. Sports are taken very seriously at US colleges, with Northwestern having a 50,000 capacity stadium. It's crazy to see the people that live down the hall or are in the same class as you play on national television every weekend.

'I've had little difficulty adjusting to life here, which I feel is largely because of the strong community aspect at Northwestern. I live in an all freshman dorm, which made the process of making friends really easy, and the clubs and societies I've joined have become little families also. As soon as people hear your accent, they initially remember you as "the British kid". While this can be annoying at times, it's a good way to start off conversations and people are always interested to learn more about your background.'

Jordan's top tips

Application process

'The application process for US colleges is very different to the system in the UK. The process is a lot more holistic – they consider you more as a rounded individual and not just grades on paper. It's comprised of many different components including admissions essays, standardised tests, a list of your extra-curricular activities, and letters of recommendation from your teachers.'

Resources

'One of the best sources of information is the Fulbright Commission, who I received amazing support from as a participant of their Sutton Trust US programme. Additionally, attending events such as College Day or university information sessions allows you to get a feel for what the different schools are like, and often provides you with an opportunity to meet the person who might end up deciding your acceptance!'

Choosing a university

'While it's tempting to only apply to well-known Ivy League schools, you should always conduct thorough research. It's important to keep open-minded – not everyone is a perfect match for Harvard or Yale and that's fine. It can be useful to write up a list of things you want from your university experience, and use that to try and find the perfect fit. The US has over 4,500 different universities, so just because you haven't heard its name before doesn't mean it's not a respected institution.'

Making friends

'Most universities will set up a Facebook group for their incoming students, which can be useful for getting to know a few people before you arrive on campus. Additionally, get involved as early on as possible! Joining clubs and taking part in extra-curricular activities are a great way to meet people with like-minded interests. If your university has Greek life, you may want to consider joining a fraternity or sorority. Some colleges will have fraternity and sorority houses on campus. Together, these groups are called the "Greek" system because each house is named after two or three letters of the Greek alphabet. You may have seen or heard of them in movies but their media portrayal is usually inaccurate. They provide great opportunities for social outlet, philanthropic events and community service, as well as helping to ensure all of their members succeed academically.'

Northwestern University is a leading research university, with twelve individual schools and colleges, and campuses in Evanston and Chicago. It is ranked 25th in the Times Higher Education World University Rankings 2015–2016.

Profile: Fulbright Commission

If you're thinking about studying across the pond, you're in good company: in 2014–2015, over 10,700 students from the UK were studying at a US university, and no other European country sends more students to the US.

Each year the US-UK Fulbright Commission surveys students when they collect their visas from the US Embassy in London, to find out why they chose to study in the States. The following reasons are always popular responses:

Quality and reputation of US universities

Although university rankings should be taken with a grain of salt (they may not reflect the points most important to you!), half of the top 10 universities in the 2015–2016 QS World University Ranking were US institutions.

With over 4,500 institutions offering undergraduate degrees, students can also choose from a large pool of universities, compared to 130 universities in the UK. From such variety of institutions, there's bound to be one that's a great fit for you.

Liberal arts

Half of the students Fulbright survey list that they are undecided about their degree subject. The liberal arts curriculum is a real selling point for students who don't know what they want to do for the rest of their lives at the age of 18.

A liberal arts education gives students a broad, well-rounded education, and allows them flexibility in exploring their academic interests before specialising in a major. If you have a passion for something and it is not offered, you might even be able to create your own curriculum and degree.

Opportunities to experience campus life and extra-curricular activities

Whereas UK universities focus on independent learning and more so on academics, on a US campus your learning and development is encouraged outside of the classroom.

American universities aim to educate the whole student by providing opportunities for extra-curricular involvement, community service, internships, sport, leadership and the arts. If there isn't a club you're interested in, you can create your own. Some actual clubs at US universities include the US Quidditch league and a humans vs zombies game of tag; both of these were founded by students and are now played at hundreds of colleges nationwide!

Funding opportunities

The availability of scholarship funding is a big draw for international students: 38% of Fulbright's pre-departure survey respondents list a scholarship as their primary source of funding.

Undergraduate scholarships are often offered to students based on merit, extra-curricular achievement, financial need or any niche personal characteristic. Just being an international student makes you stand out, so if you look hard enough there's probably a scholarship for you.

Internationalise your CV

A study conducted by the UK Higher Education International Unit found that 'mobile students' (those who study abroad) had lower unemployment rates and higher quality jobs than non-mobile students (*Gone International 2016*).

International students in the US also have the opportunity to gain work experience during their studies via work experience and internships, and can work in the US for up to one year after graduation on the Optional Practical Training permit; graduates in STEM subjects can stay on for up to three years.

WHAT ARE YOU WAITING FOR?

If you are planning to study in the US for a full degree, come along to Fulbright's USA College Day Fair, which takes place every September, and meet reps from over 150 US universities, or attend a Fulbright seminar on undergraduate study (www.fulbright.org.uk).

The Fulbright Commission also partners with the Sutton Trust on an all-expenses-paid programme (us.suttontrust.com) to give bright, state school students a taste of life at an American university. The initiative is centred on a one-week summer school in the US with introductory events and application support in the UK before and after.

Chapter 7
Studying in Canada

If you're looking to get more for your money than in the UK and considering a country with a good quality of life where you may be able to stay on afterwards, Canada has a lot to offer. In 2012, as many as 1,056 UK students were out there enjoying the benefits, according to a study published in 2016 by UNESCO Institute for Statistics (Global Flow of Tertiary-Level Students, UNESCO Institute for Statistics (UIS), 2012, www.uis.unesco.org/datacentre). The Canadian federal government is keen to recruit international students to its shores, with plans to double its international student body to 450,000 by 2022 and increase the number of international graduates remaining in Canada as permanent residents (European Parliament (ed.) (2015). *Internationalisation of Higher Education*. Study upon the request of the Committee on Culture and Education. Retrieved from www.europarl.europa.eu/RegData/etudes/STUD/2015/540370/IPOL_STU(2015)540370_EN.pdf).

The education system

The education system in Canada is run by a separate Ministry of Education in each province or territory. Each region has consistent standards and it is fairly easy to move between them. Courses are taught in English or French, although some institutions, such as the University of Alberta, teach in both languages.

The academic year runs from September to May and is divided into two semesters. Fall term runs from September to December and winter term follows from January to May. Some institutions offer a trimester system, with an additional summer term starting from May onwards, though there may be more limited programme choice at this time. Although it is possible to join courses in the second (and sometimes third) term, September intake is the most common.

University study

More than 10,000 undergraduate and postgraduate degree programmes are available at a range of public and private (not-for-profit) universities and university degree-level colleges. The majority of universities in Canada are public. Canada's education system is considered to be of high quality, with significant government investment; according to OECD's Education at a Glance 2015, Canada spends 4.1% of total public expenditure on tertiary-level education, which is higher than the OECD average of 3% (OECD (2015) *Education at a Glance 2015: OECD Indicators*, OECD Publishing, Paris, DOI: http://dx.doi.org/10.1787/eag-2015-en). In addition, Canada is ranked among the top OECD and G8 countries for academic research, with more than a third of its research conducted at Canadian universities. Bachelor's, master's and doctoral degrees are comparable in level to those from the UK.

Canada has seven universities in the top 200 of the Times Higher Education World University Rankings 2015–2016, with three of its institutions featuring in the top 50.

How to find a course

The official Study in Canada portal (www.studyincanada.com) is a good starting point for your research: you can use the site to search for courses, universities and scholarships, and it also includes links to the individual institutions.

Also explore www.universitystudy.ca, which features university profiles and advice on how to plan for study in Canada.

Accreditation and quality

You can check that your chosen institution is accredited by using the Directory of Educational Institutions in Canada. You can find this at www.cicic.ca (Canadian Information Centre for International Credentials). The listing includes all public and accredited institutions, as well as some private establishments.

Undergraduate study

Bachelor's degrees in Canada take three or four years to complete. In some cases, an honours degree is part of the degree programme; in other cases, it is taken as an extra year of study. Generally, it takes four years of study for an honours degree.

If you wish to study for an honours degree, you will need a high level of academic achievement: universities will usually stipulate the minimum average required in order to be eligible to continue on to an honour's degree. In addition, you may be required to take certain compulsory courses.

Four-year applied bachelor's degrees offer a more vocational option, combining academic study with the development of the more practical or technical skills needed for employment. Applied degrees are usually offered in Canadian polytechnics and technical institutes, though some are also available at certain universities and university colleges.

If you're looking to incorporate work experience, co-op programmes are similar to sandwich courses in the UK, providing the opportunity to work as well as gain academic credentials.

At most institutions, this typically involves alternating terms of study with terms of work. However, under a recent ruling that came into effect in June 2014, as an international student, you will only be able to work as part of a co-op or internship programme if the work is considered an essential part of your academic, professional or vocational training, and you will need to obtain a work permit in addition to a study permit (see page 255). If you intend to apply for a co-op programme, it is worth checking your eligibility to work with your chosen institution before beginning your application.

It is also worth noting that certain competitive fields, such as medicine, may not always be widely available to international students; your university will be able to advise you of any issues.

Differences from education in the UK

A key difference in Canadian education is that the degrees tend to be much more general than you would expect in the UK, particularly when compared to England, Wales and Northern Ireland. Although there will be certain courses (modules) you must study to achieve your major, you will have the option to choose electives from a range of additional subjects. For example, if you study history at the University of Waterloo, 40% of the classes you take are history courses; for the remaining 60%, you have the option to choose electives from other subjects, as well as including a minor in an additional area of interest.

> **"** My best subject in school was maths and so that's what I decided to study. However, I have always had a wide range of interests so I wanted the flexibility to do other things as well. **"**
>
> *Lauren Aitchison, University of Waterloo, Canada*

Three-year bachelor's degrees tend to be more generalised than honours degrees, which usually focus on a specific area of study.

Higher education in Canada takes place in universities, university colleges and community colleges. Some universities are research-intensive, with others focusing purely on teaching, in contrast to the UK, where all universities tend to carry out both teaching and research. The institution's website (or the institution's staff) should reveal what type of institution it is.

Community colleges

Community colleges tend to offer applied (rather than purely academic) studies, smaller classes (university classes can be large, particularly in years one and two), more co-op opportunities, and lower tuition fees. Canada's community colleges are also sometimes known as institutes, institutes of technology, technical colleges, CEGEPS (in Quebec), regional colleges or colleges.

Some community colleges also offer associate degrees, allowing students to transfer to a university degree through established links with partnering four-year universities. The system is somewhat akin to the system in the USA, whereby students typically study for two years on a community college programme before transferring to complete the final two years of a bachelor's degree at a university. Canadian transfer programmes are sometimes known as collaborative or joint programmes, with some programmes offering students the opportunity to receive a diploma or college certificate in addition to a bachelor's degree.

Entry requirements

Much as in the UK, each university sets its own admissions requirements and publicises the minimum qualifications required. High-school graduation in Canada is at a similar level to A levels or Advanced Highers in Scotland; universities will generally be looking for applicants educated to this level. Community colleges may have slightly lower entry requirements. Your institution will be able to tell you more, including whether they have any additional requirements, e.g., for competitive or specialist subjects.

If you intend to study in French, the institution will talk to you about the level of French they require and whether an assessment of your skills will be necessary.

Postgraduate study

Postgraduate courses are available at some, but not all, universities in Canada and include master's and doctoral degrees. Postgraduate study in Canada includes coursework, although less than at undergraduate level, alongside research. The courses tend to be based around seminars and will involve large amounts of structured reading, particularly in the early years.

Most master's degrees take from one to two years to complete and don't always require the completion of a thesis. Doctoral degrees (for example, PhDs) typically last from three years, with a thesis forming an essential component of the qualification. It is sometimes possible to move straight from an undergraduate honours degree to a doctoral degree. In these cases, the doctoral degree will often incorporate the master's degree.

What we know as 'postgraduate study' in the UK is more commonly known as 'graduate study' in Canada and the USA.

Entry requirements

Institutions will normally require an honours degree for progression to postgraduate study, although some exceptions are made for those with substantial work experience. Three- or four-year degrees from the UK (and other parts of the European Higher Education Area) should meet the general entry requirements for postgraduate study in Canada.

Academic recognition

Your chosen institution may already know and understand the UK qualification you are applying with; in which case, they may accept your certificates without further evaluation. If the qualification is unfamiliar, or if they are less experienced at dealing with international qualifications, you may need to pay to have your qualification evaluated. Talk to the admissions staff to see whether evaluation is required, as you may save yourself some money if you don't need this service. The Canadian Centre for International Credentials (www.cicic.ca) will provide further information on how to proceed.

Applying

Your first step when applying should be to contact the international office requesting application documentation. They should send you information about the application procedure and timescale, along with requirements for the evaluation of qualifications, the costs of study and the visa-application processes.

Undergraduate applications for universities in the province of Ontario are usually made through a centralised application service, the Ontario Universities Application Centre (OUAC), www.ouac.on.ca, though you should check with your university before applying, as some may also accept direct applications. If you apply through OUAC, you will be classed as an international (105F) student, and will be required to pay a base application fee of C$155 (£84), which allows you to apply for up to three courses, as well as a C$10 (£5.42) international service fee. It is possible to add extra choices, at $50 (£27) per course. It is also likely that you will incur additional fees set by the individual universities for transcripts and other supplementary documentation.

You will find that many individual institutions require direct application. Applications may be paper-based or online. Applications will incur a fee, often well in excess of the £23 required by UCAS. If you are applying to a number of universities in various provinces, you may have to pay more than once. Applications to community colleges should be made directly, and will also require a fee. Remember to factor in the application fee cost when working out the costs of study. Careful research and narrowing down your choices should help to reduce these costs, and the additional work required by multiple applications.

Application deadlines vary between provinces, institutions and individual programmes. International applicants are normally required to apply between December and early spring for a September start, in the autumn for January start, and around January for start dates in the summer semester. Graduate application deadlines may be earlier, particularly for the more competitive courses.

Start planning for your application a good year in advance. Bear in mind that evaluation of qualifications, the need to sit admissions tests (for postgraduate study) and the time taken for international post may slow the process down considerably. It is also important that you follow individual application deadlines and submit all the required documentation for each application that you make, as admissions staff may take longer to process an application if it is incomplete. You should expect a decision around four or five months after the closing date, although this will also vary between institutions.

The application form

The application form itself is likely to be quite a small part of the application process, requiring basic information about the applicant's:

- personal details
- contact details
- education
- test scores
- relevant professional experience (where applicable)
- referees.

Further documents required in support of an application could include:

- transcript
- letter of intent/statement of purpose
- essay or sample of writing
- letters of reference
- proof of immigration status.

A CV, medical form and portfolio may be required for certain courses. Similarly, a criminal records check will only be required in certain cases.

There will be an initial deadline for the application and a later date for the provision of the supporting documentation. Some institutions won't consider an application until all documents are received, so send all documents promptly to improve your chances.

Transcript

A transcript is an academic record produced by your school, college or university. It might include details of your education and progress from year 10 in England and Wales, year 11 in Northern Ireland or S3 in Scotland. It will include exam and mock-exam results, internal assessment results and predicted grades; it should include any special awards or recommendations, as well as an explanation of any problems or anomalies in your educational attainment.

Letter of intent or statement of purpose

This is often a key part of the application and may determine whether you are accepted. Use the statement to explain your interests, any relevant experience and what you hope to achieve with the qualification. You need to demonstrate your suitability and your potential. Try to analyse your experiences and remember to back up any claims you make about your strengths with examples and explain any discrepancies or gaps in your education, where relevant.

At postgraduate level, you should incorporate an outline of the research you intend to undertake. Consider what interests you about this area of work, how you intend to approach the research, and illustrate how the research will fit in with the focus of the department.

The statement needs to be well written and free from spelling and grammatical errors. Two typed A4 pages should be sufficient.

Letters of reference

A letter of reference should be a positive document that provides details of your skills, strengths and achievements; a detailed, targeted letter is much more helpful than a general one. You will need to find two or three academic staff who know you well and can comment on your capabilities and really sell you.

Provide your referee with details of the courses you are applying for, along with a copy of your statement and transcript. You could suggest some of the key skills you would like them to draw attention to.

The referee may need to illustrate their own academic competence and background, and should provide specific examples of your strengths, since any claims should be backed up by relevant evidence. It may be useful for your referee to compare your achievements and skills to others that they have taught.

Give your referees around one month to compile the letters. It is helpful to gently follow them up to check that the letters have been completed. Thank them for their efforts; you may need to use their services again.

Tips, sample references and standard reference forms are available on university websites. See the University of British Columbia, www.grad.ubc.ca/prospective-students/application-admission/ letters-reference, the University of Alberta, https://www.ualberta.ca/~caps/ReferenceLetters.pdf and McGill University, www.mcgill.ca/law-admissions/undergraduates/admissions/documents/#LETTERS, for some examples.

Admissions tests

Canada does not have a standardised university entrance exam; universities have their own admissions requirements. In most cases, UK students shouldn't need to take admissions tests for undergraduate courses.

Entrance exams required by Canadian graduate schools include the GRE (Graduate Record Examination) revised General Test, which can be taken across the world (www.ets.org/gre). It is available as a computer-based test in seven UK centres and costs

US$205 (£140); and the Graduate Management Admissions Test (GMAT) for business studies (www.mba.com), which is a computer-based test that costs US$250 (£171), and which can be taken at five UK locations. Other tests include the LSAT for Law School (www.lsac.org) and MCAT for Medical School (www.aamc.org/students/applying/mcat).

Universities use the results from these tests in different ways. In some cases, the result will be a deciding factor; in others, the result will be just one of a number of considerations. Ask your chosen institution how they use the results and what kinds of scores previous applicants have achieved.

You are likely to do better in these tests if you are prepared for the style of questioning and any time limits for completion. Books and courses are available to help you prepare. You can take tests like the GRE revised General Test more than once, but the costs can end up being quite substantial if you do so.

What next?

If you are successful in gaining a place at a Canadian college or university, you will be provided with a letter of acceptance. The next step will be to apply for a study permit.

You could study ...

BSc Nursing (Hons)

Collaborative programme between Seneca College, Toronto and York University, Toronto
Four years (two+two arrangement)
Apply directly to Seneca College
Annual fees C$8,864 (£4,816)
Monthly living costs (books, accommodation and transport) C$1,000 (£543)

Bachelor of Anthropology
University of Victoria
Four years
Apply directly by 28 February
Annual fees C$17,026 (£9,248)
Annual living costs for room and board C$7,380–C$10,784
(£4,009–£5,847)

MA History
University of Alberta, Edmonton
Two years
Application deadlines set by the department
Annual fees C$9,535 (£5,176)
Monthly living costs from C$1,225–C$1,505 (£681–£817)

Visas

A study permit is required for anyone who will be studying
for more than six months in the country; you can apply
online through the Citizen and Immigration Canada (CIC)
website at www.cic.gc.ca/english/study/study-how.asp, or
on paper through the Canadian Visa Application Centre in
London (http://www.vfsglobal.ca/canada/UnitedKingdom).
When you make your application, you will be asked to
complete a visa application package and pay a processing fee of
C$150 (£81).

To gain a study permit, you will need a letter of acceptance from
your university, which must be a designated learning institution
(DLI). The letter will include a DLI number, which you will need
to put on the application form. In addition, you will need to prove
that you can pay your tuition fees, living costs and travel expenses
to and from Canada for the duration of your stay. Your passport

should be valid for the full duration of your studies, and you will also need to be in good health, and without a criminal record. Follow all instructions carefully and bear in mind that if you are submitting a paper application, the processing time is likely to be significantly longer.

If you choose to study in Quebec, you will also need to obtain a *certificat d'acceptation du Québec* (CAQ), which costs $C110 (£60). This must be done in addition to applying for a study permit from the Canadian government. You can apply for the CAQ online at www.immigration-quebec.gouv.qc.ca/en/immigrate-settle/students/index.html, though you may need to post additional forms to the immigration office. The government of Quebec usually allows up to 20 business days to process applications, not including postal delivery time.

As of March 2016, if you are a British citizen, you are also now required to have an Electronic Travel Authorization (eTA) if you intend to travel to or through Canada by air. The eTA is valid for five years, or until your passport expires. You can apply for an eTA online; the application costs C$7 (£3.79) and, in most cases, the eTA will be granted within minutes of submitting your application. When you fly to Canada, you will need to travel with the passport that you used to apply for the eTA, as the eTA is electronically linked to it.

If your chosen university or college welcomes lots of international students, the staff should be experienced in supporting applicants through the immigration procedures.

Further information on the procedures and how to apply can be found at www.cic.gc.ca/english/study/index.asp.

Costs and help with finances

Costs

Tuition fees across the provinces and territories of Canada
vary. According to Imagine Studying in Canada (the Council of
Ministers of Education), in 2015–2016, university tuition fees
ranged from around C$6,420 to over C$35,000 (£3,478–£18,962)
per year for arts and humanities programmes. Fees at community
colleges tend to be slightly lower: according to Schools in
Canada (www.schoolsincanada.com), in British Columbia, the
average annual undergraduate fees for international students at
community colleges is C$10,500 (£5,418), compared to C$13,500
(£7,312) for the equivalent university fees.

Overall, international undergraduate students paid annual
university tuition fees averaging C$21,932 (£11,879) per year
in 2015–2016, while international full-time postgraduate
students paid an average of C$14,350 (£7,772) per year
(www.statcan.gc.ca).

Some research-based postgraduate study is subsidised and the fees
can be lower than undergraduate fees. To calculate more specific
costs for the courses and institutions you are interested in, the
Imagine Studying in Canada website has a useful cost calculator
at www.educationau-incanada.ca/educationau-incanada/template-
gabarit/step-etape.aspx?lang=eng.

To compare the cost of living in Canada to the rest of the world,
try the Numbeo cost-of-living ranking at www.numbeo.com/cost-
of-living/rankings_by_country.jsp. Canada is ranked number 30 of
122 countries, indicating that it is cheaper than the UK, the USA,
Australia and New Zealand.

Help with finances

If you're looking for a scholarship to help offset the costs of international study, be prepared to start your research early, more than a year ahead. Consider how you will support yourself, as scholarships are limited, highly competitive and may not cover the full costs of your studies.

Talk to your chosen university about any scholarships they offer and take a look at the Canadian government's website as a starting point, https://w03.international.gc.ca/scholarships-bourses/scholarshipnoncdn-boursenoncdn.aspx?lang=eng&menu_id=7.

Scholarship opportunities for international undergraduates are limited. At postgraduate level, scholarships include the Vanier Canada Graduate Scholarships (www.vanier.gc.ca/en/home-accueil.html) and Trudeau Scholarships (www.trudeaufoundation.ca/en/programs/scholarships).

Another option worth considering is the International Student Identity Card (ISIC) Global Study Awards, which offer successful applicants a £10,000 grant to help towards the cost of tuition fees. Although the number of awards are limited and the selection process is competitive, the awards are open to students studying abroad on any undergraduate or postgraduate programme at a higher education institution, provided they are aged 18 or over and meet certain conditions; for full details, see www.isic.org/the-global-study-awards-expand-your-horizon.

Other sources of information and funding include:

- **Erasmus+ Master Loans:** http://ec.europa.eu/education/opportunities/higher-education/masters-loans_en.htm

- **Top Universities:** www.topuniversities.com/student-info/ scholarship-advice/scholarships-study-canada
- **Scholarships Canada:** www.ScholarshipsCanada.com.

Cultural differences

Canada is considered to be a tolerant and multicultural society and it welcomes students from across the world. Canadian culture shares much with its neighbour, the USA, but there are differences. The province of Quebec is French-speaking and culturally quite different from the rest of the nation. Parts of Canada show a particularly British influence, including Toronto and Victoria.

Adjusting to the sheer size of Canada can be a shock, as well as getting used to the long, cold winter in much of the country.

> **❝** I knew it was cold in Canada but the UK really doesn't prepare you for a Canadian winter. I wish I knew to invest in a good winter coat and pair of snow boots! **❞**
>
> *Lauren Aitchison, University of Waterloo, Canada*

Citizenship and Immigration Canada has some helpful information on culture shock, as well as on adjusting to life and the weather in Canada at www.cic.gc.ca/english/newcomers/after-life.asp.

Working while studying

Full-time degree-level students can work on campus at their university or college without a work permit, though you will need a Social Insurance Number (SIN) before you can start work. Under recent regulation changes to the International Student Program, students are now allowed to work off campus without a work permit for up to 20 hours per week during term-time, and full time during the holidays, provided they have an SIN.

Citizenship and Immigration Canada should tell you all you need to know about working while studying, co-op programmes and internships, and working after graduation, www.cic.gc.ca/english/study/work.asp.

Staying on after study

The Canadian authorities have a number of programmes that allow students to stay on in Canada after completion of their studies. Remember that these schemes change from time to time and may even have changed by the time you complete your studies.

Post-graduation work permit programme

Graduating students can apply for a permit of up to three years, depending on the length of their studies: see www.cic.gc.ca/english/study/work-postgrad-who.asp.

Canadian experience class

Graduating students have the opportunity to apply to stay on in Canada permanently; you will need to meet various conditions, including at least one year's full-time (defined as 30 hours per week or more) Canadian work experience in a managerial, professional or technical occupation, or the skilled trades. It is important to note that any work experience that you gain while you are still a full-time student, such as co-op work placements, will not qualify as suitable work experience under this scheme. See www.cic.gc.ca/english/immigrate/cec/apply-who.asp for details.

Provincial nominee programme

If you are considered to offer the skills, education and experience to make an immediate economic contribution to your province or territory, you may be able to gain residence under this scheme, www.cic.gc.ca/english/immigrate/provincial/apply-who.asp.

Pros and cons of study in Canada

Pros

- Good quality of education.
- High investment in research and development.
- Opportunities to stay and work after graduating.
- Possibility of emigrating after graduating.

Cons

- Certain competitive fields may not always be widely available to international students.
- Different systems in place in the individual provinces.

Student story
Laura Bowker, McGill University, Canada (exchange)

'I made a fairly last-minute decision to apply for an exchange program at McGill University in Montreal, Canada and so I was fairly unprepared for the experience! I had never really considered studying abroad before I was told about the exchange programs on offer, although I have always loved travelling and experiencing new cultures. I can honestly say it has been one of the best decisions that I have made and I have loved experiencing the Canadian and Quebecois lifestyle of Montreal.

'When I looked into applying to McGill University I was immediately attracted by the opportunity to live in a bilingual city and experience a totally different climate. The mix of cultures, diversity and bilingualism really makes Montreal an incredibly creative city, and I found this to be very inspiring and enjoyable. The weather, which is characterised by four defined seasons, with hot summers and very cold, snowy winters, has given me the opportunity to do such a wide variety of activities, from skiing and ice skating to kayaking and hiking. It's been fantastic being able to embrace such extreme weather and experience so many new things.

'I found academically McGill was fairly different to my regular university, Edinburgh. There is a very competitive and driven atmosphere around the university, and the policies of almost continuous exams and testing, with mid-term exams dotted throughout the semester as well as finals and assignments means that you have to work incredibly hard. It's definitely challenging and a little stressful at times, but the teaching staff are generally excellent and there is a very good support network for international students and academic advising.

'At McGill there are a number of university residences, but these tend to be exclusively for first-year students. Many international students and Canadians live in these for the first year. Most people in the upper years live in apartments around the city. In Montreal the accommodation is excellent. There is such a large student population that there are people constantly advertising flexible sub-letting or apartment leases and the price here tends to be much cheaper than most UK city rents. I lived in the Plateau/Mile-End area of Montreal, which is such a relaxed and convenient part of the city, close to lots of restaurants, bars, and the Mont Royal Park. I would definitely recommend living somewhere like this, as being slightly further outside of the university bubble gives you a chance to get to know another area of the city and allows you to escape university when work is getting overwhelming!

'I have absolutely loved living in Montreal, where I've been able to experience both the Canadian and Quebecois cultures. As well as this, Canada in general has a very high immigrant population, which makes the cities very diverse and interesting. Montreal's Little Italy and China Town, for example, are definitely highlights and reflect the variety here!

'The biggest difference in terms of lifestyle has definitely been the weather. The extreme cold temperatures dictate the lifestyle in the winter months. Canadians are amazing at embracing the weather and finding so many fun things to do in the cold, like skiing, ice skating, snowshoeing, dogsledding and so many more! I was definitely a little scared about the weather to begin with, but as long as you are prepared with a good coat and boots, and embrace all the outdoor activities, it is amazing fun!'

Laura's top tips

Visa
'Applying for a visa to study in Montreal was a fairly long process. It required applying for a Canadian Study Permit and a Provincial document specifically for studying in Quebec (CAQ). I would recommend starting this process as soon as possible. It's very time-consuming to complete all the documentation and the processing time was a couple of months. It's not something to leave last minute!

'Another factor to consider before studying abroad in North America is health insurance. The policies vary between universities, but most require you to take out the university's health insurance policy, which can be fairly expensive. Just make sure you are mentally prepared for a hefty payment in the first week!'

Resources
'Before I came to Canada I read a couple of guide books, a number of blogs online and articles about living in Canada. These definitely gave me a couple of hints and tips, but it's really impossible to get an idea of the place before you arrive. Although it's great if you can find out a bit of information, speaking to someone who has studied abroad is probably the most useful thing to do. Otherwise, the best advice I would give is just to arrive with an open mind and be ready to embrace lots of new and different things!'

Living costs

'The cost of living this year in Canada has been very good value as the pound has been very strong against the Canadian dollar. Nevertheless, apart from renting prices, which are significantly lower than most UK cities, most things are fairly similar in price to the UK. Sadly, transport between cities or domestic flights are much more expensive than I expected, but the distances are so vast that it is hardly surprising.'

Making friends

'McGill offered a number of great orientation events, which were great ways to meet new people and get to know your way around the university and city. The most anticipated is "Frosh" – a fresher's week equivalent, which consisted of a week jam-packed with activities and nights out. This was an excellent way to meet lots of new people.

'The university also offers a buddy program for international students and has a very active international student society which runs trips throughout the year. These are both excellent ways to settle in and meet lots of people who are also adapting to the new culture and university.

'I took part in lots of different societies and activities at McGill, from playing on a basketball team and writing for the newspaper to volunteering in a community café. My favourite society that I got involved with was the McGill Outdoors Club, which was an amazing way to meet lots of people and see lots of the beautiful Canadian countryside. I went on many weekend trips, including dogsledding in Northern Quebec, camping on a frozen lake, cross-country skiing, hiking in the summer and staying at the club's country house. Many of my most memorable moments were spent in the Canadian countryside with this club and I would definitely recommend joining an outdoors club as a cheap way to travel and see the countryside.'

Travel and transport

'There is very good transport around Montreal. There is a Metro, which covers most of the city, and very regular bus services. The OPUS card, which is a travel card that can be used on the buses and metro, has student discounts for monthly subscriptions.

'During the summer months, the city's cycle paths become very busy especially with the Bixi bikes (bikes which you can rent for 30 minutes that are stationed all around the city). This is a lovely, convenient and safe way to get around the city, as it is very well geared up for cyclists.'

Working while studying

'There are a number of part-time jobs that are available on campus, as well as many volunteering opportunities. Unfortunately, on an exchange year-long study permit you are restricted to only working on campus but many other students work in the city alongside their studies.'

Staying on after study

'The university has excellent career facilities and an internship office dedicated to advising and helping students to get work or experience for life after university. Again it is difficult for exchange students as many of these opportunities are limited to full-time students or people on longer visas.'

McGill University is an English-language university with a student population from over 150 different countries and two campuses in Montreal. It appears at number 38 in the Times Higher Education World University Rankings 2015–2016.

Chapter 8
Studying in Australia

What makes UK students choose to travel halfway round the world to experience study in Australia? Perhaps it's down to the combination of good-quality education, great lifestyle and reasonable entry requirements. Many UK students are already convinced, with 1,678 of them enrolled in Australia in 2013, according to a 2016 study published by UNESCO Institute for Statistics (Global Flow of Tertiary-Level Students, UNESCO Institute for Statistics (UIS), 2013, www.uis.unesco.org/datacentre).

> Australia has nine institutions in the top 200 of the Times Higher Education World University Rankings 2015–2016, and one in the top 50.

The education system

A significant difference between the UK and Australia is the academic year; in Australia, this runs from February to November. Universities tend to run a two-semester year, with semester one running from February to June and semester two from July to November. It is possible to start most courses in July, although some courses, including medicine and dentistry, are only available to start in February. The long summer holiday runs from December to February.

University study

The style of teaching tends to be slightly different from that in the UK: in Australia there is a focus on practical learning, to encourage independent thought and discussion. The approach is less formal, but equally challenging. You will need to share your views on subjects and may even be assessed on your class participation. In fact, you will probably be assessed in a range of different ways, in recognition of the fact that individual students learn in different ways.

Independent study and the development of critical thinking are encouraged, much as in the UK. You might find that you have more contact hours and a closer link with the lecturers than you would generally have in the UK.

Nearly all of Australia's universities are public, with only a few private universities. Undergraduate study can be offered at both pass and honours level, with the latter usually involving an additional year of study, following completion of a three-year bachelor's degree.

How to find a course

Start your search with the official Australian government site, www.studyinaustralia.gov.au. Study in Australia also includes a mini-site for students from the UK at www.studyinaustralia.gov.au/uk. Other options include Hotcourses Abroad (www.hotcoursesabroad.com) and Study Portals (www.studyportals.com).

Accreditation and quality

It is fairly straightforward to ensure that you will be studying with an approved provider. The institutions that are approved to offer degrees and other higher education qualifications can be found on the AQF (Australian Qualifications Framework) Register at www.aqf.edu.au/register/aqf-register.

Australia also has an Act in place to support international students, which stipulates a student's right to receive current and accurate information about the course, fees and type of study from their institution before they apply. In addition, institutions taking on international students must support them adequately, which includes helping them to adjust to life in Australia and meeting their learning goals. Go to http://cricos.education.gov.au to discover the list of institutions that meet these requirements.

> **❝** I find it seems to be more personal than at UK universities. Our class is quite large, but somehow you still manage to feel a personal connection with the lecturers; they really try to get to know you and give you great feedback on assignments and how you're going throughout the year. **❞**
>
> *Kadie O'Byrne, Murdoch University, Australia*

Academic recognition

If your institution takes lots of international students, they may understand your UK qualifications and accept you without the need to compare their standard to those offered in Australia. If the qualification is not known to them, they may ask you to have your qualifications assessed.

Undergraduate study

Undergraduate study takes three to four years in Australia, with a strong emphasis on coursework. Certain courses, such as medicine, can take up to six years. Unlike the UK, ordinary or pass degrees are the norm, generally taking three years. Assessment for undergraduate degrees in Australia is continuous, so all marks achieved count towards the final degree result.

Access to an honours degree is reserved for those who have achieved particularly highly. Grading for honours degrees is similar to the UK system of first, upper-second, lower-second and third-class honours, although some institutions offer First Class Honours with University Medal for outstanding academic merit. A bachelor's degree (honours) would normally take at least four years and requires independent research and the completion of a thesis.

In addition, some universities offer a fast-track system, which allows students the opportunity to reduce the length of their degree by up to a year and begin work early.

The system allows for more flexibility than you get in much of the UK. You choose a major and study a fixed number of relevant courses, but you will also have the chance to study a range of elective courses in different subjects. You might start off majoring in one subject and end up graduating with a major in a different subject, based on your interests and abilities as you proceed through your studies.

> A degree with honours is achieved after completing an ordinary bachelor's degree with high achievement. It is different from an honours degree.

Vocational education

Technical and Further Education (TAFE) colleges offer Vocational Education and Training (VET) qualifications, which are based on collaborative partnerships between governments and different industries, and are designed to prepare you for an industry or trade. VET qualifications include AQF advanced diplomas, which take two to three years to complete.

Another option is a two-year associate degree, which serves as a foundation for a particular area of study, and is designed to help students develop basic employment-related skills. Associate degrees are offered at universities and TAFE colleges, some of which offer pathways to progress to a bachelor's degree or to continue in specialist industry training.

Entry requirements

If you have passed three A levels or equivalent study, then you should meet the general entry requirements for degree-level study in Australia. Certain university courses require particular grades and specific subjects to have been studied previously, while some courses will require a selection test or audition. On the whole, grade requirements tend to be slightly lower than in the UK. Programmes such as medicine and dentistry are competitive, requiring high-achieving applicants with some relevant experience. Associate degrees or advanced diplomas may have lower entry requirements, although they may require specific experience or relevant previous study.

> **66** The grading process is different. Instead of getting a first, 2:1, 2:2, you are awarded high distinction, distinction, credit or pass on each of your assignments, exams or units. **99**
>
> *Vicky Otterburn, Murdoch University, Australia*

Postgraduate study

A range of different graduate qualifications are available, including graduate certificates and diplomas, master's degrees and doctorates.

- **Graduate certificates** (one semester) and **diplomas** (two semesters) are the shortest postgraduate options. They are of a similar level to postgraduate certificates and diplomas in the UK and can be used as a bridge to the study of a new subject at postgraduate level.
- **Master's degrees** are delivered by coursework (taught master's); by research; or a combination, and generally take one year after a bachelor's (honours) degree, or two years after an ordinary or pass degree.
- **Doctor of Philosophy (PhD)** takes from three years.

The length of your postgraduate study depends on your academic background and the subject you choose to study.

Entry requirements

The successful completion of an undergraduate degree is the standard entry requirement for postgraduate study in Australia. For some courses, you may also be required to demonstrate relevant work experience or previous research.

Entry requirements vary between institutions and their departments. Your institution will be able to tell you more.

Applying

Each state in Australia runs its own centralised admissions service but, in the vast majority of cases, international offices require direct applications. Alternatively, some students opt to apply via an Australian educational agent (see page 99).

Closing dates fall in the autumn for courses starting in February. You need to apply to university in good time to give yourself a chance to get a visa and to sort out all the other aspects of the move overseas. Some postgraduate research programmes (PhD,

MPhil) have rolling applications. Certain courses, such as medicine and dentistry, require a much earlier application; likewise, if you're applying for a scholarship as well, you may need to start the process much earlier. Ideally, you should be preparing for your application a good year in advance.

The application form

Contact your chosen institution requesting information about the application process and an application form. Application forms can often be completed online. If paper-based, the application might be sent directly to the institution. Alternatively, you may choose to deal with an agent or local UK representative, depending on the requirements of the university or college.

The application process is more straightforward than the UK system. When applying directly to an institution, you will choose a first preference for your course, along with second and third options. The institution may charge you a fee to apply, ranging from A\$50–A\$100 (£27–£53). Certain fees may be waived when applying online or through some educational agents.

Other documents

If you are making an undergraduate application, you will need to supply your GCSE and A level certificates or equivalent. If you are applying before you have received your final-year qualifications, you will also be required to provide an official letter from your school or college with your predicted grades. If this is the case, any offers you receive are likely to be conditional; once the results are released, you will then have to provide proof of your qualifications.

If you are applying to a postgraduate coursework programme, it is likely that you will need to supply academic transcripts with details of any qualifications gained, along with your bachelor's completion certificate. Before making a formal application for a master's by research or a PhD programme, you will first need to make contact with a potential supervisor to receive provisional approval for your intended research proposal.

Some courses, but not all, require a personal statement and an accompanying academic reference. For postgraduate applications, you may also have to submit a CV.

Admissions tests

In some cases, an admissions test will be required. Your institution will tell you more.

If a test is required, make sure that you are prepared. Although you may not be able to revise, preparing yourself for the style and time constraints of the test can make a big difference.

Undergraduate admissions tests

Applicants to medicine, dentistry and health-science courses at certain universities may be required to sit either the UMAT (Undergraduate Medicine and Health Sciences Admission Test, www. umat.acer.edu.au) or the ISAT (International Student Admissions Test, www.isat.acer.edu.au). The UMAT consists of a three-hour written test, which can be taken in London. The test costs A\$250 (£133) to register and, if you are taking the test in the UK, you will also have to pay an overseas testing levy of A\$185 (£98). The ISAT is a three-hour computer-based test and is available to take in centres across the UK. It costs A\$315 (£215) to register.

Postgraduate admissions tests

Postgraduate tests used in Australia include:

- **Law School Admissions Test (LSAT):** www.lsac.org
- **Graduate Australian Medical Schools Admissions Test (GAMSAT):** www.gamsat.acer.edu.au.

> If an interview is required as part of the admissions process, you may be interviewed online or over the phone.

What next?

If your application is successful, you will receive a letter of offer. In order to confirm your offer, you will need to sign and send an acceptance of offer to your chosen institution. Once the offer is accepted and the required deposit is paid (generally the fees for one semester), you will be emailed an electronic confirmation of enrolment (eCoE), outlining your course start date, total tuition fees and the length of your programme. You will need this document to apply for a visa.

You could study ...

Bachelor of Oral Health
University of Melbourne
Three years
Apply by late December
Annual fees A$36,544 (£18,839)
Annual living costs A$16,000–A$28,200 (£8,249–£14,539)

Master of International Relations (master by coursework)
Australian National University, Canberra
Two years
Apply by 15 December for February start
Annual fees A$37,104 (£19,145)
Weekly living costs from A$370–A$570 (£191–£294)

Doctor of Engineering
University of Queensland, Brisbane
Eight units; contact the faculty for programme duration

Rolling applications; flexible start date

Annual fees A$0

Annual living costs A$17,160–A$21,945 (£8,885–£11,325)

Visas

In order to apply for a student visa, you will need your eCoE and the ability to financially support yourself throughout the course; this includes the cost of tuition fees, return air fare and A$18,610 (£9,860) in living costs per year; remember: you may need more money than this to live on.

A further condition is adequate health insurance while you are in Australia. You will also need to meet certain health requirements and may be required to show evidence of good character.

> The streamlined visa process (SVP) means that applications for degrees at participating universities require you to provide less evidence and are processed more quickly.

The type of visa required will depend on the course you intend to study. You will need to apply for a Higher Education Sector visa (subclass 573) if you are enrolled on one of the following courses:

- bachelor or associate degree
- graduate certificate or graduate diploma
- master's degree by coursework
- higher education diploma or advanced diploma.

If you are studying for a master's degree by research or a doctoral degree, then you will need to apply for a Postgraduate Research

Sector visa (subclass 574). For VET courses, you should apply for a Vocational Education and Training Sector visa (subclass 572). If in doubt, the international office at your institution will be able to advise which visa category you should apply for.

This information is a basic introduction to the visa process; contact the Australian High Commission in London (www.uk.embassy.gov.au) for the latest application procedures and fees information. You should be able to apply online and fees are currently set at A\$550 (£291), with visa application charges reviewed on 31 July each year. You shouldn't apply more than 124 days before your courses starts. You should normally expect your application to be processed within four weeks, though online applications often take considerably less time. Ask your institution if you need further support; they are likely to have experience in this process.

Further information on applying for a study visa can be found at www.border.gov.au.

Costs and help with finances

Even the cheapest Australian undergraduate degrees cost more than those on offer in England, while the most expensive courses far exceed English fees. Scottish, Welsh and Northern Irish students will pay considerably more in Australia than at home. While Australia is not a cheap option, it does have some great benefits in terms of quality of education, lifestyle and opportunities.

Costs

Fees vary between different universities. According to www.studyinaustralia.gov.au, you can expect to pay annual tuition fees as follows:

- **bachelor's degree:** A$15,000–A$33,000 (£7,947–£17,480)
- **vocational education and training:** A$4,000–A$22,000 (£2,119–£11,653)
- **master's degree:** A$20,000–A$37,000 (£10,594–£19,598)
- **doctoral degree:** A$14,000–A$37,000 (£7,416–£19,599).

Lab-based courses and those requiring specialist equipment are likely to be at the higher end of the fee scale, with courses in arts or business towards the lower end. Courses like medicine and veterinary science will be significantly higher. Remember to consider the cost of books, materials and field trips too.

> All students in Australia pay a student services and amenities fee (SSAF) for campus services and student societies. In 2016, the maximum limit was set at A$290 (£154). Some universities incorporate this within tuition fees for international students, so check with your institution whether an additional payment is necessary.

Australia is currently listed at number 13 out of 122 countries on a cost-of-living ranking for 2016 at www.numbeo.com/cost-of-living/rankings_by_country.jsp, making it comparable to living in the UK, which is placed at number 12.

It is a requirement of the visa that you have adequate health insurance; the cost of overseas student-health cover (OSHC) starts at a few hundred pounds per year. According to the Australian Department of Health and Ageing, the average cost of minimum cover for a single traveller is A$437 (£231) for 12 months. Visit www.studyinaustralia.gov.au/global/live-in-australia/insurance for more details.

The following average weekly costs are provided by
www.studyinaustralia.gov.au:

- **accommodation:** A$85–A$440 (£45–£233)
- **groceries and eating out:** A$8 –A$280 (£42–£148)
- **utilities (including internet):** A$55–A$195 (£29–£103)
- **public transport:** A$15–A$55 (£8–£29)
- **entertainment:** A$80–A$150 (£42–£79).

According to Study Options, you should aim to budget for
A$18,000–A$28,000 (£9,531–£14,825) per year for living
expenses. To find out about finances and budgeting in Australia,
go to www.moneysmart.gov. au/managing-your-money.

Help with finances

If you're hoping for a scholarship to help fund your studies in
Australia, you need to start early and get ready to prove yourself,
as competition is fierce. Scholarships are hard to come by and
often don't cover all the costs, so you will need to think about
how you will support yourself. You can make a start by using the
scholarship database on www.studyinaustralia.gov.au, and talk to
your university about any scholarships that they offer.

You could also take a look at the following websites:

- www.australiaawards.gov.au
- http://britain-australia.org.uk/about/strategic-partners/
  northcotetrust.

Cultural differences

You will soon discover how multicultural Australia is; with more
than one in four of its population born overseas, you are sure to
come across other British people. Adjusting to Australia includes

adjusting to its extremes of weather and its vast size. Find out about the climate in the different states and territories when you are deciding where to study.

The way of life in Australia is a bit different too; things are generally more informal and the good weather means that there is more time to enjoy life outdoors.

> **"** The Australian lifestyle is great! Everyone is so friendly, welcoming and laid back. Sport is a big part of the Aussie lifestyle; there are heaps of regular sports clubs and great facilities to use all year around. In the summer, people have BBQs regularly; you don't rush around because of the heat and spend a lot of time at the beach or around a pool with friends. There are lots of music festivals and events on offer. **"**
>
> *Vicky Otterburn, Murdoch University, Australia*

Working while studying

The opportunity to start working as soon as you start your studies is a definite benefit of study in Australia. For new students gaining a student visa, there is no need to apply for permission to work. Subclass 572 and subclass 574 visa holders can work for up to 40 hours per fortnight in term-time, and unlimited hours during holiday periods. Students enrolled in master's by research or doctoral degrees (visa subclass 573) can work unlimited hours once their course commences. Remember: there will be serious consequences if you break the conditions of your visa. The Australian Government Department of Immigration and Border Protection (www.border.gov.au) has up-to-date information.

There are a range of opportunities in pubs, bars, restaurants and shops, but you will need to balance your study and your work. The national minimum wage is currently A$17.29 (£9.15) per 38-hour week, although some junior employees (employees under the age of 21) may get paid less than this.

You will need a Tax File Number (TFN) from the Australian Taxation Office (www.ato.gov.au) to work and to open a bank account.

Staying on after study

Australia is keen to welcome international students and has a number of initiatives in place to facilitate staying on after study.

The Temporary Graduate visa (subclass 485) allows international students who have recently graduated from an Australian higher education institution to stay in Australia for a minimum of 18 months to work, travel or study, provided they hold an eligible visa and meet the study and qualification requirements.

The Temporary Graduate visa has two streams: the Graduate Work stream and the Post-Study Work stream. Under the Post-Study Work stream, students can apply for a subclass 485 visa if they have received a higher education degree from an Australian education provider. The visa is valid from two to four years, depending on the qualification used to apply for the visa:

- **bachelor degree, bachelor (honour's) degree, master's by coursework degree, master's (extended) degree:** two-year validity
- **master's by research degree:** three-year validity
- **doctoral degree:** four-year validity.

The Graduate Work stream is for students who have completed courses that lead to a degree, diploma or trade qualification. The course studied should be closely related to the student's nominated occupation, and this occupation must be one of the occupations listed on the skilled occupations list (SOL); for a current list of designated occupations, see www.border.gov.au/Trav/Work/Work/ Skills-assessment-and-assessing-authorities/skilled-occupations- lists/SOL. The visa is valid for 18 months from the date that it is granted.

For those considering staying on a more permanent basis, the Graduate Work stream can act as a pathway for Australia's skilled migration programme, which targets those who can contribute to the economy. The requirements and occupations needed vary, so choosing a course of study because it is on the skilled occupation list is not a guarantee of success; the list may well have changed by the time your course is complete. For the latest details, see the Department of Immigration and Border Protection website at www. border.gov.au/Trav/Work/Work.

Pros and cons of study in Australia

Pros

- Strong reputation for higher education.
- Reasonable entry requirements.
- Good pay for part-time work.
- Possibility of emigrating if you have the right skills.
- Cost of living is comparable to living in the UK.

Cons

- High cost of fees.

Student story
Joshua Jackson, SP Jain School of Global Management (Singapore and Sydney, Australia)

Josh Jackson took a big step when he decided to study abroad.

'I wasn't sure what I wanted to do for university. The headmistress of my school announced one morning in assembly that an institution was offering the possibility of 100% scholarship on fees and accommodation for four years. The Global Bachelor's of Business Administration course required two years' study in Singapore and ended with two years in Sydney, Australia.'

Getting a scholarship to cover his tuition fees resulted in a huge saving. 'The full cost of study would be about US$20,000 (£13,817) a year.'

Josh found the application process to be fairly straightforward.

'I had to write a short essay about myself. After that there was a written task with three questions that I needed to complete in a certain amount of time. Following that, I had an interview on Skype with one of the professors. The interview was very short and informal as I had met the professor around six months before on a week-long "bridge to BBA" event the university ran. This was a five-day event where students were invited to stay in university accommodation, meet the staff and spend some time in SP Jain and Singapore.

'The university sorted out the visa for Singapore for me. A few days after we arrived, the university staff took us to the immigration office where we were given the visa. For Australia, we had to apply for the visa ourselves but the university provided us with a code we needed once we had paid the tuition fees. A few days after the application went through, I was instructed to have a medical at one of a small number of panel doctors in the UK. Around seven working days after the medical, my visa was granted and I was able to fly over.

'Sorting out of the Singapore visa was the single most useful thing the university did. They also put me in touch with a current student who could answer my questions and the head of the student council emailed all the new students to give them some information before they came.

'Since I arrived, I feel the university does not help very much. They helped us get health insurance in both countries and the former dean and student counsellor were very helpful to the students in every way possible, but other than that we are very much on our own. The most important aspect of this is that although the master's degree graduates often get 100% placement, there is currently no facility in place to help us get jobs when we graduate, which many find very concerning.'

Josh has coped well with adjusting to life on two new continents.

'In the years I have been away I have had about two nights where I felt homesick, but other than that I have enjoyed the experience greatly. Some of my peers have felt very out of their comfort zone and struggled somewhat, but there are people from almost all round the world so finding someone quite similar to you is not too hard.'

He explains about some of the differences in teaching and learning that he has experienced. 'Due to the small size of the institution, I actually have a very close relationship with all of my professors. Classes rarely, if ever, exceed 30 students, whereas I have friends in the UK who have lectures with 400 or more students. I think this is a huge benefit, as well as the fact many professors teach master's degree students as well and so are very highly qualified and knowledgeable.'

Joshua's top tips

Accommodation

'Staying on-campus is always useful at first for making friends. Staying off-campus is usually cheaper, sometimes by quite a long way, but normally less convenient.

'I have stayed on-campus in both countries. In Singapore, the city is so small and transport so cheap, it doesn't matter where you stay, but in Sydney the city is very expensive. I stay in Wentworth Point, near the Olympic Park, and it is very removed from the city centre. Travelling up to central Sydney takes over an hour, and almost two hours to reach the east coast of the city.'

Food
'The cuisine in Singapore is a huge mix of different cultures, mostly traditional Asian Chinese but also influenced by Indian and Western food. They also have most of the large fast-food chains as well (McDonald's, Subway, KFC, etc.). Traditional Singapore hawker centres are a great place to go to eat like the locals. The food is cheap and quick but good and tasty as well, almost like a Singaporean version of fast food!'

Insurance
'Our school provided us with health insurance policies in both Singapore and Sydney. In Sydney it was mandatory to have health insurance to get the visa.'

Living costs
'Singapore was very cheap compared to where I live in England. At the time I was there, it was around two Singapore dollars to one British pound, but you could get a fast-food meal for around S$5. Going out to the movies and drinking was also cheaper.'

'Australia is about as expensive as London, as far as I can tell. I buy almost everything non-branded, eat at home every day and rarely go out drinking.'

Financial support for study
'I have a 100% scholarship on my tuition fees, but pay for accommodation. This is conditional on the basis that I get within the top 25% of the class throughout the year.'

Working while studying

'In Singapore I did not have to work, but I was told the pay was not very good as there is no minimum wage. Working in Australia is pretty good though. I am able to work 20 hours a week during term-time and an unlimited amount during the holidays. The pay is far better than England for unqualified jobs. However, there do seem to be a few licences around that you need to get before working. For example, I needed to pay A$100 (£51) to get a "Responsible Service of Alcohol" (RSA) licence.'

Making friends

'Making friends was never that hard. Everyone is in the same position, away from home and starting a new chapter of their life. Many had never studied away from home before, and almost everyone had never studied in a different country to their home.'

Lifestyle and culture

'The lifestyle in Singapore is very metropolitan, busy, and Asian; they are more traditional, hierarchical and family oriented. It is definitely a hybrid between typical Western and Eastern lifestyles, a good stepping stone between England and Malaysia, for example.

'Australian lifestyle and culture is very like England's, but more relaxed and with a slightly heavier influence on sport and relaxation.'

Travel and transport

'Public transport in Singapore was very good and cheap. Taxis were cheap as well and very useful when you couldn't use public transport.

'In Sydney, though, the transport is not as good and quite expensive. The buses are still quite costly, especially for a student. Getting to the city is quite a hassle and taxis are very expensive.'

Options for after you finish your studies

'I am not very sure about options after I finish, though both places seem a little easier to get a job after graduation than England. The pay in Singapore is not that great in comparison, but in Australia you get paid very well and there are more job opportunities than in England.

'The best things about studying overseas have been experiencing a new culture and travelling; seeing a completely different way of life, cuisine and society has been truly amazing. As I am in each place for two years, I really get a feel for it as opposed to going on holiday somewhere for a few weeks. The travelling has been amazing as well. Going from Singapore to Indonesia, Malaysia and Thailand is as simple as visiting France, Germany or Spain from England, and often cheaper! There are so many travel opportunities in Australia as well that I am very much looking forward to experiencing.

'Overall, studying abroad is completely what you make of it. You really have to go out there and immerse yourself in the place you are studying to fully enjoy it. If you keep yourself to yourself and only look at why it is worse than home, you won't enjoy it.'

SP Jain (www.spjain.org) was originally established in Mumbai, India in 1981 and now has campuses in Dubai, Sydney and Singapore and achieves high global rankings for its MBAs.

Chapter 9
Studying in New Zealand

New Zealand might seem like a long way to go for an education, but many international students choose the country for its safety, quality of life and the option to settle after studies. According to a survey published in 2016 by UNESCO Institute for Statistics (UIS), 537 UK students were studying there in 2013 (Global Flow of Tertiary-Level Students, UNESCO Institute for Statistics (UIS), 2013, www.uis.unesco.org/datacentre).

New Zealand is a little larger in area than the UK, but with a population of only 4.5 million.

The education system

As in Australia, New Zealand's academic year runs from late February or early March to November. The academic year incorporates two semesters, each lasting 12 weeks; you can expect breaks mid-semester and at the end of semester one, with a longer summer break after semester two (from November to February or March). It may be possible to join certain courses in July or as part of a summer school between November and February.

At all levels, students in New Zealand are encouraged to develop independent thought and defend their ideas in discussion and debate. Most taught courses are assessed by means of exams and classroom activities, which could include essays, assignments, presentations, projects and practical work. Make sure that you get involved in class activities; your participation may be assessed here too.

All eight of New Zealand's universities are publicly funded. There are also a range of other institutions with degree-awarding powers: polytechnics, colleges of education and wānanga.

- **Polytechnics, or institutes of technology,** originally specialised in technical or vocational studies, but now offer a range of subjects and research activities. A degree from one of these institutions is equal to a degree gained at one of New Zealand's universities.
- **Colleges of education,** for the most part, offer studies in the fields of early-years, primary and secondary education.
- **Wānanga** provide mainly vocational educational opportunities that include Māori tradition and culture.

New Zealand also has a number of private training establishments (PTEs), which tend to offer more specialised courses, though some offer degrees up to master's level. Certain PTEs also have articulation agreements with universities, whereby students study for a diploma at a PTE, which then offers a pathway to continue on to a degree at a partnering university.

How to find a course
Take a look at New Zealand Education (www.studyinnewzealand. govt.nz) to search for programmes up to doctoral level at universities, institutes of technology and polytechnics, and PTEs.

The site also features a scholarship search option, as well as useful information about study and life in New Zealand.

Accreditation and quality

New Zealand has strong quality systems for education. In order to verify that your course or provider is accredited, you can search for approved qualifications and recognised institutions at the New Zealand Qualifications Authority (NZQA) website (www.nzqa. govt.nz/qualifications/courses/results.do and www.nzqa.govt.nz/ providers/index.do respectively).

> Two of New Zealand's eight universities can be found in the Times Higher Education World University Rankings 2015–2016 top 400, with one of its universities featured in the top 200.

As an international student so far from home, you need to know that you will be well supported. The New Zealand Ministry of Education has a code of practice that all institutions accepting international students must follow. As of 1 July 2016, a new code will replace the existing code of practice: education providers will be required to accomplish ten outcomes by following set processes. Some of the key outcomes include the following.

- **Marketing and promotion:** any marketing and promotion of services provided to prospective international students should be clear, sufficient and accurate, so that you are able to make informed choices about what is on offer at a particular institution.
- **Managing and monitoring agents:** official representatives from institutions should provide you

with reliable advice and information on studying, working and living in New Zealand, and engage with you in an honest and professional manner.

- **Offers, enrolment and contract:** institutions should support you to make enrolment decisions that are well-informed and appropriate to your educational goals. They should also ensure that you have all the information you need before entering into a legally binding contract with them, and that proper documentation is kept.
- **Orientation:** this outcome sets out your right to take part in a well-designed and age-appropriate orientation programme, so that you have access to all the information and advice you may need at the start of your course.
- **Safety and wellbeing:** this outlines your right to live and study in a safe environment and receive adequate support to ensure your wellbeing.
- **Dealing with grievances:** this allows you to have access to proper and fair grievance procedures, should things go wrong.

The code should help you to make an informed choice on where to apply and give you a realistic idea of the level of support you can expect once you arrive.

Undergraduate study

Bachelor's degrees in New Zealand tend to take three years to complete, although some subjects take longer: up to six years for a Bachelor of Medicine. Students must successfully complete each year before moving on to the next. High achievers may opt for an additional year of study to gain an honours degree, or choose a course of at least four years with honours already incorporated.

The lecturers are fantastic and so approachable. I feel as though I can ask them anything.
David Moseley, Otago Polytechnic, New Zealand

You can often be flexible in the direction your academic studies take you, giving you the opportunity to try out a range of subjects. It is not unusual for the major subject you choose when you apply to end up being different from the one you graduate in.

Your university will guide you through the process of choosing the right core and elective subjects to achieve a major in your desired subject.

Stage 1 or 100-level courses are taken in the first year; stage 2 or 200-level courses in the second year; and stage 3 or 300-level courses in the third year. Some 200-level and 300-level courses may require you to have studied certain courses at the previous level in order to enter on to the higher-level course. Honours courses are stage 4 or 400-level.

It is possible to transfer credit and move between different institutions at tertiary level.

Vocational education

Qualifications in technical and vocational education are available at polytechnics, institutes of technology, private training establishments, or in the workplace through industry training organisations (ITOs). In addition, some opportunities are available through universities and wānanga. Level 6 national diplomas are relatively comparable to HNDs or foundation degrees in the UK. If you decide to move from a national diploma to a relevant degree, it may be possible to transfer credit or to gain exemptions from the initial stages of the degree programme.

Entry requirements

Entry requirements in New Zealand tend to be lower than in the UK, as the smaller population means less of a demand for places. The grades required often reflect the academic level you will need to cope with the demands of the course. In most cases, you will need to have gained three A levels, or equivalent; some universities ask for three Cs at A level, and there are additional grade requirements for certain courses.

At the University of Auckland, New Zealand's highest-ranking university, students need to achieve a minimum of CCC at A level (excluding General Studies) to be considered for entry. There are additional course-specific requirements: for example, a minimum of CCC for Bachelor of Education (Teaching); BBC for Bachelor of Architectural Studies, and ABB for Bachelor of Engineering (Honours). The university is not currently accepting international applicants for direct entry to Bachelor of Medicine and Bachelor of Surgery, Bachelor of Optometry or Bachelor of Pharmacy; instead, applicants will be considered based on first-year results from BSc Biomedical Science or Bachelor of Health Science, the UMAT score (for Medicine), and an interview (for Medicine and Pharmacy). Students wishing to study law must first be offered a place on another bachelor's degree, with entry to law based on the entry requirements for the degree for which they are initially accepted.

If you are applying with alternative qualifications to A levels, contact the university's international office via www.auckland.

ac.nz/en/for/international-students/is-contact-auckland-international.html.

Postgraduate study

At postgraduate level, you might choose to study for a:

- postgraduate certificate
- postgraduate diploma
- master's degree
- doctoral degree.

All of these are of a comparable level to the same qualifications in the UK. Postgraduate certificates take one semester to complete, with postgraduate diplomas taking one year. There are three main types of master's degree in New Zealand:

- **by thesis or primarily by thesis:** typically involves one year of study, with a research project (thesis, dissertation, research paper or scholarly creative work) forming a substantial component of the degree
- **by coursework and thesis:** usually takes two years to complete, and includes a research project and coursework
- **by coursework:** takes one to two years and consists of coursework, project work and research.

Doctorates would normally take three years to complete.

If you are not ready for postgraduate study, perhaps because of your achievements at undergraduate level or maybe because you are changing subject, you could consider a graduate diploma.

Entry requirements

An undergraduate degree from a recognised institution is required to undertake postgraduate study in New Zealand. You generally need a master's degree in a relevant subject to join a doctoral programme, although applicants with a first-class bachelor's (honours) degree may also be considered.

Distance learning

New Zealand has a range of distance-learning providers offering education at degree level, including the Open Polytechnic of New Zealand (www.openpolytechnic.ac.nz) and Massey University (www.massey.ac.nz/massey/learning/distance-learning). Most tertiary institutions offer blended learning, delivering their education in a range of different ways (including online) to meet students' needs.

Applying

Institutions in New Zealand require direct application, so the first step should be to contact the international office at the universities where you would like to study. They will provide all the information you need on how to apply and show you how to access the relevant application forms. They may charge an application fee. Some students choose to use the services of an agent, rather than dealing directly with the institutions.

Ideally, you should start the research process more than a year in advance, to allow time to apply for scholarships, apply for a visa and make the arrangements to move. You should plan to make contact with the universities at least six to eight months beforehand. Closing dates for applications to start in semester one (February) normally fall between September and December; to join programmes in semester two (July), you should apply by April or May. Restricted-entry or competitive courses often have an earlier closing date and some may only have a February intake.

The application form

The application forms tend to be a lot shorter and simpler than the UCAS form in the UK. You will need to provide personal details, information on your previous and current academic studies, and you may be asked to give details of your employment history or future career plans. You will need to list a first, second and (in some cases) third choice of degree, along with details of your intended major(s).

Applications are paper-based or online. If they are online, you will still need to allow time for certified or witnessed documents to be posted or couriered to New Zealand.

Other requirements

Other documents required include academic transcripts (with details of education and qualifications) and certificates. Academic references and written statements may be requested, along with portfolios and other evidence for certain courses. The institution will also ask for a copy of your passport. Copied documents often need to be certified or witnessed by someone in the legal profession or in another position of responsibility.

In addition, postgraduate applicants may need to provide two references and a CV, and may be asked to submit a research proposal.

In some cases, an interview over the phone or online may be necessary for undergraduate and postgraduate applicants.

Academic recognition

If your qualifications are unfamiliar to the international office, you may need to pay for an International Qualifications Assessment through the New Zealand Qualifications Authority: www.nzqa. govt.nz/qualifications-standards/international-qualifications/apply-for-an-international-qualifications-assessment.

What next?

If your application is successful, you will receive an offer of place, confirming details of your course, including the start date. The next step will be to apply for a visa.

You could study ...

BA Classical Studies, Greek and Latin
Victoria University of Wellington
Three years
Apply by 1 December for February start
Annual fees NZ$24,657 (£11,769)
Annual living costs NZ$18,000–NZ$25,000 (£8,592–£11,934)

Master of Cyber Security
University of Waikato, Hamilton
One-and-a-half years
Apply by 1 December for March start
Annual fees NZ$29,300 (£13,941)
Annual living costs NZ$18,000 (£8,570)

PhD Accounting
University of Auckland
Three to four years
Applications accepted throughout the year
Annual fees NZ$6,698 (£3,196)
Annual living costs NZ$20,000–NZ$25,000 (£9,544–£11,930)

Visas

Once you have accepted a place and paid your tuition fees (or the appropriate deposit), you can start applying for a visa. For short-term courses of up to three months, you should apply for a visitor visa. For courses longer than three months, you will need to apply for a student visa and supply the following supporting documents:

- the offer of place from your chosen institution (the institution must be registered with the New Zealand Qualifications Authority; see www.nzqa.govt.nz)
- scholarships or award letters (if applicable) giving details of your programme of study
- if you're under 18, you'll need a written guarantee from your institution or an authorised person that there is suitable accommodation for you in New Zealand
- evidence that you have sufficient funds for living costs; if your programme is 36 weeks or less, you will need access to NZ$1,250 (£589) per month; for courses over 36 weeks, you will need access to NZ$15,000 (£7,070) per year (bear in mind that you may need more than this to live on)
- a return airline ticket to the UK, or proof that you have the funds to purchase one
- police certificate (if you are planning to study in New Zealand for more than two years)
- passport (this must be valid for at least three months after the end of your intended stay in the country).

You will also need to take out adequate health and travel insurance to cover you during your residency in New Zealand. In addition, you may be required to provide a General Medical Certificate or a chest X-ray Certificate. PhD students have domestic student status, and are therefore not required to give evidence of adequate insurance when applying for a visa.

Applications can be made online, on paper via your local Visa Application Centre (VAC) (www.ttsnzvisa.com/gb-en/Home) or through your institution, if it is listed as a provider on Students Online (see www.immigration.govt.nz/migrant/stream/study/application/educationproviders).

Fees will vary depending on how you make your application, and are currently charged as follows:

- **online:** NZ\$270 (£127)
- **via the VAC:** £155 (which includes an £18 service fee)
- **via your education provider:** £72 (which includes an £18 service fee). It is important to note that your institution is likely to charge a supplementary administration fee for this service.

> **❝** I found the experience of applying for a visa for New Zealand a little daunting at first, especially as there were several different types of visa which you could apply for. However, with helpful advice from my tutor at the University of Birmingham and from properly reading through the information provided on the website, the process was pretty simple. You had to prove that you had enough money to fund yourself for the year, which could be challenging for some, but because I had savings from a part-time job it was fine for me. I applied for my visa quite early on and it took about three weeks for it to arrive; however, I know of some people who had some problems, such as the date of return on the visa being wrong and the visa not actually being placed in the passport! So it is really important to make sure that you apply for your visa well ahead of leaving for the country, but also to check the visa information once you get it back. **❞**
>
> *Madeleine Prince, Cawthron Institute, New Zealand*

When you apply for a visa for an undergraduate or postgraduate degree lasting over two years, if you hope to work, tick the boxes under 'variation of conditions' requesting permission to work up to 20 hours a week during the academic year and full time during the Christmas and New Year holidays.

For full details of how to apply, rules and regulations and the latest fees, go to Immigration New Zealand (www.immigration. govt.nz). Further information can be found at the New Zealand High Commission in London (www.mfat.govt.nz/en/countries-and-regions/europe/united-kingdom/new-zealand-high-commission). You should allow four to six weeks for processing, although many applications are processed within 25 days.

Most international offices have lots of experience in helping students through these processes. They will know the problems that previous applicants have encountered and should support you to make a successful application for a visa.

Once you have a visa, you will need to follow certain requirements in order to retain it, such as attending your course and achieving certain standards. Your visa will last for a maximum of four years, subject to certain conditions: see http://www.immigration.govt.nz/migrant/stream/study/canistudyinnewzealand/allaboutvisas for more details.

As of December 2015, the New Zealand government is trialling a Pathway Student Visa pilot over the course of the next 18 months, in a bid to make New Zealand a more attractive study destination for international students. The Pathway Student Visa is valid for a maximum of five years, and allows international students to take up to three consecutive programmes of study at selected institutions on a single visa. Participating institutions are able to offer a range of consecutive programmes, either exclusively at their own institution, or in collaboration with other providers; for a full list of institutions, see www.immigration.govt.nz/community/stream/educate/resourcecentre/about+pathwaystudentvisapilotproviders.htm.

If you are eligible, you will need to provide evidence that you have enough to cover the tuition fees for your first programme of study or first year of study (whichever is shorter), and that you have access to sufficient funds to pay your remaining tuition fee balance. In addition, you will need to show evidence that you are in a position to pay living costs of NZ$15,000 (£7,070) for the first year of study, and that you have access funds to support yourself thereafter. More information on the scheme can be found on the Immigration New Zealand website at www.immigration.govt.nz/migrant/stream/study/application/pathwaystudentvisas.htm.

Costs and help with finances

New Zealand is unlikely to offer a cheaper option for education at undergraduate level; some of the cheapest university undergraduate fees in New Zealand are comparable in cost to the most expensive in the UK. At postgraduate level, the costs can be higher than in the UK, although there is an incentive to study PhDs, making New Zealand a very attractive proposition.

Costs

Individual tertiary institutions set their own fees, which will vary depending on the course you choose. According to Study Options (www.studyoptions.com), annual tuition fees for undergraduate study can be NZ$20,000–NZ$29,000 (£9,427–£13,667). Fees for courses at polytechnics or institutes of technology may be lower than NZ$18,000 (£8,483) per year, making them a more affordable option.

Postgraduate tuition fees for international students can be as much as NZ$34,000 (£16,024) per year. However, international PhD students pay the same fees as students from New Zealand, starting at around NZ$5,700 (£2,686) per year.

Although you will be required to prove access to NZ$15,000 (£7,070) per year for visa purposes, Study Options suggests budgeting NZ$15,000–NZ$20,000 (£7,070–£9,433) per year for living costs if you are studying on the South Island, and NZ$18,000–NZ$25,000 (£8,490–£11,796) for the North Island. In comparison to the rest of the world, New Zealand is ranked number 14 of 122 countries on a 2016 cost-of-living ranking at www.numbeo.com/cost-of-living/rankings_by_country.jsp; the UK is listed just above at number 12.

Remember to budget for medical and travel insurance; international students are legally obliged to hold this throughout their period of study in New Zealand.

Help with finances

A range of scholarships are available, although you will need to compete with other applicants. Apply early, follow all the guidelines and be prepared to supplement any scholarship with other sources of funding; most scholarships will not cover all costs.

Talented international PhD students can apply for the New Zealand Doctoral Research Scholarship, a fully-funded government scholarship that is awarded for academic merit and the benefits that a candidate's proposed research will bring to New Zealand.

Successful applicants receive the scholarship for up to three years, and benefit from full tuition fee support, a stipend of up to NZ$25,000 (£11,796) per year and medical insurance cover up to NZ$600 (£283) per year. The scholarship is available to applicants from all disciplines undertaking study at any of New Zealand's universities. For more details and how to apply, visit http://enz. govt.nz/our-services/scholarships/nzidrs.

From mid-2016, you may also be able to apply for the Commonwealth Scholarship and Fellowship Plan (http://cscuk. dfid.gov.uk/apply/scholarships-uk-citizens). Alternatively, you can search for scholarships at www.studyinnewzealand.govt.nz/ how-to-apply/scholarships. This searches options including national and university-specific awards. Talk to your university or polytechnic about the range of scholarships they administer.

Cultural differences

New Zealand is a multicultural nation with an informal way of doing things. More than one in seven New Zealanders is Māori, so their language and culture forms an important part of the national identity. In New Zealand, you can expect an outdoor lifestyle with the opportunity to get involved with sports and a range of cultural activities.

Although there will be similarities to the UK, don't assume that life will be the same; there will be cultural differences. It is helpful to find out about the culture and way of life in New Zealand in order to prepare yourself for a successful transition. Talking to other people who have already made the move can be helpful. There are many websites for expats that might help in this process. Your university's international office may be able to help too.

Working while studying

If you have ticked the relevant boxes on the student visa application (variation of conditions), you may be allowed to work up to 20 hours per week during the academic term, and full time during the summer holidays. Make sure you have permission before you start working and follow the visa requirements to the letter. Your right to work can normally be found on your student visa. You can apply for a variation of conditions at a later date, if necessary. If you are studying for a master's by research (thesis) or doctoral degree programme, you will be eligible for unlimited work rights.

> **"** Obviously getting a part-time job is useful; however, the reason you are on this year abroad is to study. I would advise making studying your top priority; make sure that the part-time job doesn't get in the way of that (or even in the way of socialising with your new-found friends). Sometimes a part-time job can hinder other exciting opportunities such as visiting other parts of the country at the weekend. It all depends which you feel is more important. **"**
>
> *Madeleine Prince, Cawthron Institute, New Zealand*

Don't assume that you will find work immediately. It can be hard to find the right job that fits in with your studies and visa requirements. You will also need to consider how you balance your academic studies and your working life. Take a look at Student Job Search for opportunities in your area, www.sjs.co.nz. You will need an Inland Revenue Department (IRD) number before you can begin work; find out more at www.ird.govt.nz/how-to/irdnumbers.

Staying on after study

If you hope to stay on in New Zealand after finishing your studies, there are a number of schemes currently in operation. The government is keen to retain young people with the right skills and knowledge to contribute to the New Zealand economy. If you hope to emigrate, you may decide to choose your subject based on skills-shortage areas at the time you apply; don't forget that these lists are subject to change and may well be different by the time you complete your studies.

If you don't have a job offer, you have the following options.

- **Post-study work visa**
  Recent graduates from tertiary institutes in New Zealand can apply for a visa of up to 12 months, giving them time to search for a skilled job (and to work on a temporary basis while searching). Among other requirements, you will need to provide evidence that you can support yourself financially; the minimum amount stipulated is NZ$4,200 (£1,983). On finding a skilled, long-term job, you can apply for a visa under the Study to Work category for two to three years.
- **Skilled migrant category visa**
  This is a points-based residence visa, with points gained for a job offer, experience, qualifications and so on.

There are a number of options if you are offered a job considered to be in a shortage area.

- **Essential skills visa**
  The essential skills visa allows those with a job offer to work in New Zealand on a temporary basis (provided a New Zealander cannot be found to do the job).

- **Long term skills shortage list (LTSSL) work category**
  If offered a job on the LTSSL, you can apply for a
  30-month work visa; after two years, holders of this visa
  can apply for a resident visa.
- **Skilled migrant category visa**
  A job offer will enhance the points you can gain on this
  points-based residence visa.

For information on all these options and more, see www.
immigration.govt.nz/migrant. The information is complex and
subject to change. Your university may be able to put you in touch
with relevant sources of support for this process.

Pros and cons of study in New Zealand

Pros

- Range of internationally recognised qualifications.
- Support for international students.
- Reasonable entry requirements.
- Possibilities to stay on and work afterwards.

Cons

- High tuition fees.
- Far from home.

Student story
Anwar Hussain Nadat
University of Auckland, New Zealand

Anwar Hussain Nadat had wanted to be a primary teacher for some time
when his research into suitable courses led him a little further away than

he'd first anticipated. 'I started to look at the courses available in the UK and, the more research I did, the more I felt that these courses were not what I was looking for. I then decided to look at courses abroad and targeted countries which would also allow me to be qualified in the UK. I wanted to broaden my horizons and the chance to experience a whole new setting and adventure was too good to refuse.'

So what convinced Anwar that New Zealand was the right setting for him? 'I love the natural side of the earth and enjoy watching the landscapes, which New Zealand has plenty of. I also have relatives in New Zealand and knowing you have familiar faces around provides a security net which wouldn't have been available elsewhere. It is a big move so I researched New Zealand over the course of a year to make sure that it was the right fit for me.

'I knew I had to find a university in Auckland, as this is where my relatives are based. Once I learned that University of Auckland is the most highly ranked university in New Zealand, I started to focus on this institution and found out about their Graduate Diploma in Primary Teaching. I used an organisation called Study Options who are based in the UK and help prospective students to apply for universities in Australia and New Zealand. I also enquired with my relatives in Auckland, as they had studied at the university. This all helped to give me an overall picture which convinced me that this was the right institution for me.

'The cost is a little bit more than in the UK. The PGCE course in the UK costs £9,000 and last year the Graduate Diploma was NZ$31,000, roughly working out to £15,000, so £6,000 more in fees. However, as an international student it is compulsory to have both health and travel insurance, which is added to your course fee along with the student services fee, so in total it cost me NZ$33,080 which was about £16,000 as the exchange rate was high. Overall it adds up to about £7,000 to £8,000 more.

'The application process was straightforward, although it did take a number of months. Study Options were fantastic in assisting me with my application. They sent me an application which I filled in in May. They checked through the form and then sent it on to the university. There was no application fee, which was a bonus. In June, the university notified me that my application was being processed. In July, I was asked to complete a maths and literacy test online. I found the maths test to be very similar to the Professional Skills Test we have in the UK; however, the literacy test was different as I was given an article to write a summary about, rather like a mini essay.

'After this, the application process became very slow and I did not hear anything back until October when I was given a conditional place based on passing an interview and having a clean police check. I had to obtain a Police Certificate for immigration from ACRO, and this has a small cost to it.

'I completed my interview via Skype around mid-October and it lasted roughly 30 minutes. I had previously asked the university what to expect so I was able to prepare. Finally, after seven months I got the final confirmation of my place. The university does have an online application portal, which was very helpful to know how far along your application was. Study Options took a lot of pressure and worries off me, as they found the answers to any enquiries I had.'

Anwar went through the fast-track visa scheme, so getting a visa ended up being a bit quicker than getting a place on the course. 'I needed one year's visa and I received it within 10 days; however, there was a lot of preparation behind it. The full year's fee has to be paid in full and the receipt needs to go with the application. This means that you don't have the option to spread your costs. As my course also has an early start date in January (rather than a normal start date in late February), any future student would have to have the money ready by at least November to get the visa in time. If the visa is not in place, the university cancel your place. Immigration New Zealand also ask for evidence that you have sufficient money to sustain you during your study – NZ$15,000 (£7,087) for the whole year or NZ$1,250 (£591) a month.'

In addition to support from Study Options, Anwar also received help from the University of Auckland. 'I received a lot of key information and support via email. I received a list of books and resources that I had to buy as well as details of where to buy them. I was sent an online orientation module to complete, and this was very helpful as it included local transport and how to access your timetables and accommodation.

'The Faculty of Education also sent me an itinerary of the induction so I knew exactly what I had to do and where I had to be, which is always helpful when arriving into a new country and institution.

'The university also gave information on how to open a bank amount. ANZ, one of the major banks, offers an international student account and actually have a branch on the university campus. I was able to open the bank account here in the UK and deposit money into it. It was a major relief not to carry that amount around with me during the flight and have it safe and ready waiting for me in NZ.

'I am pleased to say that I have so far not had any difficulties in adjusting to life in New Zealand. As the language is the same and there are similarities in culture, it's just like being home, plus you get the chance to watch plenty of UK TV programmes.

'The education is a lot more practical and also a lot is focused on self-building. The NZ curriculum is very flexible and the child's achievement is at the heart of it, which feels different compared to the results-based approach in the UK. I have started my placement in a school and it has reminded me of the times when I was in school and when learning was fun.'

Anwar's top tips

Living costs
'You generally need in excess of NZ$20,000 (£9,451). Accommodation in Auckland is expensive and students pay roughly NZ$5,000 (£2,363) a year in accommodation. There is the option of renting one-bedrooms outside the main CBD; however, a train or bus would be needed to get to the main CBD.'

Food
'Compared to prices in the UK, it works out the same or, in some cases, a little bit more expensive. There are plenty of restaurants and takeaways but these can be expensive.'

Insurance

'As part of my course fees I paid for both health and travel insurance, as this is the requirement of the New Zealand government. If you do not have these, your visa application can be delayed and the university can withdraw your offer.'

Transport

'There is a massive import of Japanese cars, so it is easy to get hold of a second-hand or new car. The transport system is not the greatest and you can see the work and effort that has been put behind it to raise its profile. A journey in a car that would take 15 minutes takes one hour in a bus. Everyone prefers to drive.'

Financial support

'Some universities do offer doctorates at the same price to both domestic and international students.'

Working while studying

'You are allowed to work 20 hours per week on your visa, but due to the nature of my course and its intensity, I have not been able to find the time. There are plenty of companies who will hire international students.'

Lifestyle and culture

'The local New Zealand people are very friendly and I have been able to make new friends and settle in quickly. The lifestyle and culture is very relaxed compared to the UK and you also have a feel of living in a UK of the past.'

Although he's only been away for a short while, Anwar is really enjoying his time in New Zealand. 'I would not mind staying here for a few more years, perhaps applying for teaching jobs in Auckland. As part of our course we have workshops helping us to attain teaching posts near the end of the year, and the international office helps us with getting registered in New Zealand, which is helpful to know.'

He believes the experience of studying abroad is already starting to pay off. 'I am benefitting from the opportunity to explore and gain a new understanding of the perspectives of life and culture. Home is always where the heart is, but it's also good to step outside the box and see things differently and this is something I have been able to do. I hope to use this experience to make me a well-equipped individual who can offer a different perspective to everyday life.'

University of Auckland is New Zealand's largest university, with over 40,000 students. It is a top 200 university in the Times Higher Education World University Rankings 2015–2016.

Chapter 10
Studying in Asia

There are plenty of reasons to consider studying in Asia: Asia's economy is continuing to grow faster than other regions, investment in universities in Asia has been huge over recent years, and its universities are fighting for position in the world league tables. Fourteen Asian universities appear in the Times Higher Education World University Rankings 2015–2016.

Hong Kong

Hong Kong is a special administrative region of China, offering a cosmopolitan lifestyle and a gateway to China. As Hong Kong was under British rule for many years, English is still an official language. Street signs and announcements on public transport are in English, Cantonese and often Putonghua (Mandarin).

Now under Chinese rule, Hong Kong has its own currency and political system and a separate identity from the rest of China.

The Hong Kong Special Administrative Region (HKSAR) government is keen to attract international students by growing the country's status as a 'regional educational hub'; to this end, they have introduced a number of initiatives, including doubling admission quotas for international students, creating scholarships for outstanding non-local students, and relaxing employment and immigration restrictions.

Higher education in Hong Kong

Hong Kong offers a four-year bachelor's degree. Both ordinary and honours degrees are available, along with two-year associate degrees and diplomas at a lower academic level. Some associate degrees and diplomas at community colleges offer students a pathway to progress to a four-year bachelor's degree in a two+two arrangement. Master's degrees will take one to two years, and doctorate degrees a minimum of three years to complete.

If you are interested in opportunities in China, you will find that degrees from Hong Kong are compatible with Chinese qualifications. Beginners' courses in Cantonese and Putonghua will be available; some programmes even offer the chance of a year in Beijing or Shanghai.

The academic year runs from early September to May, with orientation activities taking place in late August. The year is split into two equal semesters. Hong Kong features 20 degree-awarding institutions, composed of a combination of nine public and eleven private establishments. Higher education is split between universities, polytechnics and technical institutes, and specialist colleges. There is also an Open University, which offers a wide range of distance learning and face-to-face programmes at undergraduate and postgraduate level.

To find out more about studying in Hong Kong, go to Study HK (http://studyinhongkong. edu.hk/eng). The website also features a list of courses and institutions; see http://studyinhongkong.edu. hk/en/hong-kong-education/programme-list.php.

Applying

Entry requirements vary, but satisfactory performance at A level should meet the general requirements for undergraduate-level study. For example, the University of Hong Kong (currently placed below King's College London and above the University of Manchester in the Times Higher Education World University Rankings 2015–2016 top 200) asks for a minimum of three passes at A level (not including English or Chinese language) to meet the general academic requirements. There may be additional subject requirements and you will need a pass in GCSE English Language. The University of Hong Kong also looks for evidence of second-language ability at GCSE, and state that they 'value all-roundedness'.

An honours degree is required for entry to postgraduate study.

Application deadlines vary, but may be as early as December or as late as May for a September start, with some institutions offering an early and a main round for applications. Applications should be made directly to your chosen institution, and are likely to include:

- personal statement
- reference
- predicted grades and details of previous educational achievement
- research statement (for postgraduate research).

You are likely to have to pay an application fee, and you may also be asked to attend an interview or sit an entrance exam.

Costs

According to Study HK, annual tuition fees range from HK$90,000–HK$265,000 (£7,955–£23,422).

Accommodation in university halls of residence is reasonably priced, but space comes at a premium in Hong Kong and private rental can be astronomical. Study HK suggests on-campus living accommodation costs from HK$5,000 to HK$15,000 (£442–£1,326) per semester, while off-campus accommodation costs a similar amount per month (HK$8,000 to HK$15,000). Most of the public universities are able to offer on-campus accommodation for international students, usually in shared dormitories, for at least two years of study. However, student demand is very high, so it is advisable to contact your university's accommodation office as soon as possible once your place to study has been confirmed.

> **66** Accommodation is small (this is Hong Kong after all, where space is in short supply); however, you get used to it and it is all the space you need. **99**
> *Warren Mitty, Hong Kong Polytechnic University*

When weighing up living costs (excluding accommodation), Study HK estimates, 'HK$30,000–HK$50,000 (£2,653–£4,421) per year for additional costs, including food, leisure, transportation, and personal items, depending on how extravagantly you plan to live.' Hong Kong comes in at number 10 of 122 countries on a cost-of-living ranking for 2016, making it marginally more expensive than the UK, which is listed at number 12 (www.numbeo.com/cost-of-living/rankings_by_country.jsp).

Scholarships are available, although opportunities are limited and most, although not all, are restricted to those displaying academic excellence. See Study HK for a list of scholarships or talk to your institution for further details.

Three of Hong Kong's 20 degree-awarding institutions can be found in the Times Higher Education World University Rankings 2015–2016 top 200, with one institution featuring in the top 50.

You could study ...

BSc Mathematics

Hong Kong University of Science and Technology

Four years

Apply by 15 November (early round) or 3 January (main round)

Annual fees HK$140,000 (£12,388)

Weekly living expenses (excluding accommodation) HK$600–HK$1,000 (£53–£88)

Master of Arts in the field of Literary and Cultural Studies

University of Hong Kong

One year

Apply by 1 April

Annual fees HK$146,000 (£12,911)

Annual living expenses from HK$64,200 (£5,371)

Visas

Once you have been accepted and have found a place to live, you can then apply for a student visa. This should be arranged through your university, which will normally act as your local sponsor to support the visa application. They will submit various documents on your behalf; however, there are certain documents that you will need to provide yourself, including:

- application form for entry for study in Hong Kong (ID 955A); this can be downloaded from the Hong Kong Immigration Department website

- a recent photograph (you'll need to affix this to the second page of the ID 955A form)
- copy of your passport
- your university acceptance letter
- photocopy of evidence of financial support, showing that you can meet the cost of tuition and living expenses independently of any public funds (there is no specific amount required by the Hong Kong Immigration Department; your university will be able to give you an idea of appropriate amounts to cover academic and living costs).

For more information on visas, go to www.immd.gov.hk. The application can take up to eight weeks to be processed. Normally, if you are studying on a full-time tertiary programme that is locally accredited, your visa will be valid for the duration of your studies (up to a maximum of six years), subject to the validity period of your passport. Your institution will be able to support you through the process.

Working while studying

Although a student visa doesn't normally allow work alongside study, there may be opportunities to take internships, campus-based work or work during the holidays. Talk to your university about these procedures and whether you can apply for a 'no objection letter' allowing certain conditions of employment.

After you complete your degree, you can apply for a 12-month stay without a job offer.

Pros and cons of study in Hong Kong

Pros

- High proportion of highly ranked institutions.
- A gateway to China.

- English as an official language.
- Chance to experience a different culture.
- Modern, efficient and cheap public transport.

Cons

- Private accommodation is small and expensive.
- Air pollution and humidity.
- Densely populated.

Japan

According to a study published in 2016 by UNESCO Institute for Statistics (UIS), in 2013, 407 UK students chose Japan as their study destination (Global Flow of Tertiary-Level Students, UNESCO Institute for Statistics (UIS), 2013, www.uis.unesco.org/datacentre). The Japanese government is keen to attract more international students and is investing in higher education and extending the study options available in English.

The Global 30 group of universities was set up to boost the number of international students in Japan, and offers scholarships for tertiary-level study. So far, 13 universities have been admitted to the scheme, and award a range of degrees taught in English:

- Doshisha University
- Keio University
- Kyoto University
- Kyushu University
- Meiji University
- Nagoya University
- Osaka University
- Ritsumeikan University
- Sophia University
- Tohoku University
- University of Tokyo

- University of Tsukuba
- Waseda University.

Find out more, including links to all these universities, at www.uni.international.mext.go.jp.

Higher education in Japan

Currently, most institutions in Japan require proficiency in Japanese, but there are some exceptions. A number of Japanese universities offer master's and doctoral degrees in English, although options are more limited at undergraduate level. JASSO (Japan Student Services Organisation) has a list of university degree courses offered in English; see www.jasso.go.jp/en/study_j/search/daigakukensaku.html#no7.

There are far more private than public universities; Japan also has some international universities and overseas universities with campuses in Japan.

> Two of Japan's universities are featured in the Times Higher Education World University Rankings 2015–2016 top 200.

The academic year starts in April and is run as a two-semester system, April to September, and October to March, with holidays at intervals throughout the year. It should take you four years to complete a bachelor's degree; the first one to two years offer more general studies, while the final two to three years allow you to specialise. Certain courses, such as medicine and dentistry, will take up to six years to complete. Study at master's level tends to take two years, with a further three years required for a doctorate.

Applying

Normally, 12 years or more of formal education will be sufficient for entry to university in Japan. You should apply directly to your chosen university; requirements for supporting documents vary from university to university, but may include:

- university application form
- CV
- one or two essays
- copy of A level certificates (or equivalent), or certificate of predicted grades
- academic transcript
- letter(s) of recommendation
- medical certificate.

In addition, you may be required to sit an entrance exam or attend an interview.

Costs

Study in Japan (www.g-studyinjapan.jasso.go.jp) suggests average monthly costs, including fees, of JPY138,000 (£851). The cost of living in Tokyo will be higher, so you should consult individual universities for local costs. The Study in Japan website also has lots of information on scholarships, living and accommodation costs.

University accommodation is substantially cheaper than private rented accommodation, so check whether your chosen university will guarantee accommodation for you. In private accommodation, in addition to rent, there is a returnable security deposit, *shiki-kin*, and a non-refundable 'thank-you' deposit, *rei-kin*, which can amount to around four months' rent (and sometimes more). In addition, according to JASSO, most apartments are not furnished, meaning that if you opt to rent in the private sector, you may find that you incur significant start-up costs.

Japan has a reputation for being expensive; it is ranked number 11 out of 122 countries on a 2016 cost-of-living ranking (www. numbeo.com/cost-of-living/rankings_by_country.jsp), placing it just above the UK.

You could study ...

Bachelor Economics
Keio University, Minato
Four years
Apply by 29 February
Annual fees JPY745,000 (£4,821) (including admission, registration and facilities fees)
Annual living expenses (excluding accommodation) JPY900,000 (£5,824)

MA in International Peace Studies
International University of Japan, Niigata (private)
Two years
Apply by 15 February for April entry
Annual fees JPY2,100,000 (£13,577) (including admission fees)
Minimum monthly living expenses JPY104,000 (£672)

Visas
You will need a student visa in order to study in Japan; your university will act as a sponsor for the visa process and should obtain a Certificate of Eligibility for you. Once you have the certificate, you will need to take the original and a photocopy to the Embassy of Japan in London for processing, along with a valid passport, a signed visa application form (available to download at www.uk.emb-japan.go.jp/en/visa/CoE.html), and a passport-sized photograph taken within the last six months.

Once you have submitted the required documents, it will normally take four working days to process your application. The period of stay for a student visa is granted for set periods of time: four years and three months, four years, three years and three months, three years, two years and three months, two years, one year and three months, one year, six months or three months.

Working while studying

In Japan, student visa holders need the approval of their university and the immigration office to be able to work. As a general rule, once you receive approval, you are permitted to work up to 28 hours a week during term-time, and up to eight hours a day during the holiday period.

For information on study in Japan, go to www.studyjapan.go.jp/en.

Pros and cons of study in Japan

Pros

- A culture that combines tradition and cutting-edge technology.
- Drive to increase numbers of international students.

Cons

- Language barrier outside the classroom.
- Relatively few Western students at present.
- The need to factor in additional fees for study and accommodation.

Malaysia

Malaysia has hundreds of higher education institutions to choose from and strong links with the UK. Many overseas universities have chosen to base campuses there, including institutions from the UK, such as the University of Nottingham, Newcastle University (Medicine) and the University of Reading. This means you can receive an accredited degree issued by a UK institution, while also having the opportunity to experience a new culture and benefiting from much lower living costs.

Other institutions offer degrees incorporating UK qualifications. These mainly take place in private colleges, and are known as '3+0' degree programmes, allowing students to pursue a full-time UK degree entirely in Malaysia. For example, BEng (Hons) Electrical and Electronic Engineering from INTI International College, Penang is awarded in collaboration with Coventry University.

Higher education in Malaysia

Institutions with degree-awarding power in Malaysia include 20 public universities; a number of private higher education educational (IPTS) institutions (universities, university colleges and colleges); and foreign universities with a local campus. The academic year in Malaysia begins in September; certain courses also have intakes in January or May. In Malaysia, a bachelor's degree takes three to four years to complete, with the exception of courses such as medicine and dentistry, which take five years. A master's degree will take between one and three years and can be coursework-based, research-based, or a combination of the two. A minimum of two years' subsequent study can lead to a doctorate.

Courses taught in English tend to be restricted to private or international universities at undergraduate level. At postgraduate level, there should be English-medium options at public universities too. Only selected private institutions approved by the Ministry of Home Affairs and the Ministry of Education are open to students from overseas; you will need to check that your chosen university has the appropriate permissions to recruit international students. In addition, private higher education institutions in Malaysia must offer courses that are endorsed

by the Malaysian Qualifications Agency (MQA); you can search
for accredited courses and institutions using the Malaysian
Qualifications Register on the MQA website at www.mqa.gov.my.
All public universities are accredited by the MQA and can recruit
from overseas.

Study Malaysia (www.studymalaysia.com) has a course search,
along with useful information about education, costs and the
country itself.

Applying

International applicants will need to apply directly to their chosen
institutions, either online or via a paper application. Application
procedures will vary from institution to institution, though it
is likely that you will have to provide details of your previous
education, which may include submitting academic transcripts.
A personal statement is also likely to be a key component of the
application, and for postgraduate applications, you may also
need to submit a research proposal. You should apply by the
required closing date and at least six months before you are due to
commence your studies.

Costs

Tuition fees vary from institution to institution. Study Malaysia
suggests that undergraduate fees range from RM43,000–
RM100,000 (£7,534–£17,508) (for pharmacy) at private
universities and from RM50,000–RM450,000 (£8,760–£78,841)
(medicine) at overseas university branch campuses. NB These costs
are for the entire programme, not per year. The average annual
undergraduate tuition fee is RM20,000 (£3,504).

Postgraduate research degrees at public universities cost from
RM1,800–RM6,000 (£315–£1,051) per year at master's level, and
RM2,700–RM8,000 (£473–£1,402) for PhDs.

The fees for a UK degree might be only slightly lower in Malaysia, but if you choose to study overseas, you will benefit from a lower cost of living and an international experience. Living costs are considerably lower than in the UK, with a suggested budget of RM1,200 (£210) per month. Malaysia is rated number 94 out of 122 countries on a cost-of-living index for 2016 (www.numbeo. com/cost-of-living/rankings_by_country.jsp), making it one of the cheapest countries featured in this book. Information on funding and scholarships can be found at https://studymalaysia.com/scholarships, the Ministry of Higher Education (https://biasiswa. mohe.gov.my/INTER), and from your institution.

You could study ...

BSc Quantity Surveying
University of Reading Malaysia Campus, EduCity, Iskander Puteri
Three years
Apply two months before the programme starts (intakes in January and September)
Annual fees RM42,290 (£7,291)
Monthly living expenses RM2,000 (£345)

Master of Performing Arts (Drama)
University of Malaya, Kuala Lumpur
From one-and-a-half years
Apply by April for September intake
Annual fees RM16,000 (£2,759)
Monthly living expenses RM1,000 (£172)

Visas
International students need a student pass to study in Malaysia. Once you accept your offer, your university will apply for a student pass on your behalf; you should pay the visa processing

fee and any other fees at this stage. Once the student pass is granted, you will receive a student pass approval letter. You will need to take this with you when you travel to the country, in order to be issued a visa on point of entry to Malaysia. A representative from your university will meet you when you arrive at the airport to help clear you through immigration, so it is important that you liaise with your university first to confirm your travel plans. More information is available from the Education Malaysia Global Services (EMGS) website, http://educationmalaysia.gov.my, a subsidiary of the Ministry of Education Malaysia.

Working while studying

If you're looking to work part time to support your studies, you will first need to submit an application to your university, together with an application fee of RM120 (£13). Your university will forward your application to the Malaysian Immigration Department, after which you will be invited to an interview. If your application is approved, you will be able to work up to 20 hours per week during semester breaks, festive holidays and holiday periods longer than seven days. As an international student, you can work in restaurants, hotels, petrol stations and mini markets; your university is required to report your academic progress to the Immigration Department every three months, so you will need to demonstrate satisfactory academic achievement and attend your classes in order to retain your right to work.

Pros and cons of study in Malaysia

Pros

- Reasonable tuition fees for Malaysian degrees.
- Opportunity to gain degrees from USA, UK and Australia in a country with a low cost of living.
- Chance to experience a different culture.
- Tropical climate.

Cons

- No world-renowned Malaysian universities.
- Need approval of your institution before you can work during term-time.
- Not all universities are open to international students.

Singapore

Neighbouring Singapore may be small, but it is a hot spot for financial services, an important trading centre in the heart of Asia and home to the world's busiest port. Its education system is well recognised around the world and comparable in level to education in the UK. English is widely used, particularly for education and business, and most courses are taught in the language.

Higher education in Singapore

The academic year runs from the beginning of August to early May and is divided into two semesters, with some intakes available in January for certain courses. Bachelor's degrees are available at ordinary level (after three years' study) and with honours (after four years). Most master's degrees take one to two years, with a minimum of two years and a maximum of five years required to complete a PhD.

Singapore has five autonomous public universities:

- National University of Singapore
- Nanyang Technological University
- Singapore Management University
- Singapore University of Technology and Design
- Singapore Institute of Technology (which provides an industry-focused university education).

There is one government-funded private university, SIM University, along with a number of other private institutions,

polytechnics and international universities with a campus in
Singapore.

Singapore might only have a handful of universities, but two
of them can be found in the Times Higher Education World
University Rankings 2015–2016 top 200. This includes the
National University of Singapore, which is placed at number
26, making it the most highly ranked Asian university.

To find out about university options, you could start with
Ministry of Education Singapore, www.moe.gov.sg/education/
post-secondary, where you'll find a useful guide on higher
education. Contact Singapore (www.contactsingapore.sg) has lots
of information on living in Singapore.

Applying

At undergraduate level, universities will be looking for good
passes in three A levels, so you should be aiming to apply with
grades at C or above. In some cases, particularly if you're
applying before you know your results, the universities will
require the SAT or ACT admissions tests. (For more information
on the SAT and ACT, see the US-UK Fulbright Commission
website, www.fulbright.org.uk/study-in-the-usa/undergraduate-
study/ admissions-tests.) According to the Complete University
Guide (www.thecompleteuniversityguide.co.uk), Singapore has
decided to cap the number of places for international students;
as such, places are limited and entry is likely to be competitive,
meaning that meeting the minimum entry requirements will
not necessarily guarantee you a place on the course for which
you apply.

Bear in mind that if you are applying with predicted grades, your admission may not be confirmed until August, meaning that you may possibly have to miss the start of term, which might include the orientation week and the first few weeks of classes. Most Singaporean universities will not allow international students to defer their place.

At postgraduate level, you are likely to need a 2:1 in an honours degree combined with the GMAT (www.mba.com) or the GRE revised General Test (www.ets.org/gre) admissions tests for specific subjects. See individual universities for entry criteria and test requirements.

Applications should be made directly to the university's admissions or international office. As part of the application, you might have to write a short essay on your achievements or reflect on any positions of responsibility. Postgraduate-research applicants may need to write a research proposal. At both undergraduate and postgraduate level, it is likely that you will need to provide references.

The university will charge you an application fee. You can apply from September or October onwards, with most applications closing in February.

At the National University of Singapore, you will not be eligible for competitive courses like dentistry and medicine if you apply with predicted grades. If this is the case at your chosen university or with your chosen course, wait until you have your actual grades to make the application; this might mean waiting for the next intake, but can also result in exemption from certain admissions tests.

Costs

Tuition fees in Singaporean universities are high, but are
subsidised by the government through the tuition-grant scheme.
This scheme is open to international students on the condition
that you work for three years after graduation for a Singaporean
company; this can be deferred for specific reasons, including
further study. You can find out more at the Ministry of Education
website (www.moe.gov.sg) or from your university.

The National University of Singapore (ranked above King's College
London and the University of Manchester on the Times Higher
Education World University Rankings 2015–2016 top 200) charges
annual fees for undergraduate degrees ranging from S$29,350–
S$141,100 (£14,833–£71,533) for medicine and dentistry. These
fees fall to between S$17,100–S$55,450 (£8,675–£28,131) when the
tuition grant is included.

At postgraduate level, Nanyang Technological University
suggests typical fees of S$16,700 (£8,472) for master's and DPhil
programmes; this includes the tuition grant (or service obligation).
Additional fees may be payable for the students' union, exams and
health services.

Scholarships are available to search on the Ministry of Education
website (www.moe.gov.sg) or can be discussed with your
university. In addition, you may be eligible to receive a tuition fee
loan, which covers up to 90% of the subsidised tuition fees payable
by Singaporean students, providing you are paying subsidised
fees and meet certain requirements. For more information, see
www.dbs.com.sg/personal/loans/education-loans/tuition-fee-loan.

The National University of Singapore estimates on-campus living
costs of S$8,625 to S$13,000 (£4,376–£6,596) per year, which

includes accommodation, food, transport within Singapore, books and supplies, and any personal expenses.

Singapore falls at number 7 of 122 countries listed on a cost-of-living ranking (www.numbeo.com/cost-of-living/rankings_by_country.jsp), so is considered somewhat more expensive than the UK at the moment.

You could study ...

BFA in Art, Design and Media
Nanyang Technological University
Four years
Apply from 1 October
Annual fees S$17,100 (£8,696) with tuition grant; S$31,460 (£15,999) without
Estimated monthly living expenses from S$1,300 (£661)

Master of Public Health
National University of Singapore
From one year
Apply by February for August intake
Annual fees S$42,800 (£21,765) with tuition grant; S$76,200 (£38,750) without. Financial aid available
Estimated monthly living costs from S$1,100 (£559)

Visas
You will need a Student's Pass to study in Singapore. Your university will register you on the Immigration and Checkpoints Authority online registration system (SOLAR), and you will then need to complete an online application (eForm 16). The application should be made at least one month (but no more than two months) before the start of your course. There is no required amount of money that you need to provide evidence of, so you should talk to your university about an advisable amount.

If your application is successful, you will be issued with an
in-principle approval (IPA) letter, which incorporates the visa.
You will need this letter to enter Singapore. Before you arrive
in the country, you will need to book an appointment at the
ICA Student's Pass Unit for completion of formalities, in order
to receive your Student's Pass. You will need to bring certain
documents to the appointment, including your passport, a recent
passport photograph, and a signed printout of the eForm 16. It
may be possible to complete formalities via your university; where
applicable, your university will be able to advise you on the time,
date and venue for offsite enrolment.

Find out more at the Immigration and Checkpoints Authority
(www.ica.gov.sg) or the High Commission for the Republic
of Singapore in London (www.mfa.gov.sg/content/mfa/
overseasmission/london.htm).

Working while studying

You can work up to 16 hours per week during term-time without
a work permit; this is subject to certain conditions and the
approval of the university or polytechnic that you are studying
in. You would need to talk to your institution to request a letter of
authorisation.

On graduating, if you are successful in finding a job, you will need
to obtain an employment pass before you can start working. For
more details, see the Ministry of Manpower (www.mom.gov.sg).

Pros and cons of study in Singapore

Pros

- Chance to experience another culture.
- Modern city-state with a high standard of living.
- Tropical climate.

Cons

- Densely populated.
- Competitive entry.
- Need approval of your university before you can work in term-time.

China

The Chinese government is investing heavily in its higher education and is keen to attract international students; currently, around 41,000 international students are studying in China, according to the Complete University Guide (www. thecompleteuniversityguide.co.uk). The growth of China as an economic force in recent years means that awareness of Chinese culture and language is likely to be an important asset.

The British government is also keen that UK students develop their understanding of China; its Generation UK project offers internships and scholarships towards short-term study in China. Find out more at www.britishcouncil.org/study-work-create/ opportunity/study-abroad/china.

> Two of China's universities, Peking University and Tsinghua University, feature in the Times Higher Education World University Rankings 2015–2016 top 200.

Higher education in China

The academic year runs from September to mid-July, and is typically divided into two semesters, with some universities offering a spring intake for certain courses. The application deadline for courses starting in September usually falls in late

July; however, international students are advised to apply earlier, ideally between February and April.

Bachelor's degrees normally take four years to complete, master's degrees take two to three years, and doctorates take from three years; all are similar in level to those offered in the UK.

Traditionally, the style of teaching in China has been more teacher-centred than in the UK. However, you may find that this is less of an issue on English-taught courses aimed at international students.

A good place to start your search is Campus China (www.campuschina.org). You can also search for degree programmes on the CUCAS (China's University and College Admission System) website, www.cucas.edu.cn. Once your search brings up a list of courses, you can select those taught in English. Study in China (www.csc.edu.cn/Laihua/indexen.aspx) also holds a list of English-taught programmes in Chinese higher education, as well as information on scholarships. You'll find more opportunities at postgraduate level rather than at undergraduate level.

Applying

A level study is generally required for undergraduate courses, with a bachelor's degree (plus two references) required for master's study, and a master's degree (plus two references) for doctoral study.

Applications can be made directly to universities or online through CUCAS. If applying through CUCAS, additional documentation (copy of passport, academic transcripts and police certificates (or criminal records check), for example) can be scanned or clearly photographed for submission. CUCAS charges a service fee of US$50 to US$150 (£34–£103). The exact fee depends on your chosen institution. If you are accepted, your institution will then issue an admissions notice; you will need this to apply for your visa, and you should allow up to six weeks for the notice to be issued.

Costs

CUCAS advises of tuition fees around US\$3,300–US\$9,900 (£2,262–£6,786) per year and average monthly living expenses of around RMB4,500–RMB5,000 (£475–£528) in metropolitan areas, such as Shanghai or Beijing. Costs in many other cities are likely to be lower, at around RMB1,500–RMB3,500 per month (£158–£369). Some sources suggest higher average costs than this and costs will vary depending on the type of lifestyle you want to lead. China is listed as number 61 of 122 countries on Numbeo's cost-of-living ranking for 2016 (www.numbeo.com/cost-of-living/rankings_by_country.jsp), making it one of the more reasonable countries for cost of living featured in this book.

> **❝** The city of Ningbo itself was much cheaper than the UK and the cost of living was a fraction of what I would spend in the UK. **❞**
>
> *Lewis McCarthy, University of Nottingham Ningbo, China*

Full and partial scholarships are available through the China Scholarship Council (www.csc.edu.cn/Laihua). You may also be eligible for a Chinese Government Scholarship, provided you meet certain requirements. There are a range of government scholarships available at both undergraduate and postgraduate level; for more details and information on how to apply, visit www.csc.edu.cn/laihua/scholarshipdetailen.aspx?cid=97&id=2070. Alternatively, you can search for scholarships through CUCAS (www.cucas.edu.cn).

There are age restrictions for international students hoping to study higher education and apply for certain scholarships in China.

- Undergraduate applicants should be under 25.
- Master's degree applicants should be under 35.
- Doctoral applicants should be under 40.

You could study ...

BA in Journalism Studies

Tsinghua University, Beijing

Four years

Apply by 7 March

Annual fees RMB26,000 (£2,751)

Monthly living expenses RMB3,250–RMB4,450 (£344–£471)

Master in Public Policy

Peking University

Two years

Apply by 31 March

Annual fees RMB29,000 (£3,071)

Annual living expenses RMB50,000 (£5,290)

Visas

The type of visa that you apply for depends on the length of your study programme. For study in China up to 180 days, an X-2 visa is required; if you will be studying in China for more than 180 days, you will need an X-1 visa. You can apply through the Chinese Visa Application Centre; currently, applications cannot be made online, so you will need to make an appointment at one of their UK offices, which are located in London, Manchester and

Edinburgh. The Visa Application Centre advises applying at least one month, but no more than three months, in advance of your planned travel date. For more details, go to www.visaforchina.org.

Working while studying

You may be permitted to work part time during your studies, or undertake an internship on campus, provided that you receive permission from your university and the Chinese immigration authorities. In order to be eligible to work, you will need a Consent Letter from your university, and a Certification, which must be issued by the company for which you intend to work. The police station will then mark your visa 'part-time work'. It is important \to note that once your application has been approved, you will not be able to apply for a different job in another company.

Pros and cons of study in China

Pros

- An increasingly powerful world economic force.
- Investment in higher education.
- Chance to experience a new culture.

Cons

- Language barrier outside the classroom.
- A new setting for international students.
- Issues around censorship and political restrictions.

Qatar

If you're interested in the Middle East, but prefer the familiarity of a UK or US degree, you could take a look at Qatar. Qatar's Education City is a huge complex of education and research facilities just outside Doha and includes universities from the USA, France and the UK, in addition to Qatar's Hamad bin Khalifa University. Find out more about Education City at the Qatar Foundation for Education, Science and Community Development at www.qf.org.qa or at Education City at www.myeducationcity.com.

As it is a hub for elite international universities, your experience will vary according to which institution you choose. You can opt for a UK degree or choose a degree from another country. The tuition fees, style of teaching and who will award your degree will be determined by your chosen university.

> **❝** My visa was organised by UCL Qatar and was very straightforward, apart from some mandatory health checks and appointments, which all expatriates moving to Qatar must undertake after they arrive in Doha. Support upon arrival was particularly helpful, starting with a 'meet and greet' at Doha airport, and followed by lots of induction activities. **❞**
>
> *Benedict Leigh, UCL Qatar*

Applications should be made directly to your university. With the exception of students studying at the UCL campus, students in Education City may be eligible to apply for interest-free, need-based loans, which are awarded by Qatar Foundation through the Hamad Bin Khalifa Financial Aid Programme; for more information, see www.hbku.edu.qa/en/DynamicPages/index/105/FinancialAid. In addition, the universities have scholarship opportunities in place to support the cost of studying and living in Qatar; at UCL, for instance, the UCL Qatar Award for Cultural Heritage is available to talented students from low-income families, and can include cover for tuition fees and living costs, as well as a stipend. Your university will be able to inform you of any scholarship opportunities when you make your application.

Student life is likely to be different in Qatar, where the sale of alcohol is limited and modest dress is expected. Social activities might be more focused on campus activities, cultural events and shopping malls rather than all-night clubbing.

Qatar is listed at number 24 on Numbeo's 2016 cost-of-living rankings (www.numbeo.com/cost-of-living/rankings_by_country. jsp), making it cheaper to live in than the UK, Australia, New Zealand and the USA.

You could study ...

Bachelor in Biological Sciences
Carnegie Mellon University Qatar, Doha
Four years
Apply by 1 March
Annual fees QAR186,865 (£35,290)

MA Museum and Gallery Practice
UCL Qatar, Doha
One year
Apply by 1 June
Annual fees QAR99,900 (£18,875)
Approximate monthly living expenses, excluding accommodation QAR1,500 (£283)

Pros and cons of study in Qatar

Pros

- Investment in higher education.
- Opportunity to mix with a diverse student body with students from over 60 countries.
- Chance to experience a new culture.

Cons

- Different student life.

Also worth considering ...

If you're interested in studying in Asia, another option worth exploring is South Korea. English is widely spoken and taught in South Korea, which has a high standard of living, including a low unemployment rate and top-rate public services, as well as generous scholarship opportunities for international students. Four South Korean institutions feature in the top 200 of the Times Higher Education World University Rankings 2015–2016. To find out more, visit the Korean Ministry of Education website at www.niied.go.kr/eng/index.do.

Student story
Lewis McCarthy, China

'I thought studying overseas would be a great opportunity to spend time living in a different country and culture. I decided not to take a gap year after my A levels and thought that by taking a degree that included a year abroad, I could combine the experiences of gap year travelling with academic study.'

He was interested in China from the start. 'I chose to learn about China as it is a very different culture to the UK and Europe – the country is also growing in economic and political influence. I believe an understanding of China enhances my career prospects and differentiates me from other graduates.

'I looked at various universities and a range of courses, but it was Nottingham's degree in Management with Chinese Studies that fitted me best. A key factor was that Nottingham has its own campuses in China and Malaysia, the opportunity to study at those was too good to pass up.

Crucially, I could study at a world-class British university abroad, while other universities only offered programmes abroad at "partner" universities. A further important consideration was that it was a three-year course, rather than the four-year courses offered elsewhere. This meant I potentially saved a year's worth of student borrowing.'

This wasn't the only way that Lewis managed to cut the cost of learning. 'At Nottingham's campus in Ningbo, the accommodation was around half the price. The city of Ningbo itself was much cheaper than the UK and the cost of living was a fraction of what I would spend in the UK.'

Application for his year out was straightforward, with everything either dealt with or supported by the University of Nottingham. Even applying for a visa wasn't too problematic. 'The application was a relatively long-winded process, but the staff in the Chinese visa centre were exceptionally helpful. Even though I had not filled in part of my form, they telephoned me and, with my permission, completed it on my behalf so it didn't need to be sent back to me again. They also processed and mailed the visa and passport back quickly.'

When he first arrived in China, he found that he wasn't quite as prepared as some fellow students. 'I felt Nottingham could have provided more support, I think part of the problem was that my course was officially part of the Business School, not the School of Contemporary Chinese Studies. I got the impression when arriving that those on the Chinese Studies course had been given more guidance and clues as to what to expect.'

But Lewis didn't let this hold him back and he adjusted well to life in China.

'When I first arrived, everything seemed so new, different and interesting that it felt more like a holiday than living somewhere else. By the time that feeling had worn off, I was already settled and accustomed to most things. Still, I know some people who did experience homesickness, miss certain food and get irritated by cultural differences: people not queuing and no concept of personal space, for example.'

Lewis went on to have such a positive experience in China as an exchange student that, after graduating, he went back to China to study Mandarin at Shanghai Jiao Tong University. 'Living in Shanghai was considerably more expensive than Ningbo; however, it was still cheaper than the UK. Rent in Shanghai is roughly half that in London. The cost of study in Shanghai was £2,000–£3,000 – however, the Chinese government offered various non-means-tested scholarships that covered all of these costs plus accommodation, as well as providing a small stipend for living.

'The university application process was simple: I applied by downloading forms via their website, filled them in and emailed back. Once they had confirmed that they had space on their course, I paid some fees via a bank transfer and that was it!

'Shanghai didn't provide much support. I was emailed welcome packs, but beyond that it was up to me. This was not a problem. The city is cosmopolitan and easy to navigate, there were many helpful students on campus who assisted me when I asked or looked lost.

'On the Chinese language course you are left to your own devices, although the school does occasionally have events that you can attend. That said, the staff and teachers were all very helpful; they were forthcoming in offering their contact details in case we (the students) ever needed help or things explaining in Chinese. On campus there were also sports facilities that were free to use without the need to book, such as a running track, football field, tennis courts, outdoor gymnasium, etc.'

There were some differences to get used to, particularly the style of teaching. 'The teaching differs hugely: the emphasis is on rote learning; a lot of information may be covered in a lesson and you are expected to put in several hours outside class time to learn and memorise what is covered in class.'

Lewis has faced a few negative experiences along the way. 'Pickpocketing, having food stolen while on a train and witnessing mass brawls have all occurred in the two years I have spent in China. However, providing you are aware of risks and use some common sense you should be fine. There are risks in any country. On the whole, China is probably the country that I have felt safest in for travelling, living and walking home late at night.'

Lewis's top tips

Accommodation

'If you search for private accommodation in China, as I did the second time I went there to study, be prepared to look at many houses each day with estate agents whisking you off by car or bike for viewings. If possible, try to be clear about what you want and where you want to live. There should be someone in the office who speaks a little English, otherwise you can use Google or Baidu Translate.'

Food

'Don't be squeamish! As long as you're not vegetarian, be willing to try everything. The food is possibly the biggest thing to get used to in China. It is nothing like Western versions of Chinese food. Expect to see all body parts of animals (nothing is wasted) and lots of different tastes and types of cooking. In China, it is customary to share several dishes per meal rather than have a single dish each.'

Living costs

'If you are making food yourself, try to buy meat and vegetables from the same place as the Chinese do – usually markets – it will be infinitely cheaper than Western supermarkets, which have imported products that are generally very over-priced.

'If you want to live a Western lifestyle in China, be prepared that it might cost more than you think, and potentially more than it would in the UK. Rent and travel will be much cheaper but buying Western food and drinking in (some) bars could be more expensive; maybe this is more of a problem in Shanghai, rather than other cities. I didn't find it a problem in Ningbo.'

Scholarships

'China Scholarship Council (www.csc.edu.cn/Laihua) and Hanban (http:// english.hanban.org) offer some excellent scholarships.'

Working while studying

'There is always demand for English teachers and it pays anywhere between £10–£20 an hour. Just check the conditions of the visa you are on.'

Lifestyle and culture

'Chinese culture stretches back nearly five thousand years and the Chinese are very proud of their culture. Reading about the culture and history is a good way of preparing yourself and understanding some things when you arrive; just expect it to be different from how you imagine. It is very different from the UK.

'The lifestyle is great, a bit of disposable income can go quite far in China and you can go out for meals and eat at nice restaurants relatively cheaply. Foreigners are well respected within China and you should not have problems with locals; many will be warm and chatty, eager to make new friends.'

Travel

'You don't need to speak as much Chinese as you think to be able to travel in China. All of the tourist areas will have English translations and if you travel to areas that are off the well worn track, passersby will often help you if you seem lost.

'It is a country the size of a continent, so be aware that customs and lifestyles may be marginally different in other places across China. The food will certainly change, as each region has its own preferred tastes and delicacies.'

Options for after you finish your studies

'There are work options, such as teaching after you study. It is also fairly easy to find work in international or Chinese companies. A grasp of Mandarin will put you in a much stronger position, but it is not always deemed compulsory.

'During the time abroad, you will be exposed to so many different opportunities and possibilities that you would not receive at home, travelling to different areas and regions, eating local delicacies, work opportunities, homestays with local friends, etc.

'Meeting new people will also give you different perspectives on your own views and a much better insight into local culture, history and customs than can be taught in class. Meeting new people doesn't simply extend to those of the locality that you are studying in either; some of my closest friends now are compatriots and international students who I studied abroad with.'

Lewis recommends www.echinacities.com and www.shanghaiist.com to help you find out more about life in China.

Chapter 11

Studying in the rest of the world

You might imagine that you wouldn't find students from the UK studying right across the globe, yet this is not the case. Although a less common choice than Australia or the States, some UK students opt for countries like South Africa or Brazil as their place of learning. This chapter introduces you to some of the countries you might not have considered for your studies.

South Africa

Why South Africa? The Rainbow Nation offers diversity, culture and an outdoor lifestyle combined with a great climate and low cost of living. According to a study published in 2016 by UNESCO Institute for Statistics (UIS), in 2013, 434 UK students took advantage of what the country has to offer (Global Flow of Tertiary-Level Students, UNESCO Institute for Statistics (UIS), 2013, www.uis.unesco.org/datacentre).

Higher education in South Africa

Higher education is offered at universities, universities of technology, and comprehensive universities. Traditional universities offer academic study, while universities of technology focus on practical or vocational options; comprehensive universities offer both. There are a variety of private universities in South Africa. English and Afrikaans are both used as languages of instruction.

Bachelor's degrees take at least three years (up to six years for medicine), with an additional year of study needed to achieve an honours degree. A master's degree takes at least one year, while doctorates require a minimum of three years' research.

The academic year runs from February to November. Universities South Africa (http://www.universitiessa.az.za has links to all the public universities, where you can browse the courses on offer.

> South Africa has one university in the Times Higher Education World University Rankings 2015–2016 top 200, and two in the top 400.

Applying

Applications should be made directly to your chosen institution by the deadline they specify. The institutions will often charge an application fee. If you are making an undergraduate application, your institution will advise you how to get a certificate of exemption to validate your international qualifications. Two A levels in approved subjects at grades A to E plus three passes at GCSE in approved subjects (including English) should meet the general requirements for undergraduate programmes in South Africa. One of the subjects offered must be in a second language. For Scottish students, four passes in Scottish Highers plus one National 5 should be sufficient. There will be additional requirements for specific subjects. Applications can take up to eight weeks to process, and you will be required to pay a fee. For further details, see the South African Matriculation Board website (www.he-enrol.ac.za/qualification-country). A bachelor's (honours) degree should meet the general entry criteria for a master's degree.

While postgraduate-research programmes may have flexible application dates, you will still need time to apply for a study visa and to prepare for the move. South African post can be slow, so you should apply as early as possible. Closing dates for undergraduate and taught postgraduate courses vary; expect to apply in the autumn if the course starts in February, maybe earlier if you're also applying for a scholarship.

Costs

Fees vary depending on what you study and where. For example, at the University of Cape Town, international undergraduate fees start from around ZAR25,000 (£1,188) for the first year, increasing to up to ZAR64,370 (£3,059) for certain health science courses. In addition, full-time international students are required to pay an international term fee, which is a regulated annual fee. In 2016, the international term fee for undergraduate degrees was ZAR46,290 (£2,150). The university also charges an administrative service fee; in 2016, this was set at ZAR3,275 (£156). The university estimates living costs of around ZAR17,000 (£808) per month, which includes rent, food, transport, personal expenses, books and stationery (per semester). The international office at your chosen university will be able to tell you more about which costs you are likely to incur.

> 66 My tuition fees were more than in the UK as I was an international student. However, that was more than compensated for by the relatively low cost of living in Cape Town compared to London. For this reason, my overall cost of living and studying in Cape Town for a year and a half was about 50% less than it would have been had I studied in London. 99
>
> *Nick Parish, master's student, South Africa*

In a 2016 cost-of-living ranking produced by Numbeo
(www.numbeo.com/cost-of-living/rankings_by_country.jsp),
South Africa is listed at number 104 of 122 countries, making
it the cheapest country featured in this book.

You could study ...

Bachelor of Social Work

University of Johannesburg
Four years
Apply by 30 September
Tuition fees charged per module; annual average fees
ZAR102,280–ZAR110,330 (£4,763–£5,137)
Annual living expenses from ZAR48,685 (£2,264)

MA in Neuropsychology

University of Cape Town
One year
Apply by 31 October for February start
Annual fees ZAR87,775 (£4,094)
Monthly living expenses ZAR17,000 (£808)

Visas

Once you have received a written offer, you will need to apply for
a study visa at one of the South African Visa Facilitation Centres,
which are situated in London, Manchester and Edinburgh. There
is a £35 processing fee and an expected turnaround time of 32
working days if you submit your application in London, and 34
days if you apply in Manchester or Edinburgh. You will need to
prove that you can support yourself financially (you must show
evidence of a minimum monthly income of ZAR8,500 (£404) to
cover basic food and accommodation, though if you are under 25,
your parents can sponsor you). In addition, you will be asked for a
medical report and a police certificate (or criminal records check),
as well as proof of medical cover. The visa should be valid for the

duration of study, and it should allow you to work up to 20 hours per week.

Pros and cons of study in South Africa

Pros

- Great climate.
- Low cost of living.
- Outdoor lifestyle.

Cons

- Crime rate.

The Caribbean

A number of UK students head off to the Caribbean for their studies, particularly for medical or dental programmes, with over 70 medical schools listed there. Many opt for international universities with a base in the Caribbean that prepare students for a medical or dental career in countries like the USA, Canada or the UK. This list includes St George's University Grenada, Ross University, the American University of the Caribbean, and Saba University School of Medicine. St George's recruits from the UK and prepares students for medical practice in a number of countries, including the UK, whereas the other institutions tend to have more of a North American focus.

At St George's University, if you choose to study medicine, you could be looking at total fees over four years of US$246,000 (£168,634). You'll also need to budget for living expenses of around US$2,500 to US$3,000 (£1,714–£2,057) per semester if you live on campus. There are scholarships on offer which may assist with costs. The university has intakes in August and January, and you should apply directly.

There are also local universities offering courses, most notably the University of the West Indies (UWI), a regional university representing 17 countries, with four sites across the Caribbean. Its fees at undergraduate level are calculated using a pay-by-credit system, and are around US$15,000 (£10,281) per year, with the exception of medicine, which is around US$28,000 (£19,191).

Undergraduate degrees tend to take three to four years, followed by a two-year master's degree and a three-year PhD. Make sure you check the validity of any professional qualification with the relevant professional body; for instance, if you intend to practise medicine in the UK, you should check requirements with the General Medical Council. For a list of relevant professional bodies in the UK, visit the website of the National Contact Point for Professional Qualifications in the UK at www.ecctis.co.uk/uk%20ncp.

Unfortunately, there isn't one single source of information to find recognised universities in the Caribbean. You could use the High Commission websites in the UK; for example, the Jamaican High Commission in the UK, at www.jhcuk.org/citizens/universities, lists UWI, University of Technology, and Northern Caribbean University. You could also use accreditation organisations, such as the University Council of Jamaica, the Barbados Accreditation Council, and the Accreditation Council of Trinidad and Tobago. You can find contact details for these and other accreditation bodies at CANQATE (Caribbean Area Network for Quality Assurance in Tertiary Education), www.canqate.org/Links/RelatedLinks.aspx. Once you are sure that your university is recognised and accredited, you can then consult their website for the latest information on courses, fees and how to apply.

You could study ...

BA Literatures in English

University of the West Indies, Cave Hill Campus, Jamaica
Three years

Annual fees BBD$33,000 (£11,380)

Living expenses not provided, hall fees from BBD$6,100 (£2,103)
per academic year

MBA (Entrepreneurship & Marketing)

Northern Caribbean University, Manchester, Jamaica

Two years

Fees per credit US$420 (£290)

Living expenses not provided, accommodation with meal plan from
US$3,300 (£2,278) per academic year

Pros and cons of study in the Caribbean

Pros

- Tropical climate.
- Low cost of living.
- Chance to gain medical training relevant to more than
  one country.

Cons

- A range of education systems on offer with no single
  reliable source of information.
- High costs for medical and dental studies.

Hopefully, the information about these countries will have
whetted your appetite and given you a starting point for
your research. Of course, the countries profiled here are
not the only options open to you; many other countries are
keen to attract students from the UK. If you are interested in
studying elsewhere in the world, you can use the information
in this book (see Chapters 2, 3 and 4) to help ensure that the
education you opt for is the right choice for you.

Student story
Justin Axel-Berg, University of São Paulo, Brazil

'I originally left the UK during the financial crisis after I had graduated and was unable to find a job that I wanted. Instead, I qualified as an English teacher and started travelling. I always had the intention of returning to study and when the opportunity arose I took advantage of the fact that there was a top-class university on my doorstep.

'I decided I wanted a change from Asia, which I know well and have lived in before, and Australia, in which I studied during my degree. Brazil has a dynamic and exciting economy with lots of opportunity for foreigners. It has a deserved reputation for being friendly, exciting and warm.

'The Universidade de São Paulo (USP) has consistently been rated the best institution in Latin America, with a very strong research tradition and excellent reputation. All degree courses in federal and state universities in Brazil are completely free to all applicants, with a good chance of receiving a scholarship for living expenses while you study through one of the funding bodies.

'In order to do anything in Brazil, Portuguese language is a pre-requisite, and that includes, for the time being anyway, university. The university offers language courses to foreign students while you study, which are of good quality, and they have an online distance-learning programme, so you will be able to pick up some Portuguese at home before you leave. It's not an insurmountable challenge, but it is a challenge nonetheless. People are always willing to help you out with it and will happily share class notes with you in case you missed anything. Essays can be submitted in English if you prefer.'

Justin found the application process to be fairly straightforward. 'I had to sit the GRE exam, which I did in London. I then wrote up a research proposal and a CV and sent it via email along with the application form.

The procedure does vary from course to course, so it's best to check their website.

'While I was waiting for my documents to arrive I was in constant contact with the university by phone and by email, and they took a real personal interest in getting me to Brazil safe and well.

'The process of applying for a visa was quick, but a little bit complicated. Firstly you must register and complete a form on the Ministry of Foreign Affairs website before booking an appointment at the consulate. Unfortunately, my university acceptance letter was caught in a postal strike so I was rather delayed in getting documents sorted, but once I got to the consulate they were friendly and helpful and the whole process took well under a week from giving them my passport to receiving my visa. Once you arrive in Brazil you then have to go to the police to register and get your Brazilian ID card (RNE), which takes about six months to arrive.'

Justin praises the academic support he has experienced since starting at the university. 'My academic advisor is excellent, and here they tend to take a much more hands-on approach to support than in the UK. He is constantly sending me interesting events to attend or things to read. I would say that education in Brazil is much more tutor-led; Brazilian students have their hands held much more than in the UK. There is also more of a focus on personal and career development alongside research than in the UK.'

Although he is an experienced traveller and has studied overseas before, Justin did have to make some adjustments. 'There are always little things that surprise me. Although Brazil is superficially very European, in reality it most definitely isn't. People's outlook on life is different, what people say versus what they mean is very different. Also the fact that, in a polite way, Brazil functions in a kind of irrational bureaucratic chaos can be difficult to adjust to; things simply don't work in the way that you expect.'

On the whole, there have been very few negative experiences. 'Perhaps a few too many afternoons sitting in the *policia federal* trying to register my documents. Despite São Paulo's violent reputation, it's really quite a safe place. I've lived here for three years now, travelling all over the city at all times of night and day, and never come to harm anywhere.'

Discovering the latest information about study in Brazil can be a challenge.

'The information is unfortunately a bit scattered at the moment as UK and international students are so few. It's best to contact the university and ask for information. Gringoes (www.gringoes.com) is a good guide to living in Brazil with a very supportive forum.'

Justin's top tips

Accommodation

'USP cannot guarantee accommodation because of the size of the student body, but private-sector provision is excellent and catered towards students in either "*republicas*" (shared houses) or individual kitchenettes or studio flats both next to the campus and further into the city. It'll be very hard to sort anything out before you arrive though, so plan on starting in a hostel for a couple of weeks'.

Food

'Brazilian food is delicious, heavy on meat and beans, as represented by the famous *feijoada* (bean and meat stew). Fresh fruit juices are everywhere and made of a vast array of things you'll never have heard of. São Paulo also has the best sushi outside of Japan as a result of the huge Japanese population, and the Italian food and especially the pizzas are fantastic.'

Insurance

'As a student you may use the public healthcare system. It is probably recommended to have your own private insurance too, but personally I haven't bothered, and every time I've needed the doctor I've been well looked after.'

Living costs

'São Paulo is not a cheap city to live in. People come to Brazil expecting the third world and finding the first. Expect to spend up to BRL700–BRL1,000 (£138–197) per month on a room. I pay more than this because I live in my own apartment in the city. Food is often roughly the price of the UK, although savvy shoppers buy in street markets where it is much lower. Alcohol is reasonably priced. All electronics and other non-consumables are absurdly expensive; bring your mobile phone and laptop with you from home.'

Financial support for study

'Both CAPES and FAPESP give generous scholarships which will go a long way towards supporting you as you study. They are widespread and not terribly difficult to get. The university also offers postgraduates the opportunity to monitor and assist courses in return for money.'

Working while studying

'Working is not possible on a student visa, although there is a burgeoning market for international students tutoring English privately all over the city.'

Making friends

'It's Brazil: everyone wants to stop and chat with people passing by. It's extremely easy to make friends and Brazilians are very welcoming, warm people who treat foreigners very well.'

Lifestyle and culture

'Brazil is a lot more laid-back than the UK and a lot more informal and relaxed. People live for the beach, and it is easily accessible from SP at the weekends. São Paulo is the cultural capital of Brazil and the amount of art, especially street art, is phenomenal, as is the range of music and fashion available in the city. There is something here for everyone, but you might have to search for it.'

Travel and transport

'The traffic is terrible. Really bad. However, the buses are very regular, clean, safe and cheap, and the metro, although limited, will cover everywhere you will want to go as a foreigner. It is also cheap, quick, safe and very clean.'

ABROAD

Options for after you finish your studies

'Brazil is expanding rapidly, and has technical needs in almost every field at the moment. It also has a specific need for bilingual people with some expertise. If you're planning to do almost anything in Brazil, a qualification from USP will get you there.

'Living in beautiful Brazil, being exposed to another culture in a deep way not open to most travellers or even expats and learning to view the world through another culture is fascinating and an experience I wouldn't trade for the world.'

University of São Paulo is the highest ranked university in South America in the Times Higher Education World University Rankings 2015–2016.

Chapter 12

Further research and resources

Before you go

UK National Academic Recognition Information Centre (NARIC)
www.ecctis.co.uk/naric/individuals
Information on the comparability of international qualifications

**National Contact Point for Professional Qualifications in the
United Kingdom (UKNCP)**
www.ecctis.co.uk/uk%20ncp

Foreign and Commonwealth Office
www.fco.gov.uk
Find an embassy or seek travel advice by country

Prospects Study Abroad (postgraduate focus)
www.prospects.ac.uk/postgraduate-study/study-abroad

U-Multirank
www.u-multirank.eu
Compare international universities based on your own chosen
criteria

iAgora

www.iagora.com/studies

Students review and rate their international universities

STeXX

www.stexx.eu

Students review and rate their worldwide universities

The Association of Commonwealth Universities

www.acu.ac.uk

Citizens Advice

www.citizensadvice.org.uk

For information on how studying overseas might affect your status in the UK

HM Revenue and Customs

www.hmrc.gov.uk

Information on tax when you return to the UK

International course search

Find a master's/MBA/PhD

www.findamasters.com

www.findanmba.com

www.findaphd.com

International Graduate

www.internationalgraduate.net

Search for master's, MBA and PhD opportunities worldwide

International university league tables

The Times Higher Education World University Rankings

www.timeshighereducation.co.uk/world-university-rankings

QS Top Universities

www.topuniversities.com/university-rankings

Academic Ranking of World Universities

www.shanghairanking.com

Financial Times Business School Rankings

http://rankings.ft.com/businessschoolrankings/rankings

Costs and funding

Numbeo

www.numbeo.com/cost-of-living/rankings_by_country.jsp

Cost-of-living comparison

Expatistan

www.expatistan.com

Cost-of-living comparison between cities worldwide

Professional and Career Development Loans

www.gov.uk/career-development-loans/overview

International Student Identity Card (ISIC)

www.isic.org

Student discounts worldwide

Student Finance England

www.gov.uk/student-finance/overview

Student Awards Agency for Scotland

www.saas.gov.uk

Student Finance Wales

www.studentfinancewales.co.uk

Student Finance Northern Ireland
www.studentfinanceni.co.uk

Commonwealth Scholarships
http://cscuk.dfid.gov.uk/apply/scholarships-uk-citizens

Insurance

European Health Insurance Card (EHIC)
www.nhs.uk/NHSEngland/Healthcareabroad/EHIC/Pages/about-the-ehic.aspx

Endsleigh Insurance
www.endsleigh.co.uk/personal/travel-insurance/study-abroad-insurance

STA Travel Insurance
www.statravel.co.uk/study-abroad-travel-insurance.htm

Blogs and diaries

Third Year Abroad, The Mole Diaries
www.thirdyearabroad.com/before-you-go/the-mole-diaries.html

The Fulbright Commission Student Blogs
www.fulbright.org.uk/news-events/uk-student-blogs

University of Southampton Study Abroad and Exchange blog
http://studyoverseas.soton.ac.uk/welcome-to-our-blog

Durham Students Abroad
https://durhamstudentsabroad.com

The University of Nottingham in North America
http://universityofnottinghamnorthamerica.blogspot.co.uk

Short-term study overseas

Study China

www.studychina.org.uk

INTO China

www.intohigher.com/china

IAESTE

www.iaeste.org

Fulbright Commission

www.fulbright.org.uk/study-in-the-usa/short-term-study

Summer schools at US universities

EducationUSA

https://educationusa.state.gov/your-5-steps-us-study/research-your-options/short-term

Third Year Abroad

www.thirdyearabroad.com

Distance learning

International Council for Open And Distance Education (ICDE)

www.icde.org

Study Portals (search for distance-learning courses worldwide)

www.distancelearningportal.com

Distance Education Accrediting Commission (USA)

www.deac.org

Educational agents and marketing consultancies

A Star Future

www.astarfuture.co.uk

Study Options (for study in Australia and New Zealand)
www.studyoptions.com

The Student World Fair
www.thestudentworld.edufindme.com

Degrees Ahead
www.degreesahead.co.uk

Mayflower Education Consultants
www.mayflowereducation.co.uk

PFL Education
www.preparationforlife.com

M & D Europe
www.readmedicine.com

PASS4 Soccer Scholarships
www.pass4soccer.com

Study-International (for study in Australia, Cyprus, Latvia, the Netherlands, New Zealand, Poland and the USA)
www.studygo.co.uk

Admissions tests
Scholastic Assessment Test (SAT)
www.collegereadiness.collegeboard.org/sat

American College Test (ACT)
www.act.org

Undergraduate Medicine and Health Sciences Admission Test (UMAT)
https://umat.acer.edu.au

International Student Admissions Test (ISAT)

www.isat.acer.edu.au

Special Tertiary Admissions Test (STAT)

https://stat.acer.edu.au

Graduate Management Admission Test (GMAT)

www.mba.com/global

Graduate Record Exam (GRE) revised General Test

www.ets.org/gre

Dental Admissions Test (DAT)

www.ada.org/en/education-careers/dental-admission-test

Law School Admissions Test (LSAT)

www.lsac.org

Medical College Admission Test (MCAT)

https://students-residents.aamc.org/applying-medical-school/
taking-mcat-exam

Graduate Australian Medical Schools Admissions Test (GAMSAT)

www.gamsat.acer.edu.au

Health Professions Admission Test (HPAT)

www.hpat-ireland.acer.edu.au

Studying in Europe

Study Portals
www.studyportals.eu
Search for courses and scholarships worldwide

PLOTEUS (Portal on Learning Opportunities throughout the European Space)
www.ec.europa.eu/ploteus/en

A Star Future
www.astarfuture.co.uk/what_to_study.html
Search for courses taught in English in Europe and beyond

EUNiCAS
www.eunicas.co.uk
Search for courses taught in English

EURAXESS
www.ec.europa.eu/euraxess
Research opportunities in the EU

PromoDoc
www.promodoc.eu/study-in-the-eu
Doctoral study in the EU

European Commission, University in Europe
www.ec.europa.eu/youreurope/citizens/education/university

European Commission, Study in Europe
www.ec.europa.eu/education/study-in-europe

Eurodesk
www.eurodesk.org.uk
Information on European work, study, funding, travel and volunteering

Europass

www.europass.cedefop.europa.eu

Documents to make your qualification and skills easily understood across Europe (CVs, diploma supplements and so on)

European Youth Portal

https://europa.eu/youth/country/76_en

European and national opportunities and information to young people living, studying and working in Europe

Erasmus+ study abroad

www.britishcouncil.org/study-work-create/opportunity/study-abroad/erasmus

Austria

www.oead.at/welcome_to_austria/education_research/EN

Belgium

www.highereducation.be (Flemish community)

www.studyinbelgium.be (French community)

Czech Republic

www.studyin.cz

www.msmt.cz (Scholarships)

Denmark

www.studyindenmark.dk

www.optagelse.dk/admission/index.html (Danish Co-ordinated Application System, KOT)

www.su.dk/english/su-as-a-foreign-citizen (State Educational Support, SU)

Estonia

www.studyinestonia.ee

Finland

www.studyinfinland.fi

www.studyinfo.fi (applications to bachelor's and master's degrees taught in English)

France

www.campusfrance.org/en

www.lmde.fr

Germany

www.study-in.de/en

www.hochschulkompass.de (HochschulKompass, institution search)

www.daad.de/deutschland/en

www.uni-assist.de (centralised admissions service)

www.daad.de (German Academic Exchange Service, DAAD)

www.uni-assist.de/index_en.html (uni-assist, application service for international students)

Hungary

www.studyhungary.hu

Ireland

www.educationinireland.com

www.icosirl.ie (Irish Council for International Students)

www.citizensinformation.ie

www.qualifax.ie (course search)

www.postgradireland.com (postgraduate search)

www.cao.ie (Central Applications Office – undergraduate admissions)

www.pac.ie (Postgraduate Applications Centre)

Italy

www.study-in-italy.it

Latvia

www.studyinlatvia.lv

Lithuania

www.lietuva.lt/en/education_sience/study_lithuania

www.skvc.lt/en/content.asp?id=235 (Lithuanian Centre for Quality
Assessment in Higher Education)

The Netherlands

www.studyinholland.nl

www.studyinholland.co.uk

http://info.studielink.nl/en/studenten/Pages/Default.aspx
(Studielink for applications)

Norway

www.studyinnorway.no

www.nokut.no (Norwegian Agency for Quality Assurance in
Education, NOKUT)

Poland

www.studyinpoland.pl

Portugal

www.studyinportugal.edu.pt

Slovakia

www.studyin.sk

Slovenia

www.slovenia.si/en/study

Switzerland

www.studyinginswitzerland.ch

www.swissuniversities.ch/en/higher-education-area/studying/
studying-in-switzerland

Spain

www.mecd.gob.es/portada-mecd (Ministry of Education, Culture and Sport)

www.uned.es (National Distance Education University (UNED), for evaluation of qualifications)

Sweden

www.studyinsweden.se

Studying in the USA

Fulbright Commission

www.fulbright.org.uk

EducationUSA

https://educationusa.state.gov

College Board

www.collegeboard.org

College Navigator

www.nces.ed.gov/collegenavigator

National Association of Credential Evaluation Services (NACES)

www.naces.org

The Common Application

www.commonapp.org

Scholarships and financial aid

eduPASS

www.edupass.org/finaid/databases.phtml

International Education Financial Aid

www.iefa.org

International Scholarships

www.internationalscholarships.com

US Citizenship and Immigration Services

www.uscis.gov

Studying in Canada

Study in Canada

www.studyincanada.com

Universities Canada

www.univcan.ca

Canadian Information Centre for International Credentials

www.cicic.ca

Citizenship & Immigration Canada

www.cic.gc.ca/english/study/index.asp

Immigration Québec

www.immigration-quebec.gouv.qc.ca/en

Statistics Canada

www.statcan.gc.ca

International Scholarships

http://istudentcanada.ca/inbound/find-a-canadian-program

www.ScholarshipsCanada.com

Studying in Australia

Study in Australia
www.studyinaustralia.gov.au
www.studying-in-australia.org

Australian Qualifications Framework
www.aqf.edu.au

Australian High Commission in London
www.uk.embassy.gov.au

Department of Immigration and Border Protection
www.border.gov.au

International Scholarships
www.australiaawards.gov.au

Finances and budgeting
www.moneysmart.gov.au/managing-my-money

Australian Taxation Office
www.ato.gov.au

Studying in New Zealand

New Zealand Education
www.studyinnewzealand.govt.nz

New Zealand Qualifications Authority
www.nzqa.govt.nz/search

Universities New Zealand
www.universitiesnz.ac.nz/studying-in-nz

Student Job Search

www.sjs.co.nz

Immigration New Zealand

www.immigration.govt.nz

New Zealand High Commission, London

www.mfat.govt.nz/en/countries-and-regions/europe/united-kingdom/new-zealand-high-commission

Inland Revenue Department

www.ird.govt.nz/how-to/irdnumbers

Studying in Asia

Hong Kong

Study in Hong Kong

http://studyinhongkong.edu.hk/eng

Hong Kong Immigration Department

www.immd.gov.hk

Malaysia

Study Malaysia

www.studymalaysia.com

Singapore

Contact Singapore

www.contactsingapore.sg

Ministry of Education

www.moe.gov.sg

Immigration and Checkpoints Authority
www.ica.gov.sg

High Commission of the Republic of Singapore, London
www.mfa.gov.sg/london

Ministry of Manpower
www.mom.gov.sg

China
Campus China
www.campuschina.org

China's University and College Admission System (CUCAS)
www.cucas.edu.cn

Ministry of Education of the People's Republic of China
www.moe.edu.cn

China Scholarship Council
www.csc.edu.cn/Laihua

Chinese Visa Application Centre
www.visaforchina.org

Japan
Study in Japan
www.studyjapan.go.jp/en

Global 30 (Top 13 universities in Japan offering degree programmes in English)
www.uni.international.mext.go.jp

JASSO (Japan Student Services Organisation)
www.jasso.go.jp

Embassy of Japan in the UK
www.uk.emb-japan.go.jp

Qatar
Qatar Foundation for Education, Science and Community
Development
www.qf.org.qa/education

Education City, Qatar
www.myeducationcity.com

Studying in the rest of the world

The Caribbean
Jamaican High Commission, United Kingdom
www.jhcuk.org/citizens/universities

Caribbean Area Network for Quality Assurance in Tertiary
Education (CANQATE)
www.canqate.org/Links/RelatedLinks.aspx

South Africa
Universities South Africa
www.universitiessa.ac.za

South African Matriculation Board
www.he-enrol.ac.za/qualification-country

South African High Commission, United Kingdom
www.southafricahouseuk.com

Glossary

Academic transcript
A record of academic progress from around year 10 (Y11 in NI, and S3 in Scotland) onwards, including exam results, unit grades, internal assessments, academic honours and explanations for any anomalies.

American College Test (ACT)
The ACT is used to determine academic potential for undergraduate study.

Arvestus
A pass or fail assessment used in Estonian universities. Also see *eksam*.

Associate degree
A two-year programme of higher education, often in a vocational subject, such as hospitality or health, which sometimes offers a pathway to a full bachelor's degree in a two+two arrangement.

Bologna process
A system to make higher education comparable and compatible across the EHEA, through use of mutually recognised systems and a clear credit framework.

CAO
Central Applications Office, the centralised service for undergraduate applications to institutions in Ireland.

Certificate of Eligibility

The Certificate of Eligibility is used by Japanese universities and colleges as proof of admission and is needed to apply for a student visa.

Collegegeldkrediet

Student tuition fee loan offered by the Dutch government to support undergraduate and postgraduate study in the Netherlands.

Common Application

Central applications system for undergraduate study at over 600 higher education institutions in the USA.

Community college (USA)

These colleges offer two-year associate degrees, with the possibility of transferring to a university to top up to a full degree; a cheaper option than going straight to a US university.

Co-op programme

Period of paid work experience linked to a university course, rather like a sandwich course in the UK.

Core

The compulsory foundation for university study (used in North America and a number of other countries); students choose from a broad range of subjects.

Credencial de acceso

Official evaluation of secondary-level qualifications for higher education in Spain.

CUCAS

China's University and College Admissions System, a service for international students applying to higher education in China.

Dichiarazione di valore
Official letter acknowledging the suitability of the education received in your home country for higher education in Italy.

Diploma mobility
Taking an entire degree overseas, as opposed to a study-abroad or exchange programme.

Diploma supplement
A detailed transcript of attainment in higher education, recognised across the EHEA and beyond.

eCoE (electronic confirmation of enrolment)
The eCoE is issued by Australian colleges and universities as proof of enrolment and is required to apply for a student visa.

ECTS
European Credit Transfer and Accumulation System, aiding the transfer of students between institutions.

EHEA
European Higher Education Area: the countries where the Bologna process is utilised.

Eksam
Graded examination used in Estonian universities. Also see *arvestus*.

Elective

An optional course (module) taken at university, which contributes towards the total number credits needed for graduation.

English medium

Education with English as the language of instruction.

ENIC-NARIC

European Network of Information Centres-National Academic Recognition Information Centres, a resource for information on the education systems and academic and professional credentials of countries within Europe and beyond.

Erasmus+

Training and education scheme that allows students to study, train, work or volunteer abroad in 33 countries.

Erhvervsakademier

Academies of professional higher education, offering more vocational programmes, such as academy profession (AP) degrees.

eTA

Electronic Travel Authorisation, authorisation to enter and travel in Canada by air, which must be granted prior to departure.

Europass

Helps people to study, work or train across Europe, by presenting skills and qualifications in a standardised format that is easily understood in a range of countries.

Freshman year

First year (USA).

Frosh

Another name for a fresher or freshman. *Frosh* week is similar to freshers' week in the UK.

Graduate Australian Medical Schools Admission Test (GAMSAT)

Used to determine academic potential for postgraduate medical courses.

Graduate Record Exam (GRE) revised General Test

Used to determine academic potential for postgraduate study.

Junior year

Third year (USA).

KOT

The central university applications system in Denmark for English-taught bachelor's, professional bachelor's and academy profession programmes.

Letter of intent

A statement demonstrating why you should be considered for your chosen course, used by universities to distinguish between applicants. It may also be described as a letter of motivation, a statement of purpose or a personal statement.

Letter of motivation

A statement demonstrating why you should be considered for your chosen course, used by universities to distinguish between applicants. It may also be described as a letter of intent, a statement of purpose or a personal statement.

Letter of recommendation

Reference letter to a potential university, most often (but not always) from a member of academic staff who can comment on your ability and potential.

Major

Your main subject area, for example, history, engineering or nursing.

Mid-term

An exam taken midway through the academic term.

Minor

A secondary subject area or a specialism of your major.

***Nollning* (Sweden)**

The introduction of new students to university life, much like freshers' week in the UK.

***Numerus clausus* (Germany)**

A competitive system for courses that have more applicants than places. Central *numerus clausus* refers to courses that are restricted nationwide, while local *numerus clausus* is for courses where places are limited at a particular university.

***Numerus fixus* (the Netherlands)**

A fixed number of places are available on a course.

OECD

Organization for Economic Co-operation and Development.

Orientation

Events and activities for new students, like freshers' week in the UK.

Personal statement

A statement demonstrating why you should be considered for your chosen course, used by universities to distinguish between applicants. It may also be described as a letter of intent, a letter of motivation or a statement of purpose.

Polytechnic (New Zealand; Finland; Switzerland; Hong Kong; Singapore)

An institution providing professional or work-related higher education, in conjunction with business and industry; also known as a university of applied sciences.

Research-intensive or research-based university

An institution involved in extensive research activity and doctoral education.

Research proposal or research statement

The outline of an applicant's plans for research, including area of interest and rationale, used mainly in postgraduate applications.

Scholastic Assessment Test (SAT)

Used to determine academic potential for undergraduate study.

Semester

The two periods into which the academic year is divided in some countries.

Senior year

Fourth year (USA).

SIN

Social Insurance Number, a number issued by the Canadian government that grants the holder the right to work in Canada.

Sophomore year
Second year (USA).

Statement of purpose
A statement demonstrating why you should be considered for your chosen course, used by the universities to distinguish between applicants. It may also be described as a letter of intent, a letter of motivation or a personal statement.

Studielink
Central university applications service for most undergraduate courses in the Netherlands.

Study-abroad programme
A term often used to describe an exchange programme or short-term overseas study.

Studyinfo
Central applications system used for most undergraduate and master's courses taught at Finnish universities and universities of applied sciences.

Tertiary education
Education following secondary level; it includes university education, as well as other post-18 education options, such as vocational training.

UNESCO
United Nations Educational, Scientific and Cultural Organization.

University college (Denmark, Norway and Sweden)
An institution providing professional undergraduate degrees in areas such as engineering, teaching or business.

University of applied sciences (Finland; the Netherlands; Switzerland)

See Polytechnic.

Wānanga

An educational establishment in New Zealand that teaches degree-level courses in a Māori cultural context.

Index of advertisers

The definitive guide to teaching English as a foreign language

16th Edition

Are you looking for an exciting opportunity to travel and work abroad?

Covering over 600 language schools in over 100 countries worldwide, *Teaching English Abroad* will give you all the vital information you need to find job opportunities abroad, including:

- A country-by-country guide to English-language teaching opportunities
- A directory of language schools worldwide, including contact details
- Real-life accounts of teaching English as a second language
- Essential advice and tips on how to apply
- Advice for preparing and overcoming any problems

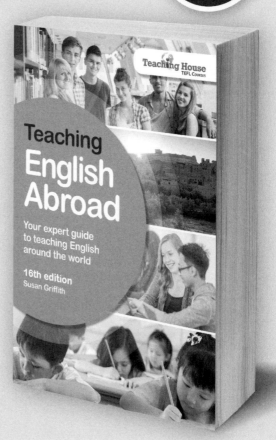

Teaching House
TEFL Courses

Teaching English Abroad

Your expert guide to teaching English around the world

16th edition
Susan Griffith

'We consider this to be our Bible!'
Managing Director, TEFL Worldwide, Prague

Get 10% off online!
Enter 'StudyAb' at checkout

trotman t

www.trotman.co.uk

Travel the world
Funding your trip
as you go

17th Edition

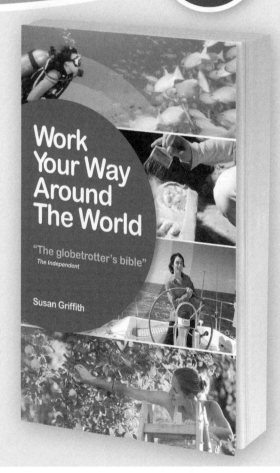

For jobs abroad, including volunteering and summer jobs, *Work Your Way Around the World* is the number one guide for the self-funded world traveller, providing all the information you need to successfully find work abroad.

This book reveals the best places to find work, how to get the necessary permits, tips for travelling safely and much more, including:

Hundreds of job opportunities across the globe

Insightful case studies from travellers who have been there and done it

Advice on applying for and securing jobs abroad

Culture and lifestyle information by country

Work Your Way Around The World

"The globetrotter's bible"
The Independent

Susan Griffith

'The Globetrotter's bible'
The Independent

Get 10% off online!
Enter 'StudyAb' at checkout

trotman | **t**

www.trotman.co.uk